The Ultimatum of Pleasure

Behavioral Economics and Social Development

Arsen Dallakyan and Karlen Dallakyan

Hamilton Books

Lanham • Boulder • New York • Toronto • Plymouth, UK

4501 Forbes Boulevard, Suite 200, Lanham, Maryland 20706
Hamilton Books Acquisitions Department (301) 459-3366

Unit A, Whitacre Mews, 26-34 Stannary Street,
London SE11 4AB, United Kingdom

Printed in the United States of America
British Library Cataloguing in Publication Information Available

Library of Congress Control Number: 2017940773
ISBN: 978-0-7618-6943-6 (cloth : alk. paper)—ISBN: 978-0-7618-6944-3 (electronic)

∞™ The paper used in this publication meets the minimum requirements of American National Standard for Information Sciences Permanence of Paper for Printed Library Materials, ANSI/NISO Z39.48-1992.

Contents

Introduction

This book represents a synthesis of a theoretical research of the new civilizational paradigm with a workbook that answers a question as to how to change one's life given the conditions that human life is increasingly dependent on incessant process of technological advancement.

Being proud of the technological achievements, the mankind today has not only progressed in terms of essential understanding of life, but has considerably moved away from it, having placed an artificial world between themselves and the nature. This world is not only the artifacts, but represents absolutely different reality invented by people, sodden into the impetuous pursuit of pleasures, including the one from the thirst of total superiority over the entire surrounding world.

Narcissistic and hedonistic eidos of the modern civilization as the reason of the unconscious pursuit of pleasure, its consequences and possible alternatives is what exactly the object of our research. What civilizational paradigms exist today that compete with each other, where can they lead the mankind, which of them we give preference to and why? How does the technological progress change the human existence? In our opinion, these are the main questions that would decide the future of the planet. Our duty is to answer these questions also because all other living beings, who appeared to be the hostages to unreasonable human ambitions, are incapable of doing anything in this case and wait for this or that decision from us.

In this work, we consider the nature, essence, cultural and historical evolution of pleasure as the main incentives of personal and social development. It is shown where the pursuit of pleasures leads the mankind to and what the threats of this race are during the era of modern (or advanced) technologies. If the primitive culture made a man a slave to his physical pleasures, the technical civilization, putting us into the dopamine dependence on high technologies, can make us slaves to the powerful elites who control the technologies.

Raymond Kurzweil, technical director at Google and known futurologist, having defined the main trends and achievements of the technical development and having split them by years, predicts the practical implementation of human immortality by 2042, and technical singularity, i.e. transformation of the Earth into the single computer by 2045. However, physical immortality doesn't mean immortality of a person as a spiritual being. For this purpose it is required to overcome the ultimatum which pleasure presents us with: "Exceed or degrade!"

The authors come to a conclusion that already today the mankind has encountered such an ultimatum. The man overcomes the principle of pleasure in decision making, becomes free from the primitive instinct and creates new humanistic culture in which pleasure is a personal encouragement of oneself for the reasonable decision. Or the man will continue torturing in stress from the endless expectation of pleasure which he won't be able to reach at all, and during the era of consumerist technical civilization (society) it will bring him down to a being-function whose only task is to provide market and social exchange.

If one has learned the mechanisms that control pleasure, it is possible not only to become the master of oneself, but also to succeed in behavioral marketing, in controlling the development of consumers and society, in general. In fact, a new civilizational paradigm is offered in a monograph, the role of marketing in its formation is disclosed, essential transformation of marketing in the 21st century is considered, and marketing focus not on the needs of the personality, but on the control of pleasure is revealed. The book presents natural-scientific and philosophical concepts of pleasure, various biological, psycho-physiological and psychological schools with their own ways of understanding the pleasure phenomenon are considered here. By means of the retrospective analysis, the evolution of human pleasure and the degree of his freedom is represented. It is shown that ascension of a man over his bio-egoistical nature is the main driver of social evolution. This is the essence of personal formation of a man, self-realization of his true self.

We presume to consider the specifics of the current situation, to show peculiarities of the modern technical civilization and the role of pleasure in it, then to pass to comprehension of the reasons to perform possible diagnosis of the problem by making a recipe of its solution. The modern society characterized by the mass consumption has only expanded the number of people who are instinctively aimed at pleasures in an unconscious pursuit of dopamine. Scientific and technical progress provides the mankind with more and more opportunities in a pursuit of pleasures that threatens a man not only with bio-psychosocial degradation, but physical death as well.

The dialectics is interesting—at first the thirst for pleasure generates new technological solutions which in turn lead to emergence of new, previously unknown pleasures. For example, the desire to derive pleasure from information led to invention of the “Internet” which subsequently led to emergence of mass dependence on it. In the pleasure captivity, people are losing a huge amount of time, burrowing their faces in the phones, but can't do anything with it. The most important thing is that these technologies, as a result of the impetuous growth of pleasure, change both human behavior and social reality. It means that the pursuit of pleasure, and not the development of production means, as Karl Marx thought, was the root motive of the social changes.

The process of historical evolution of civilizational paradigms which depends on the attitude towards pleasure is for the first time discussed in this book. Thirst for power, aspiration to wealth, sexual inclination, about which classics were talking- all this is only the tip of the iceberg. People are not conscious (aware) of their endless dependency on pleasures that gives rise to impetuously blind quest for more pleasures. The present stage of the development of technical civilization has provoked one more round in this race. A man began to feel pleasure from his own technical transformation. And moreover, which is even more terrible, from the increasing dependence on technical means. This very transformation of a man could threaten his own existence and would lead him to be a weak-willed being dominated by robotics.

The will of a man comes forth to a proscenium, as the means of his self-realization which has to face a serious fight against existential fear - the eternal guardian at the gates of personal development. There is a pressing need of a new paradigm in which development of pleasures would be driven by the reasonable will of people.

Therefore, in the first part there is comprehension of challenges of the modern civilization, first of all the technological one which has catalyzed an unprecedented pursuit of pleasure. In the second part, we analyze the place and the role of pleasure in the dominating civilizational paradigms including terrorism, having, seemingly, nothing in common with pleasure. In the third part the essence of the new civilizational paradigm offered by the authors—New humanism—is revealed.

The author of this book is the doctor of philosophy, professor and top manager, vice-president of a large corporation, who has an extensive experience of practical marketing in business world under his belt, thus it represents not only theoretical, but also a practical value.

Enjoy reading!

Chapter One

Pleasure and the Vector of Civilizational Development

1.1 PARADIGMAL DISTINCTIONS IN UNDERSTANDING OF PLEASURE

Any research requires definitions of the researched phenomena. For the purposes of this book we broadly define pleasure as a feeling of joy, of satisfaction humans receive from pleasant sensations, experiences, and thoughts. It is a positive emotion accompanying satisfaction of requirements, gratification of needs and desires.

French philosopher and psychoanalyst Jacques Lacan equates pleasure with dependence, as far as "pleasure is linked not with idleness, but with dependence or erection of desire"[1].

Many psychologists associate pleasure with a release from such erection of desire, weight, tensions, dearth of desire. It means that the pleasure provides either realization of desire or absence of it and, accordingly, absence of tensions itself. This view is in line with our idea concerning the usage in current behavioral marketing of the pleasure as a means of the consumers' dependence on their desires, or rather as a means of managing the consumers' behavior.

In his seminal work "The Use of Pleasure," Michel Foucault points out a rather unusual aspect of the pleasure as "practice of the self"[2], meaning that humans, while realizing their pleasures, form and develop themselves. However, the practice of using the pleasure for behavioral marketing purposes, in our view, can be defined as "practice of the other." It is a sort of the "pleasure engineering." Foucault further considers, in terms of human sexuality, ways of directing and regulating people's behavior by means of pleasures in various cultures. He underlines that religion, morality and rights had a special control over humans' experiencing pleasures, and to be more exact, over the ways of pleasure realization. Highlighting the strictness of the ancient laws, Foucault (1990) states,

Although the necessity of respecting the law and the customs was very often underscored, more important than the content of the law and its conditions of application was the attitude that caused one to respect them. The accent was placed on the relationship with the self that enabled a person to keep from being carried away by the appetites and pleasures, to maintain a mastery and superiority over them, to keep his senses in a state of tranquility, to remain free from interior bondage to the passions, and to achieve a mode of being that could be defined by the full enjoyment of oneself, or the perfect supremacy of oneself over oneself. (p. 304)

Today such a function of external control over pleasures is shifting more and more to marketers, who became aware of the earning power of such manipulation. However, before discussing the modern state of affairs, we will begin with the genesis of the pleasure as a concept.

1.1.1 Pleasure as the Highest Blessing

To understand such a complicated phenomenon as pleasure we invite you to travel in time to the gorgeous gardens of the Epicurean school. Here, among date palms and fig trees you can find students who arrived to the school from all corners of Greece. At the lectern you can see the Teacher himself, a son of a warrior, born in Samos, an honorable Athens citizen, a philosopher, that is Epicurus. He says that pleasure is the supreme blessing, but he frowns for some reason as if he apprehends that his words will be misinterpreted by his pupils. Although no, he does not frown, it is simply the sun that blinds him. The philosopher steps into a tree shadow and continues his lecture with a smile on his lips.

It is 307 BC, Epicurus has recently turned 35 and his dream has come true at last: he has opened his own school. Today he has finally found the time to finish a big sign and hang it on the school gates. The sign reads, "A stranger, you will feel happy here: the pleasure is the supreme blessing here." The sign turned out to be so well done that nobody could imagine the philosopher himself rather than a professional carpenter had made it.

Unfortunately, his hidden talents were not the only thing that later descendants were unable to comprehend. The genuine essence of the philosopher's school remained unclear and muddled to many people as well. Puritan critics have distorted it, presenting the decent Greek as a lustful libertine who had indulged in the cult of delights. They have ranked Epicurus among hedonists, equating the word "Epicurean" to "a beastie" who dipped in depravity and indulgence of his low needs.

Epictetus, a stoic, addressed Epicurus by saying, "Here is the life you declare as worthy: to eat, to drink, to copulate, to defecate and to snore"[3].

What did Epicurus understand as pleasure, calling it the supreme blessing? Pleasure for Epicurus is the supreme delight, goodness. "Every person aspires to avoid sufferings and seek pleasures. That is why we declare pleasure as the beginning and the purpose of a blissful life", he states[4]. Epicurus categorizes pleasures as corporeal and spiritual, short-term and long-term, natural and empty ones. Natural pleasures might be essential or not essential, where essential ones may be required for happiness, for the body, or for life itself. Epicurus remarks that not every pleasure is a blessing, but only the one, which is not followed by troubles. If long-term suffering follows a short-term pleasure, one should avoid such pleasure. We should note that Epicurus understood that the worldview of the epoch determines understanding of the content and essence of pleasure.

Epicurus considered prudence as the supreme blessing. The main thing in pleasures was moderation. The highest form of delight for Epicurus was a state of peace and calmness of mind, imperturbability, i.e. ataraxy. According to Epicurus, spiritual delight lies in imperturbable peace of a sage, in the feeling of the self, inner dignity and in rising over the destiny or fate, "It is better to be unhappy with a sense rather than be happy without any sense"[5]. "Live humbly and abstain from excesses," that is what Epicurus called for, using himself as an example: "I exult from the corporal delight eating bread and water, I spit on expensive pleasures not for them themselves, but for their unpleasant consequences"[6].

If we contemplate these statements to the accusations formulated against the school, it becomes clear why Epicurus was unable to stand the groundless distortion of his ideas and committed suicide. To be fair, there is another explanation of his untimely death from a kidney disease. Undoubtedly, the incorrect interpretations of his thoughts caused many troubles for him. However, such unfair treatment was the fate of many wise men, whose way of life was known to be different from the life of a mass man.

Only three of 300 Epicurus' letters survived, those addressed to Herodotus, Pythocles, and Menoeceus. With only three letters left as the evidence of his thought, but Epicurus' name resonates through the centuries and thus far it is impossible to start a conversation about pleasure without mentioning him. And we refer not only to his genuine theory but also the ones that sprang off from his ideas.

1.1.2 Pleasure as Contempt for Pleasure

In the 2nd century BC, during the Lamisol wars, Leosthenes, an Athens strategist, sent his troops to conquer the city of Lamia. The invader intended to take the city by an unexpected attack at night. He had a great advantage in the number of warriors. But despite all his power, the attack failed over and over again. Leosthenes had nothing to do then but besiege the castle, thus depriving its defenders of provisions, and force them to surrender. He was annoyed since he had anticipated entering the historical chronicles as a notable conqueror breaking the castle defense by storm. There are fewer honors in besiegement. Before setting the siege the commander suggested the defenders to surrender and summoned their representative to negotiate. After the negotiations to everyone's surprise quite the opposite happened: the siege was taken off. What had happened during the talks, and how did that unknown soldier, the castle defender, manage to break the aggressive spirit of the old commander?

When the aggressor suggested the city and the soldier to capitulate, the latter put his arm to the torch without saying a word. The smell of burned flesh filled the room. The soldier would not remove his hand. Leosthenes was unable to keep looking at that and averted his eyes. The soldier removed his arm only when he lost his hand. Everybody realized then that it was simply impossible to take by siege the castle defended by such warriors. Thus the term "to stand stoically" was coined and used for a whole school of philosophical thought.

The Epicureans and the Stoics lived and worked almost at the same time. Zeno, the founder of Stoicism, was a Phoenician. He was born in Kitium on Cyprus in the second half of the 4th century BC. The Stoics denied not only pleasure and delight, but also many other human urges and needs, placing the highest and only value on the virtue. They even considered it a good thing if a person was subjected to deprivation since deprivation was testing his endurance and firmness towards virtue, which was the prime goal for the Stoics. The Stoics dispraise every passion, appealing to indifference and spiritual calmness. They claim virtue as the will, which is in concordance with the nature. According to the Stoics, evil people even if they obey the laws of the Nature and God, do that under force like a dog tied to a wagon and forced to follow it wherever it moves.

One of the most famous Stoics was Chrysippus (280–207 BC). He said that a good man was always happy, whereas a bad one was always unhappy, and the good man's happiness did not differ from the happiness of God. The Stoics are also known to be rather unpretentious in everyday life as they got along with a bare minimum. Their coat served them as a tent, a bed, and clothes.

The Stoic school reached its highest point in the works of Roman philosophers, such as Seneca, Epictetus and Marcus Aurelius. Seneca (3 BC–65 AD) was a Spaniard whose educated father lived in Rome. Although, as Bertrand Russell smartly notes[7]. Seneca was less lucky with his pupil than Aristotle. Seneca's pupil was Neuron, a Roman emperor. Although Seneca despised wealth he was a rich man. After he had fallen into disgrace of the emperor

Neuron the philosopher was accused of conspiracy and condemned to death. In view of his merits he was generously allowed to commit a suicide.

Seneca writes on pleasure in his papers "On Happy Life" and "On Blissful Life." He starts his paper "On happy life" with these words, "All people want to live happily, my brother Gallio, but they vaguely imagine what the happy life consists of"[8]. Seneca emphasizes that he accepts the general rule of all Stoics: Live in conformity with the nature. He states,

Such a life is possible only if first of all, a person constantly possesses a sensible mind; then, if his spirit is courageous and vigorous, noble, hardy and prepared for any circumstances; if he cares of his physical needs satisfaction without falling into disturbing suspiciousness; if he is interested in material aspects of life in general without being tempted by any of them; and finally, if he is able to use destiny's gifts without becoming their slave (Ibid, p. 169).

Calmness and freedom are the main conditions for achieving this state: "The strong, cloudless and constant enjoyment, peace and harmony of spirit, greatness united with mildness take place of pleasures, of the insignificant, fleeting and not only vile, but also harmful delights. After all any cruelty comes from infirmity" (Ibid, p. 169). The highest blessing, according to Seneca, is the invincible strength of mind, sophisticated experience, calmness in actions together with humanity and care towards the people around. He recognizes a happy man as the one for whom "a true pleasure will be . . . contempt for pleasures" (Ibid, p. 170). Cheerful mood and mental satisfaction by his inner filling "generously reward a person for the insignificant, trite and passing desires of his frail flesh. After all that very day when he becomes the slave to pleasure, he will feel all the burden of suffering as well" (Ibid, p. 170).

Seneca further writes, "Only the person who feels neither passionate desire nor fear due to reasonability may be called a happy one" (Ibid, p. 171). Seneca formulate such an anti-hedonistic position throughout his entire paper:

As for pleasures, even let them surround us everywhere, creep with all ways, caress our souls with their delights and waste even more temptations in front of us aimed to excite all our body or only separate parts of it, none of the mortal, if he had at least a drop of human dignity left, would wish to rush about day and night in spasms of passion and, having forgotten about his soul, would live exclusively by interests of his flesh. (Ibid, p. 171)

Thus, Seneca separates happiness and virtue from pleasure, and at times even opposes them: "Virtue is something majestic, sublime, regal, invincible, tireless, whereas pleasure is something low, slavish, ailing, passing, watching and nesting in indecent places and taverns" (Ibid, p. 172).

Seneca notes the limitation of pleasure, suggesting that it dies away at the moment of the greatest delight. Then there comes disgust, and apathy follows the first devotion: "In general, there is never any stability in the event marked by spontaneity of the movement"[9]. The pleasure can be beneficial for the person if it is directed by the reason and good will. It should play the secondary, and not the dominating role, similar to the auxiliary and light-armed troops. In the other paper, "On blissful life," Seneca writes: "That very day when a person dominates sensual pleasure, he will dominate grief as well"[10]. Thus, such an important condition of a happy life as harmony with self (peace of mind) and harmony with the nature is once again emphasized.

One of Socrates' pupils, Antisthenes, founded his own school later called the Cynics. The school got its name after its best-known representative Diogenes of Sinop (from the city of Sinop), whose nickname was a Dog. And Cynos in Greek means a dog. Till Socrates' death, Antisthenes had lived in an aristocratic society and did not differ much from his friends. However, shocked either by the execution of his Teacher, or by the defeat of Athens (or both), he became almost another person, began to lead an absolutely different life, despising those values and things which he used to subscribe to and appreciate before. He despised luxury, aspiration to physical pleasures and artificial pleasures. "I will rather go crazy, than admire anything," he used to say[11].

Antisthenes' student, Diogenes, became famous for his extraordinary acts already during his lifetime. He despised wealth, material values, lived in a barrel, fraternized not only with all people, but also with animals. When crowned Alexander the Great asked Diogenes how he could help him, the latter quietly answered, "Only don't stand in my light." Diogenes searched for virtue and freedom in release from desires. When he was treated with wine once, he poured it out on the ground. The indignant owner asked him, "Why did you spoil my wine?" Diogenes answered, "And you would like me to spoil my health?" According to another legend, once a rich person brought Diogenes into his house to show how magnificently and beautifully, unlike Diogenes, he lived. Diogenes looked around and spat in the owner's face. When the owner got indignant and demanded an explanation, Diogenes said that he simply wanted to spit out, but he could not find the worst place rather than the owner's face because everything was glistening and shining clean. When Diogenes was asked why he behaved that way, he explained that he was exaggerating a situation so that his acts were more effective.

Great Plato stated that the pleasure, as well as thoughts, can be true and false. He noted that the pleasure can have a cognitive, i.e. an informative function (like thinking) since the whole person, and not an isolated sensitive part of him, is the source of pleasure. Underlining that the corporal pleasures hinder the cognizing of the truth, Plato says by Sokrat's mouth: "The true virtue is united with the mind, all the same, whether the pleasures, fears and everything of that kind annex it or not"[12].

According to another titan of ancient philosophy, Aristotle, there are two sorts of pleasures: those connected with the process of needs' satisfaction and realization of our forces, and those that are connected with improvement of our activities. The second type is the highest order of pleasure. The highest pleasure results from the active use of our vital energy. The pleasure and life are tightly united and do not allow separation. The highest pleasure, according to Aristotle, is achieved through the mental activity (the supreme human activity). Thus, Aristotle approaches understanding of pleasure as a personal subjective experience of pleasure. It is clear for him that the degree and brightness of the pleasure experience will depend on the person's psyche[13].

"Indulgency in the pleasures,—says Aristoteles,—is libertinage, and it deserves blame . . . One is called a loose liver for his suffering more than he should because he doesn't get pleasures; and one is called sensible as he doesn't suffer for lack of pleasure and for abstinence from it"[14].

Spinoza understands pleasure as a potentiality, force, "The pleasure is transition of a person from a smaller perfection to a greater one"[15].

Spencer considers pleasure as something that induces a person to act in accordance with what is favorable for him.

Consequently, as we've shown, the ancient thinkers, firstly, distinguished between the true and false pleasures, and secondly, they've put an emphasis on the necessity to control pleasures by means of reason.

1.1.3 Scientific Interpretation of Pleasure

Under the expert redaction of doctor of medicine Michael Votinov, Aachen University, Germany

From the physiological point of view, pleasure represents a way of encouragement of a person. Through the sensation of pleasure, the brain tells us that a certain action is good, and therefore is useful and, as a result, it should be remembered and repeated. The brain of a primate, as well as directly a human's one, at the time of positive experience excretes dopamine, the neuro-mediator (biochemical active agent helping to transfer nervous impulses chemically) responsible for expectation of pleasure. The more dopamine, the stronger the pleasure. In addition to dopamine, almost all human empirical and cognitive reactions have their own, already revealed by today, neuro-mediators which perform chemical conductors' functions: acetylcholine, catecholamines (adrenaline, noradrenaline and, already mentioned, dopamine), neuro-active peptides, amino acids (gamma-aminobutyric acid, glycine, glutaminic acid), histamine.

Researchers from the team of Robert Froemke, doctor of medical sciences from the Skirball Institute of Biomolecular Medicine (The Langone medical center of the New York University), found out that one of the most powerful hormones of the brain—oxytocin—plays an important role in the process of motivating the individual to definite behavior. Oxytocin is called "a pleasure hormone," sometimes "a happiness hormone." It was believed earlier that it participates in a more limited sphere of the human behavior, generally in physiological, sexual etc., but doctor Froemke's team found out that oxytocin also increases the volume of information processed by the brain and defines a response, "social" reactions of the individual. For example, it teaches the mother's brain how to react to needs of the baby.

Three brain types are singled out in the brain structure of a human: the reptilian, which is the most ancient and responsible for survival instincts; limbic or emotional; and actually the one we think with, neocortex. It is interesting that as scientists note, 95% of decisions happen in the reptilian and emotional brain. Among the hormones produced by the brain and influencing our behavior they single out serotonin, endorphin and cortisol, along with dopamine and oxytocin. Dopamine causes a feeling of expectation of something positive, this is what we call expectation of pleasure. Its action lasts only two minutes. For a continued sensation, it requires replenishment. Oxytocin causes the expectation of feeling of love, security, unification and works for six minutes. Serotonin causing feelings of superiority, status increase, victory, and acknowledgement works for one day, i.e. the full 24 hours. Endorphins causing pleasure from life, from feeling healthy, of feeling joy, last for four hours. And cortisol, which is responsible for the feelings connected with the loss of the beloved, treason, loss of the spouse, deception, and fears, lasts for the full three years! The brain learns both good and bad. In the latter case the person ceases to show activity, avoiding repeated pain. That is, the negative experience affects the brain stronger than the positive one. But our interest in this case is in the hormones connected not with deprivation of pleasure, but with providing it.

So, the brain excretes dopamine and oxytocin as encouragement for the expected pleasure, which is good for the whole organism. Like a good manager, the brain motivates the organism with some kind of an advance, "a prepayment" for the correct behavior, teaches a person how to behave properly not only biologically, but socially as well. Sometimes dopamine may not be connected with social behavior, and sometimes even contradicts it. Animals of course do not realize that and blindly follow their pleasure. But to our general regret, people often do behave the same way. Most people are unaware of the internal motivators of their decisions, they simply give in to an internal impulse.

Whereas the minority, possessing both the advanced technologies, the stocks and the latest achievements of science, learned this secret, and subordinated the development of market capitalism to it. Having taken control over all the pleasures in the world, the minority turned them into goods and started to sell them successfully, forcing the majority to forget about everything and to run in the intended direction. Of course, it did not happen in one day. Throughout all the history of human culture the attitude towards pleasure was changing. We will elaborate on the character of co-evolution of the culture and pleasure preceding today's Ultimatum of Pleasure in the following chapter.

In the meantime, let us consider various interpretations of the pleasure phenomenon.

In the 20th century psychologists and philosophers start talking about the oneness of the pleasure principle. It is distinguished only in the spheres of its application: one and the same pleasure can be caused by either a slice of chocolate or by world peace.

Neo-Freudians understand the essence of pleasure as an unconscious aspiration of a person to something that can even do much harm to the person. It is in itself a characteristic of a neurotic person. To wish passionately for something which is harmful for a person is the essence of a mental disease. And many consumers of the mass society are struck with this very neurosis. That is to wish for something which is not only unnecessary for them but also causes harm. For example, Fromm (1990) writes: "Pleasure or happiness, which exist only in a person's head, but are not a condition of his existence as a personality, I suggest to call pseudo-pleasure or pseudo-happiness. . . . There where the grief and misfortune were expected, there respectively they will be felt, but in fact they will be pseudo-sufferings. Pseudo-pleasure and pseudo-suffering are deceptive feelings; virtually they are thoughts of the forthcoming feelings, but not the original emotional experiences". (pp. 141–142)

Modern science treats pleasure as "the feeling, the experience accompanying satisfaction of a need or interest" (Ivin, 2004, p. 341). Almost all scientific sources today understand pleasure as a feeling or a positively colored emotion accompanying satisfaction of one or several human needs. Pleasure is contrasted with the feelings of tension, discomfort, pain, suffering, i.e. negative emotions or feelings.

From the psychological point of view, pleasure is a consequence of achieving the expected result within the motivational system of a person. Let's imagine a balance scale. There is a motivating factor on one side of the scale and there is the potential encouragement and benefit on the other, when people achieve the latter they receive the pleasure. On an imaginary balance scale, a motivating factor is on one side of the scale, while the other has the potential encouragement and benefit, after achieving which people receive the pleasure.

A set of motives for human behavior is being distinguished. However, to our mind, it is possible to single out four main motives:

1. safety;
2. sociality;
3. success and superiority (alpha motive) and
4. innovation.

Let us take for example a case when your motive is safety. You have found yourself in what you perceive as a dangerous city district at night. Imagine your car has broken down and you are compelled to wait for a tow truck. There is not a soul around. Danger is felt everywhere, a bottle has been broken somewhere, someone has shouted loudly. Suddenly you see a group of strong guys in leather jackets and hoods appear from the backstreet. It is a street gang. They are quickly approaching you, and you can already make out that two guys of the gang hold baseball bats in their hands. What pleasure you would experience then when at the utmost despair, you turn the ignition key and the car suddenly starts, and you speed up with slipping wheels away from this ill-fated street. Boundless pleasure will overwhelm you. You could not even imagine before that feeling of safety might give such pleasure.

Many psychologists and philosophers studied how pleasure influences the life and behavior of a person. Fechner was one of such scientists, whose ideas, as we know, strongly affected Freud. He put forward the notion of "the principle of pleasure from action"[16]. Unlike hedonistic doctrines he meant the pleasure as the reason for human actions, and not as the purpose of them.

Fechner noted that these motives sometimes might not be caught by the consciousness: "It is quite natural that if our motives are hidden in the unconscious, it also refers to pleasure and displeasure". (Fechner. Ibid. 229.) This idea of unconscious nature of many pleasures lies at the heart of the Freudian concept.

Research on the subject of pleasure conducted by Freud (1955) emphasizes an important role of pleasure in an organism's life. Freud refers to "the principle of pleasure" as one of the main regulators of mental processes and human behavior in general, calling it a life instinct. As it is known, behind pleasure there is always a desire, which the society is eager to take under control. However, in the course of socialization, according to Freud, the natural setup of the individual on pleasure is replaced by "the principle of reality"[17].

The socially-oriented Super Ego inhibits desires of a person, his aspiration to physical pleasure and forces it out to the sphere of the unconscious. This, according to Freud, is the basic reason of numerous types of pathologies.

According to Freud, the society is ultimately interested in distracting people from sexuality and directing them to work. Further developing Freud's ideas on the principle of pleasure and the principle of reality, Marcuse notes that the principle of pleasure controls unconscious processes while the principle of reality acts on the consciousness level. A subject of the principle of reality is the civilization suppressing aspiration to pleasures by education, and also by various institutes of economic and political organization of society.

Fromm further distinguishes between the physiological and mental pleasures, for instance the pleasure from reading a book or from the recognition of a person by the society. Moreover, he categorizes the mental pleasures into rational and irrational and finds the latter ones unsatisfying as they are based on such irrational phenomena like fear and anxiety. For instance, sleepiness can be either rational as a response to not getting enough sleep, or irrational as a means of suppression of anxiety and fear. The same applies to distinguishing between hunger and appetite. The former is a type of physiological reaction and the latter is, perhaps, a mental reaction to complexes, fear, and anxiety[18]. All of this should be taken into consideration by marketers in their professional applied activity.

According to Foucault, the society does not so much suppress pleasures as it creates a discourse with the purpose to regulate the experience of pleasure and, thus, strengthens its political power (Foucault.1996, p. 51).

The aspiration to pleasure is constituted in desire; the desire itself is erotic: it is purposeful, it is followed by tension, demands effort and will for the implementation and thus testifies about the ability of vital activity. The pleasure is significant as realization of the desire being directed to it. But in comparison with the desire, the pleasure can seem vain, because the peace delivered by it can symbolize death, at least death of desire; hence the "horror to be satisfied"[19]. Russian philosopher Nikolay Berdyaev, while analyzing the creation, also wrote that sublime pleasures are significant not by being pleasures themselves, but by their being sublime. Therefore, the real restriction of the principle of pleasure went the way of definition of valuable priorities: e.g., worthy life, the rights or the benefit of other people, personal perfection etc.

One more research project deserves special attention, "The Pleasure: Creative Approach to Life" by a famous American psychologist, founder of bio-energetics Alexander Lowen, who teaches a person to hear and understand one's body, speaks about the need to restore the natural corporal spontaneity and ability to express feelings for the sake of establishing harmony of the person with oneself and the world.

Lowen A. (1970) presents pleasure as a feeling inseparably linked with a full-fledged creative life because "the capacity for pleasure is also the capacity for creative self-expression" (p. 118). It is particularly current since the desire for power shared by many people suppresses the creative beginning and becomes the reason of uprising muscular tension. Lowen offers the exercises intended to help a body to regain its natural freedom and spontaneity, and to help a person to become more open for pleasure and life delights.

In other words, according to Lowen, pleasure is not only a natural state of a person, but also a necessary feeling for one's complete and balanced life. And displeasure arises due to the wrong thinking, feelings and life which lead the person to contradictions and psycho-physiological inhibitions that

W. Reich calls a psychological shell, and Fechner calls them tension. Lowen suggests removing a displeasure problem by releasing the contradiction between physical, mental and social existence of the person. Because when one of the person's components suffers, he or she cannot be satisfied and happy. Lowen suggests that one of the universal remedies to harmonize all these three spheres of the personality is creative activity, in which harmony of the personality is coming to life. As Lowen (1970) emphasizes, the biopower analysis offers a person two things: firstly, clear understanding of the fact that pleasure and delight are peculiar to a human nature and life. Neither money, nor the power, nor success are able to give it . . . . And, secondly, it is surprising, but there is a way to help the person to reach that. I consider that the biopower analysis cannot save the world . . . so far, but it allows you to feel well not only thanks to what you are doing for the sake of yourself, but also thanks to what you are doing for the relatives, for the nature and for life. One more thing: if you have these two bases to feel well, this feeling will be a real support for you in extreme old age. (p. 121)

Thus, Lowen is not limited to pure bio-energetics and physiological ego-centered pleasure, but considers it more widely, as a social feeling, focused on others as well.

The pleasure that Lowen speaks about is not simply cheerfulness, but a deep internal state. People among whom such a state is common, according to him ". . . do not include those who declare enthusiastically their devotion to life . . . they are not adherents of some idea, nor adherents of a certain dogma. But almost always they are special people" (Ibid, p. 128) They radiate an intensive feeling of pleasure and content. There is a spark in their eyes and intelligence in their moves. They look at you with interest and listen with attention. When they speak, they express their feelings and everything they say does matter. Their relaxed bodies move freely and with the ease. Their internal vital energy is quite palpable and is a reflection of their healthy skin color and a good muscular tone. Even to be in their proximity is a pleasure too. Such people realize their identity. They are original, harmonious and complete.

When a person aspires to nothing but to derive pleasure, he or she becomes a slave to his or her Ego. In the end, the person will come to experience a great displeasure. To reach the true pleasure, the person has to rise to one's "I," which itself will specify what the person should derive pleasure from. A fine illustration of this thought is the image of Faust and his struggle with himself.

The pleasure, according to Goethe, is a gift of God for those who identify themselves with life, rejoicing at its beauty and magnificence. Meanwhile, the attitude of people towards pleasure is very ambiguous. In "Faust" the devil tempts with pleasure which is not within his power to provide. All the matter is in different understandings of pleasure.

Bertram Jessup, in the preface to his translation of "Faust" writes, "The magic of the 16th century and science of the 20th are similar in the aspiration or intention to dominate and manage the life. Moreover, the importance of it had amplified greatly upon the fall of authority of the Almighty God"[20].

A human received the power of condemnation and destruction, the power that had been a prerogative of the punishing Almighty. And now with the power seeming unlimited and without the constraining forces, what can prevent a person from destroying himself? In Carretti's interpretation, "I" was replaced by "Ego" and the human did not notice it, just like Judas Iscariot, who betrayed his teacher, having given in to his internal Mephistopheles (1963, p. 468).

Lowen (1970) notes that the devil is in each of us, embodied in our ego which promises fulfillment of desires if we obey to its aspiration to dominate. He further emphasizes, that domination of the ego over the personality is nothing else but a devil perversion of essence of the person. The ego should not be the owner of the body, but only its faithful and devoted servant. The body, as opposed to the ego, strives for pleasure, but not for the power. The corporal pleasure is a source of all our pleasant feelings and positive thoughts. Take away corporal pleasure from a person, and he would be overflowed by frustration, rage and hatred. His thinking will become perverted, creative potential will run low. He will set a self-damage program (Ibid, p. 6).

Thus the importance of body-mental harmony is emphasized. The ego shouldn't dictate the body what is pernicious for the latter.

The same is fair for the body, which should not cause any mental problems by its needs. Both parts of the centaur should coexist peacefully, helping each other to derive pleasure from one and the same event. Moreover, Lowen suggests that solving this contradiction between a body and soul is possible by means of pleasure which is a creative force. Only pleasure possesses enough strength to resist the potential destructiveness of power. The key of creative life is hidden in pleasure. The opposite is also true: creativity opens a door to the country of pleasure for a person. Lowen fairly notes that the pleasure provides motivation and energy for a creative approach to life, "Any creative act, begins with pleasant excitement, passes through a stage of hard work, peculiar labor pains and finishes with pleasure of implementation. From beginning till end the whole creative process is motivated by aspiration to pleasure". (Ibid, p. 9)

Creativity is impossible without pleasure. One of the keys to pleasure is physical activity. At the heart of any experience of original joy or happiness, according to Lowen, there lies the corporal feeling of pleasure. He says that only the action giving pleasure can be cheerful and happy. "True joy and real happiness are being filled with sense through pleasure which is felt by the person in a certain situation" (Ibid, p. 10) But the opposite is not true: joy and happiness are not always pleasure.

Freedom acts as another key to pleasure. Work, and walk, and anything else could be a source of pleasure. However, all these should be chosen by a free person, according to Lowen:

> I knew many people who found pleasure in their work, but none of them could tell that it was cheerful or brought them happiness. Work is serious, it demands a certain discipline and devotion. It is aimed at the desirable result which the person seeks to achieve. But work can be pleasure if the person is ready to spend easily, freely and fully the energy which is required for its performance. Nobody will get pleasure from activity dictated by external forces or which demands more energy than the person is able to afford. (Ibid, p. 15)

Since pleasure is the flow of an outward feeling, which arose as reaction to the environment, we usually correlate it with the object or the situation, which caused this reaction. So, people associate pleasure with entertainment, sexual relations, visit to a restaurant or sports activities. Certainly, the pleasure takes place in situations that stimulate emergence of a feeling, however it would be wrong to identify pleasure with a similar situation. Entertainment can be pleasant only when a person is in the corresponding mood, and would not bring anything but discomfort if he or she needs silence and rest.

To understand the essence of pleasure, Lowen (1970) contrasts it with pain, Both are reactions of the individual to a situation. If the reaction is positive and the feeling flows outside from within, the person speaks about the Pleasure being felt. If the reaction is negative and there is no rhythmical stream of feeling, the person describes a situation as unpleasant or painful. But since the experience of Pleasure or pain is caused by what occurs in the body, any internal breakdown which blocks a feeling stream will cause pain irrespective of the external situation's attractiveness. (Ibid, p. 19)

Polar dependence of pleasure and pain is illustrated by an example when release from pain is endured as pleasure. For the same reason disappearance of pleasure sometimes leads the person to burdensome, tensed state. As Lowen affirms, "since we associate pleasure with certain situations, and associate pain with specific traumatic events, we do not realize that our self-perception is always caused by these feelings" (Ibid, p. 20).

Unlike pain, pleasure is unstable. While a good piece of a beefsteak stimulates our appetite, several pieces of a beefsteak can cause indigestion. It often happens that the same lunch that was pleasant yesterday does not please us today. The pleasure in many respects depends on the mood. It is difficult to enjoy a beautiful object when you are depressed, the same as to feel aroma of a rose with a stuffy nose. However a good mood, being an indispensable condition for pleasure, does not serve as a guarantee for pleasure at all. Harmony between the internal state and external situation is required for pleasure. And what is very important, pleasure is a consequence of our reaction to the event, and not the mere influence of this event.

Pleasure comprises a considerable unconscious component responsible for its spontaneous character. It is beyond any management. It can arise in the most unexpected situations: at the sight of a flower growing by the road, during a conversation with a stranger or when the undesired party turns into a delightful soiree. On the other hand, the pleasure can escape even under the most careful preparations for pleasant pastime. Actually, the more diligently you aspire to it, the less probably you receive it. And if a person, having reached the pleasure, grabs it with excessive greed, it disappears right before the eyes. Just like Robert Burns once wrote in one of his poems, "But pleasures are like poppies spread: You seize the flower, its bloom is shed."

The historical review of the phenomenon of pleasure showed that throughout all human history philosophers divided pleasure into two conditional categories: the highest and the lowest.

Each school assigned its own meanings to the concepts, but the main idea remained the same: the highest pleasure brings benefit to a person and stimulates his development, while the lowest one, on the contrary, harms and leads to degradation.

Only with the advent of Freudianism, psychologists and philosophers started to talk about the fact that the pleasure principle is universal, it differs only in the area where it is applied: the same pleasure can be experienced from a slice of chocolate, or peace in the world.

The fundamental position of the authors of this book is the following: a person needs to surpass the mere principle of pleasure, and not to get involved in juggling the objects of desires.

Any pleasure, no matter whether it is a passionate night with an exciting partner or protection of the best friend's honor. In the process of decision-making the pleasure has to leave a role of the main choice criterion. And to start playing the role of encouragement which was initially assigned to it. Encouragement, for presence or absence of which, the person answers.

1.2 EVOLUTION OF CULTURE AS A RESPONSE TO THE CIVILIZATIONAL CHALLENGE OF PLEASURE

Evolution of a man as a difficult bio-psychosocial being is influenced not only by the nature, but also by the culture. As an external force, it transforms the person. A man, right after his birth, is involved in a sphere which is absolutely alien to his biological organization and which like a computer program is encoding him. Further, we will consider how exactly the culture influences transformation of a person and, first of all, his attitude towards pleasure, and primarily the differences in this context between the Dionysian and Apollonian cultures[21].

1.2.1 Pleasure and Development of Material and Sensual Type of Culture

The Dionysian culture as the joyful, festive existence aimed at the satisfaction of the human vital needs received its name after Dionysus, a son of Zeus, who was considered a god of wine, blissful ecstasy and enthusiastic love. To approve the Dionysian principle means to follow sensual pleasures, to enjoy one's life. But apart from that, he is the haunted god who is suffering and dying. Everyone who follows him is compelled to share his lot.[21] It is interesting that some authors note special closeness of Dionysus to the nature and women. He is mystical, intuitive, often appears as the unwanted and restless elements, as the reason of the conflicts and madness. Dionysus often personifies an Anima in mentality of a man.

Romans' Dionysus is the god Bacchus, a god of wine and winemaking, of rage and blissful freedom. Dionysus is a son of Zeus and a mortal woman, Semele, a daughter of Cadmus, the tsar of Thebes. According to the myth, Zeus's wife Hera, out of jealousy, willing to do much harm to Semele, advised her to ask Zeus to appear in his divine guise. Semele, unsuspicious, made Zeus swear to keep his promise. Zeus could not break his oath and appeared before Semele in all the divine greatness and thus killed her, burned her with his lightning. Semele was already pregnant by that time. Zeus withdrew the child and took him out in his hip. One of interpretations of the name "Dionysus" is "Zeus's limp," another is "Divine Nis" (the mountain where Dionysus was brought up). Demented by jealousy of guileful Hera, Dionysus was very quick-tempered and constantly resorted to violence, and sometimes he even had madness attacks.

Therefore, the Dionysian culture which is focused on the maximum satisfaction of material and sensual needs is fraught with various collisions. A human, having little difference from an animal, is consumed with desire and pleasures which intoxicate him and lead to madness like wine. Pushkin's old woman from the fairy tale "Fisherman and the Golden Fish" is a vivid example of the hero of the Dionysian culture.

1.2.2 Pleasure and Development of Spiritual and Idealistic Type of Culture

Unlike the barbarous Roman culture, the Ancient Greek culture has an Apollonian character. The forefront here belongs not to material, but already to moral and mental values. The philosophy appears as the leading form of the public consciousness.

How did the Greek culture affect the perception of pleasure by people?

The pagan cosmo-centric thinking allowed the Greeks to consider themselves a part of the unified, alive and life-giving Cosmos. Philosophical systems served as the evidence to that, for example, the representatives of the Milesian school were almost idolizing the natural elements. Therefore, the pleasure in such a worldview should join to the entire cosmic-naturalistic system. An illustration of such understanding is a mythical and metaphorical image of a centaur, a creature representing synthesis of a man and a horse. What brings pleasure to a horse, can do harm to a man.

Already then the society adopted ways of manipulating the behavior of a man through dosing and distributing of pleasure. Having perfectly understood that, the Cynics in the person of their brightest and infamous Diogenes, practically refused from pleasures to keep their freedom. When Diogenes saw a boy drinking water holding his palm under the stream, he threw out his mug saying: "The boy is wiser than me because he could do with the less."

The Roman civilization, as a hedonistic civilization of excessiveness, disproved with all its existence and development the Socrates' thesis "Nothing excessive. Since moderation is the most important and the most difficult thing in life". As it is known, the slogan "Bread and circuses!" could have become the main motto of the Roman civilization. Gladiatorial fights along with orgies in the Roman baths and extensive libations, as a result of the culture orientation to wealth and the power, eventually led the Roman civilization to crash. Instead of the culture of the world, according to O. Spengler, Rome offered a city civilization. "The city,—he writes,—is one point at which all life of the great countries concentrates while all the rest withers; instead of the people rich in forms, which grew together with earth, a new nomad appears, a parasite, a resident of the big city, a man who is absolutely deprived of traditions, who had dissolved in the shapeless mass, a man of facts, without religion, intelligent, fruitless, full with deep disgust for the peasantry (and further to its highest form—the provincial nobility), therefore, is a huge step to the nonorganic end".[22] As we see from the quote, Spengler anticipates globalization processes, calling them building of the single world city. And globalization leads a pleasure to universalization, as means of manipulating people. Not for nothing Rome rose to the ruthless war against the Christianity which besides everything was trying to put all the pleasure under control of religion and morals. The Apollonian culture of the Greeks which conceded to the Dionysian civilization of Romans in turn receded before the Apollonian culture, but already of the medieval Europe, which had established in the West for more than one thousand years.

1.2.3 Pleasure in Religious Culture

Thinkers of the Middle Ages themselves often drew a picture of the gloomy "dark Middle Ages". In their descriptions, there is no joy and optimism, there is no satisfaction with life, there is no aspiration to improvement of the existing world, there is no hope for luck and wellbeing in this world. The aspiration to death, to the other world is being felt, where at least might be found true happiness, pleasure and rest. However, the situation was far more contradictory. The early Middle Ages coincided with dissolution of the Roman Empire, the Great resettlement of the people and with the deep social, economic and cultural crisis. In the IV century, there was a transition from "the Roman world" to "the Christian world", from the Dionysian culture to the Apollonian one. The Western world had appeared, as a matter of fact, from the merge of the Roman world with the barbarian one, thus it is even more contradictory. Many achievements of the ancient art were lost. One of the merits of Christianity is that it balanced the rights of all, both slaves, and masters, both Greeks, and Romans, and the barbarians. It opposed love, forgiveness and hope for the best to violence.

The Antiquity was striving for harmony of the body and soul, the Roman culture proclaimed a priority of the body, force, will to conquer, in other words the will to the power. Unlike Rome, where there was a cult of physical pleasures, the Christianity was turned to the soul, appealing for physical restrictions, asceticism, suppression of inclinations of the body. Belief, hope and love were the spiritual guides of the medieval culture. Love to the enemies meant distribution of love on all people without exception.

The culture of the "Middle Ages" was not homogeneous though. Its social structure comprised of the clergy, the feudal aristocracy and the third estate. The second estate of the aristocracy was represented mostly by the knights for whom force, courage, nobility, generosity, vanity, and love to a fairy lady were obligatory.

A knight, as a rule, originated from a good family, had to differ in beauty and attractiveness. M. Ossovskaya says that "his beauty was emphasized usually by the clothes testifying of his love to gold and jewels"[23]. A knight was required to show force, endurance, restraint and continuous proof of his glory, in other words feats were required. He could not even stay with his wife who he just had married because his friends watched him not to effeminate in inaction. A woman, whose husband was killed on a joust, could marry her husband's murderer. So the food cooked for the funeral feast commemorating the late husband could quite go to a wedding table of the "inconsolable" widow.

The attitude of knights towards goodness seems to us no less queer. There is no sense to perform good deeds if they remain unknown, Chrétien de Troyes says, approving constant care of his image. Pride was admitted absolutely justified if it was not hypertrophied and did not turn into haughtiness and arrogance. The heaviest charge for the knight was charge of a lack of courage. Noble, generous, true and reliable, he had to be able to love women truly and faithfully.

"To fight and to love" were the slogans of a knight. The love had to be mutually faithful. The knights who accepted a fidelity vow to the ladylove firmly resisted loving avowals of other women. But, if the knight did not achieve glory, the lady had the right to stop loving him.

Some researchers of the medieval culture note that praising the ladies by the knights often had more pragmatic character. The wandering hungry knights, roving from one lock to another, eulogized the hostess often richer and more famous, whose husband was, as a rule, far away, in hope for hearty reception, and probably for promotion. But, anyway, everything occurred according to a courteous style of behavior. Serving to knights' honor and duty is the main pleasure of the knight. The culture and morals in particular act in this case as means of pleasure transformation.

In the Middle Ages, there are many known cases of long-lasting correspondences between convents and friaries, where in an excited form the distant affection was expressed by people who knew they would never see each other. That is, they tried to derive pleasure from "Platonic" love. In general, the Middle Age was an era of pleasure submission by morals and religion. People started deriving pleasure not from satisfaction of their physical and biological, i.e. vital needs, but from abstention, not from satisfaction of those needs, but sometimes even from pure torture of the organism, considering that it goes for good to the soul.

Alisher Navoi's words are interesting in this regard: "Rich is not the one whose possessions are abundant, not the one, who keeps on getting pleasure of possessing wealth. Only he who is spiritually rich and who, by the grace of the Creator, has a treasure in which he finds no blemish for himself."

The person of a faith is not at all deprived of pleasure. On the contrary, he sometimes sacrifices few-second pleasures for eternal happiness, for peace and harmony in his soul.

"The human pleasure today consists in having fun,"—E. Fromm wrote. In other words, in deriving pleasure from mass consumption of goods and services." The world, according to E. Fromm's remark, is one big object of our appetite, a big apple, a big bottle, a big breast; we are suckers, eternally waiting for something, eternally hoping for something—eternally disappointed".[24]

Even in the Middle Ages, the commonalty indulged in life pleasures often without burdening themselves with restrictions. Especially bright were the celebrations with games, merriment and jokes. But nevertheless they already were not like those in Rome. Both the West and the East felt the influence of religion during the era of the Middle Ages. If we remember Augustine Aurelius, in particular his paper titled "The City of God," we will notice that he divided the whole world into "Civitas Dei"(the City of God) and "Civitas Terrestris" (the City of men). People of "the City of God" subordinate their life to the Christian precepts and after death the life in heavens is prepared for them, thus they will go to eternity. People of the City of men, proving their names, are guided by earthly feelings, indulging in earthly pleasures and therefore will not find the eternal life, falling into inexistence.

1.2.4 The Role of Pleasure in Development of a Humanistic Paradigm

The Renaissance, representing a certain return to ancient art (here comes the name—the Renaissance), offered synthesis of the Apollonian and Dionysian cultures. The pleasure again "comes back from Heaven to Earth", in other words, is proclaimed in this world. A belief in a man, his capabilities, talent, creativity regenerates. Anthropocentrism of the Renaissance replaces the Middle Ages theo-centrism. The humanistic culture which is focusing attention on the human is developing. A human personality acquires not only the supreme value, but also integrity, and even universality. It is quite enough to remember the great representatives of the Renaissance that the above stated would become obvious. Only the name of Leonardo da Vinci seems sufficient. And there are lots of them. It is interesting that educated and gifted people were especially appreciated at that time. They were treated as saints during the Middle Ages. Was not that the reason for such a leap forward in art, philosophy and science?

What was the destiny of pleasure during that great epoch? Two papers come to mind at once: "The Divine Comedy" by Dante Alighieri and Boccaccio's "The Decameron". They are completely different and even kind of opposite though. Or "Book of songs" by Francesco Petrarch and "Gargantua and Pantagruel" by Francois Rabelais. Names of the great representatives of this remarkable epoch of spiritual liberation of a man represent themselves the whole era. They are Botticelli, Donatello, Raphael Santi, Michelangelo Buonarotti and, of course, the aforementioned Leonardo da Vinci, Giotto, Giordano Bruno, Nicholas of Cusa, Thomas More, Campanella, and many, many others. A lot of works are written about each of them and still it is possible to write hundreds of books. But to us, in this case, in the context of the problem under our interest, it is important to consider how the attitude of people towards pleasure was changing and how the role of pleasure in people's lives was changing in different epochs.

We will address to great Dante's "The Comedy" which the descendants, expressing their admiration, called "the Divine Comedy". Using a religious, common for the Middle Ages, the Christian, the Catholic plot, Dante considers evolution of mankind retrospectively, from the next world. The main character, who tried to commit suicide, during his lifetime with the permission of the Lord was taken over all circles of the hell, through the Purgatory and brought to the heaven to show that human life is not limited by this world, i.e. by life on earth. The person continues to exist in the next world, already in another, in a spiritual form. And, if he had lived improperly, terrible torments would expect him. It means that realization of karma is going on here, in spiritual life.

In the Hell, as shown in "the Comedy", deep underground, sinners are suffering: suicides, murderers, tyrants, traitors, unfaithful wives and husbands, etc. In the Purgatory, on the island, ordinary people are living after death, they are pagans who are unaware of Jesus Christ. These are simple people worshipping false gods. The island is a mountain at the top of which there is the best place of the Purgatory. Here people can realize their mistake, get cleared and come to the true God and even fly up to the Paradise. In the Paradise there are souls of the true righteous. Different in their qualities they occupy different planets. On the Moon there are souls of the nuns who were violently married and therefore did not keep a virginity vow. On Mercury there are souls of ambitious figures whose life was right. Venus is a habitat of the loveful righteous. On Mars there are souls of fighters for belief. On Jupiter there are souls of fair people. Saturn is the place for contemplators. The Sun is occupied by the shining souls of wise men, theologians and philosophers. The eighth sphere of the paradise is "the Nest of Leda" in constellation of the Gemini. Here the souls of righteous persons found a shelter. In the same constellation there is the ninth sphere—the Empyrean, where the souls of babies and the blissful are resting. From here the dazzling eternal light helping to find the supreme knowledge and truth emanates. It is "the love that moves the Sun and the luminaries"[25].

Thus, a man of the Renaissance was free in a choice of the way of life, but he had to pay for that in the next world. Therefore, it is necessary to think hundred times before indulging in the earth pleasures. Not all authors though penetrated so deeply into causation of the process of pleasure experience. Boccaccio, for example, shows the usual life of people with their earthly, sometimes even sinner pleasures. Despite a certain freedom in comparison with the Middle Ages, during the Renaissance positions of the religion were strong, rigid control of the church over people's behavior still remained. The problems arising during Leonardo da Vinci's research activity, for instance, with his medical experiences, operations which he performed over corpses, previously taken out from graves, serve good evidence to that. Only interference of a high patron in the person of the king rescued the great scientist and the artist from the inquisition trial. And what did Giordano Bruno pay for? Do you think that it was for his scientific ideas, as it is usually represented in popular literature? In fact, it was for trying to defend his personality, his beliefs, like Socrates did not put up with an attempt to destroy his dignity.

And for speaking roughly to the representatives of the court. Unfortunately, the life is often the price for retaining personality and dignity. Is it pleasure to die for the honor? It is a difficult question. But to realize that you were not frightened and, despite everything, did not go to pieces and remained yourself, is apparently pleasure, indeed.

In this regard the sculpture of David by Michelangelo Buonarotti is significant. We see a beautiful, quiet, proud, and full of dignity face of David who had to fight in a deadly and almost hopeless battle with Goliath, a one-eyed Cyclops. David, as we know, personified an image of Italy, and Goliath was the enemy trying to subdue it. The serene courage of David reflects a character of the people who had tolerated honorably all burdens of multi thousand-year history. We imagine the pleasure which David felt after the fantastic victory over the Cyclops! But the ingenious artist modeling David's figure already knew the outcome of the fight and enclosed restrained pleasure from own courage in the sculpture face.

1.2.5 Pleasure and the Triumph of Rationalistic Culture

The Apollonian culture of the Renaissance is being replaced by absolutely new Faustian culture of the Modern times which is characterized by development of science and techniques. Rationalism of this epoch changed cardinally the attitude of people towards pleasures as well. Formation and development of capitalism had made pleasure mercantile and pragmatic. The science considerably pressed the religion and art and turned them into the dominating form of the public consciousness, having practically usurped the right of explaining the world. "The knowledge is power" became the leading slogan of the epoch. The focus on knowledge, meaning power became already openly declared. Again the aspiration to physical expansion, expansion of territories is observed. The people began to divide on progressive, knowing, civilized and therefore "having the right", and all others—here possible to cite Raskolnikov's words—"the trembling creatures" who should be "cultivated".

F. Bacon's empiricism, atheistic views of the French materialists of the Age of Enlightenment finally established pragmatic and physiological attitude towards pleasures. "If the God does not exist, everything is allowed" are familiar words of Raskolnikov following Nietzsche's ideas. Pleasure from life gradually substitutes for happiness. Once again the thieves' thesis starts looming on the horizon—"We live only once!" And further comes "we should take everything from life!"

With the progress of capitalism and its transformation into imperialism in the XX century, the mass psychopathological consumption in pursuit of the endlessly modified pleasures reached its peak. The pleasure became that very button by pressing which the true human existence was cut out. A man became a manipulated puppet again. This time he was manipulated not by the politicized religion, but by owners of the pleasure industry which itself served to their narrower specific goals. Capitalists gradually and steadily were turning people into the manipulated herd. The industry of pleasure became an optimum means for this purpose. It is known that the pleasure threshold is changing all the time. A fine illustration to it is the destiny of an alcoholic or a drug addict. Although it is possible to bring as an example the lives of oligarchs, and even great politicians, such as Alexander of Macedon, Caesar, Napoleon. There is no wish to put in one row with them such a personality as Hitler but those who want can do that for us.

And once a pleasure threshold moves infinitely, a man can be gradually turned into another being. Moreover, it is possible to change him both to that, and the other side. Both up and down. But the capital, rushing upwards all the time, had chosen another vector of evolution for the mass man—down. The modern industry of pleasure is an ideal means of forming a unified flock. The New Middle Ages came back—the period which Nikolai Berdyaev wrote about.

Again the Dionysian culture but already hypertrophied sets in.

The pleasure throughout all the history was a criterion of the civilization's character. Slave dependence of a man from the surrounding nature in a primitive society was changed by slavery from people during the slaveholding period, then turned into slavery from the hypertrophied religion, then turned into slavery from science and techniques during the Modern times and, at last, had developed into slavery from money during the era of capitalism. The pleasure connived at that since it was the reason of this slavery.

What is possible to oppose to that? Only the new attitude towards pleasure. Managing it consciously in order not to become operated and manipulated. To avoid destruction of all human in a person, a new, humanistic culture is required, a new era of the power of a man over pleasures, the era which we call the New Humanism. The era of a free creative person. And in this context, N. Berdyaev's words about the sense of creativity as means of spiritual release of a personality are very handy.

The mere ability to control own pleasure will bring the person to the era of a post-human. Having risen over pleasure, a man will take up the reins of evolution and further he should choose his way: to take the way to Nietzsche's Human- God or to go towards the God-Human which the eastern philosophy spoke about, and the Russian religious philosophy (Vladimir Solovyov) called for.

We will return to this question at the end of the book, and now, at your permission, we will continue our conversation about pleasure. In the following chapter we will describe pleasures-giants of the last century. We will show the influence of the most widespread pleasures of the era of consumption on the man and society.

The attitude of a person towards pleasure is influenced by the culture which surrounds him. Moreover, pleasure throughout the history was a criterion of the civilization's character. The Dionysian culture of the ancient society was cultivating physical pleasures.

The Apollonian culture of the Ancient Greece, with its emphasis on spiritual pleasure, called the man for the harmony of body and spirit. Roman civilization returned the man to the bosom of rampant, overindulgent Dionysian culture heralded with physical pleasure.

Middle Ages returned man to Apollonian culture virtually vetoing any physical pleasure. Renaissance called the man, via Apollonian culture, to physical and spiritual pleasure.

The New Era opposed the earlier schools with Faustian culture valuing rational and pragmatic attitude to the pleasure. The era of capitalism has created an industry of pleasure, turning it into a means of manipulating people who turned into mass consumers. We need a new cultural epoch, cultivating humanity and allowing a person to be himself.

1.3 PLEASURE CHALLENGES OF THE CONSUMERISM SOCIETY

Boring century?

The XXI century, in a certain sense, might be called a century of boredom. The boredom has ascended to the throne and rules the world today. It directly depends on the quantity of news, entertainments and other interesting things happening around. Paradoxically, but boredom and entertainment generate each other. The more the boredom is, the more entertainments are around us and vice versa. Boredom is like a parasite living inside of us, it just increases from the entertainments directed against it.

A black hole in the internal space

Starting from the middle of the 20th century a black hole began to grow in the society—the existential vacuum. Emptiness, multiplied by absurdity, generating together total indifference, is very well described in the works of Albert Camus, Jean Paul, Franz Kafka, etc.

In his papers "A man in search of sense" and "Suffering from a senseless life" a fine French philosopher, psychologist Viktor Frankl reveals in detail how the sense had left the life of the majority of people, and how many people had replaced it by aspiration to wealth. In E. Fromm's words, "to have" replaced "to be"

In psychology, there are lots of different definitions of boredom, but common almost for all is an idea of boredom as a result of substitution, replacement of something what a person would like to be engaged in, by what he is actually engaged in. A person may not know what he actually wants but he knows precisely what he does not want. And at the moment when he is bored, he is engaged right in that. Most often feelings and desires are inhibited by a person, and what is serving to replace them is not interesting to him. Why some children are bored at school? It happens because their real interests lie in other things. Whereas the school sometimes without finding that out, simply replaces them with the program, without any care of its being individualized. Therefore boredom is most often a result of ignoring a person's uniqueness, his interests. Moreover, such denial could originate from himself, from other people, or from the society in general. John Eastwood, a professor of the University of York, notices that boredom is an unpleasant feeling appearing when a person feels both a desire and impossibility to be engaged in any activity bringing satisfaction.

Mostly the people with a low level of responsibility, who have not reached a serious spiritual level, are bored. They most often accuse all and everything of their own boredom. "People around are stupid, the movie is awful, the girlfriend is silly "—they are used to say being afraid to admit that it was their own choice and they, having freedom, could have changed that all. These people are so selfish and narcissistic that they are not capable to admit that they are bored first of all with themselves because in their head, more precisely in their consciousness, there is nothing that would interest them. Now we see why the industry of boredom distribution is so well-developed. The society needs such futile people who are always bored to make great money on them!

There is even a special psychological theory that people need a certain quantity of incentives so that the brain has something to process. When the stimulation is not enough, a person starts to be bored. Similar to Pavlov's dogs, is not it? Thus we are stimulated with the mass culture, turning us into a mass consumer of the mass society.

Boredom can also arise due to an internal dissonance. Each of us, whatever unique he is, passes through age crises in due time, when he doubts many seemingly known things. What is this all for if there is no sense in anything and nothing changes? The feeling of existential boredom can result from alienation of a person in this absurd world. Albert Camus perfectly showed it in his story "A Stranger". The main character was not touched by anything, even the news of his mother death, even the murder committed by him and the sentence announced to him. He is a stranger in this world. The speed of deployment of senseless events in this mad world brought him into almost somnambular condition of a person who was only nominally present in this world. To speak in J. Baudrillard's words, a person himself had turned into simulacrum. A.S. Pushkin brilliantly grasped this tendency in the XIX century and revealed it in the image of the bored Eugene Onegin, and Franz Kafka brought this image to grotesque in the character of his hero in the novel "The Process", in which boredom, indifference and misunderstanding of the happenings merged into one absurd phantasmagoria.

An experiment was conducted among office employees: they were asked about their favorite day of the week. The greater majority said it was Friday. And the most depressive day for the same people was Sunday. Paradoxically, Sunday is the most depressive day for people; Sunday is the day when the greatest number of suicides happen, Sunday is the day of bad mood, despondency, not because tomorrow people must go to work but because they do not know what to do. They are bored!

On Friday they dropped off all the week's stress, all in their own way. On Saturday they finished all the stuff which was collected during the week: shops, repair, cinema, theaters.

And Sunday is empty . . . . It is unclear, what to be engaged in.

It is that very existential emptiness, a black hole, existential vacuum—boredom.

And here starts the escape from freedom that E. Fromm wrote about. Worse than Sunday it could be only the third day of vacations. When out of habit a person tries to start working, but being on vacations he does not find where to direct his energy to. He becomes nervous, irritable, grabs his phone, starts checking e-mails, answering missed calls—generally, starts spoiling his holiday for himself, and for his soul mate.

Why does that happen? Because there is no other filling in the person except for work and between emptiness and work he, of course, chooses work.

Only the emptiness would not disappear anyway. It sits to itself quietly and waits till it starts to strangle a person like a boa.

Boredom for Sale

A person does not realize what is happening with him. He only knows that he is bored. It becomes boring for us on the fifth minute of idleness. We must constantly be occupied with something. Just like sharks, if we stop we will suffocate.

What is not important at all is the kind of occupation and the main thing is not to be left in private with oneself so as to not come across the black holes all of a sudden.

That is why we have surrounded ourselves with such abundance of news, entertainments, shocks—we hope that the moment when we will be able to distract from them won't come.

Like a person who has neglected his wound is afraid to unwind the bandage and remove the dressing to see how things are there, we are afraid to come out of storming stream of events. Events, events, events, news, reviews, forecasts, photos, calls, messages, information—all these are an escape from emptiness. We are hiding in the illusory world because we are not capable to create our own real one.

This awareness would help us to beat boredom if it were not a source of incredible income. Boredom brings loads of money, being the most valuable resource, more kicking than gas which will run out soon, while the boredom will not, and judging by the trend, will only increase.

We noted earlier that pleasure appears when tension is removed. Physiologically it is provided with dopamine. When the organism gets rid of tension, a person feels pleasure. While boredom is the chief supplier of tension in our society and will remain that for many years. People very quickly become bored and they are ready then to be engaged in anything only not to suffer from boredom.

Unfortunately there are very few researches on this topic, but we presume that boredom provides an opportunity to flourish for the spheres which are bringing an income in trillions of dollars. This is not only the sphere of entertainment, not only movies, restaurants, bars, theaters, museums, exhibitions. All social networks, all shops, even car showrooms and banks work for boredom. As soon as it becomes boring for a person, he wants to entertain himself. Games, work, purchases, communication will fit for entertainment. What is required to make the economy of the country grow? To multiply boredom! So that people rush to dull it by a market exchange: money in exchange for freedom from boredom.

Oil Will End, Boredom Will Not

It is an ideal strategy of development: non-endurance of boredom will grow the stronger, the more you take yourself away from it. Having lived 3 days as a Jedi from the star wars, fighting with the aliens and extricating an intergalactic plot, it would be rather difficult to return to work of an ordinary manager. It would seem awfully boring. Probably, in the same measure as a farmer's life in the village would seem for a common manager who got used to intrigues in the office, to jokes, to lunches, to defense of projects.

Boredom has no limits, it can be raised and raised, and people will more and more frequently run away from it at least to do shopping.

Some people call it a plot. However, we should proceed from logics. And if we know that water bends around obstacles in its way, and does not start flowing back, we can easily foresee where it will turn. And so now we observe how a small stream called "world marketing" started beating from the ground, its age is only 70–90 years. During this time we have understood what it is.

Let us take some steps forward on the way of the stream to where it has not reached yet and we try to foresee how its course will lay down. We will lay out a garden there so that by the time when watering is required, the water would come here.

It is not the plot, it is the market. And if we are compelled to lay out gardens, it is better to do that along the stream.

It is better to earn money where it already is. Boredom is an underestimated potential. A man is still over liberated. And if a person is underloaded, someone is losing money. It is the time to start selling portable devices for stimulation of separate parts of the brain. For example, you put on a hat, chose "light sadness" in a catalog, entered an appropriate code like in a karaoke system, and the hat starts stimulating with current, the zone of your brain which causes light sadness.

You have wished—romantic mood—you received,

You have wished—sexual excitement—here you are pleased!

It is important to understand the idea: the pleasure from getting rid of boredom is the strongest motivator and its relevance will only grow because a man plunges more and more into dependence on external influence and new information.

Those things which used to be normal to him, in 20 years will seem devilishly boring. Thus controlling pleasure one can control social evolution. Let alone the class struggle!

1.3.1 Human Communication as Luxury

Social Networks in the Blend Pool

Usually, when people start discussing communication and its role in the modern society, they cannot avoid speaking of social networks. It is one of the most discussed marketing topics of the last decade—the nets have passed through so many execrations, so many accusations. They are accused of turning people into sociopaths, of reducing men's libido and breaking marriages, and of causing addiction, that ingenious Facebook programmers are getting the world hooked on a needle of information consumption forming addiction to that. Quite regularly articles appear saying how dangerous social nets are for children, how many perversions could be found there, how the principle of anonymity spoils people and so on and on and on.

We should underline that communication is always bilateral feedback, and giving a "like" to somebody's photo is not an example of communication.

Besides the fact that communication in the Internet does not bear that psychotherapeutic power than personal communications do, it does not bring the same volume of pleasure as a personal contact does. We consume only 15% percent of information through words, the rest we get through non-verbal means.

Communication as Food

Communication is the strongest of pleasures. Eric Berne said that the children deprived of parent embraces were more often ill and their mortality was increasing." It is possible to assume,—the psychologist wrote,—that there is a biological chain leading up from emotional and sensory deprivation through apathy to degenerative changes and death. To this extent a feeling of sensory hunger should be considered the major condition for the life of a human body, in fact as well as a feeling of food hunger".

Communication with friends and relatives he called psychological embraces, considering that they are not less important for health, by the way, not only psychological, but also physical health, than healthy food and physical culture.

Why do we get pleasure from communication? Why do even the most closed introverts after a week-long domesticity aspire to go out? They want to listen to voices, to look at people and to show themselves as well. Why is imprisonment in a solitary confinement the strictest of punishment measures?

A man is a social animal and one of the first things that he learned for survival was communications with congeners. Loneliness is a luxury which we are able to afford during the era of excesses.

Loss of Pleasure

A great number of people in Metropolitan have led to the emergence of a desire to cloister. Tiredness from communications has led to its devaluation. People started neglecting communication, avoiding it. Especially during the last ten years, since not only the number of people increased, but also the number of communications with them. Earlier "the world of an individual" consisted of 40 people, including friends, relatives, colleagues, neighbors. Today 700 people are in the friend list.

Communication became excessive. Should something of this kind happen in the primitive times, then our reflex to discharge dopamine from communication wouldn't develop. Our brain wouldn't remember it as useful and vital experience. On the contrary we surely would develop a vomiting reflex from an extra greeting.

Instead of unconscious expectation of pleasure which we experience during acquaintance or communication with already a familiar person, we would start itching, or we would have a head ache.

Formerly we used to impart extremely important knowledge: where berries might be eaten and where a neighbor got poisoned by them, where a tiger's cave is and where another tribe lives, which it is better to keep away from.

Our brain discharges dopamine to fix this knowledge and as it often happens to instincts, the world has changed, and they have not.

We continue to expect pleasure from communication with people, but, of course, we receive less and less usefulness from it.

No wonder we have ceased to derive pleasure from communication.

To return communication value. To return pleasure

The pleasure from communication is now exotic, we remember it when we meet an old friend who we have not seen for half a year, or parents, or the beloved lady when we come back from a long business trip.

Having lost the great pleasure from communication, having passed it through our fingers, people complain that their life is boring and poor.

And all these happen in the times when in a phone of almost everyone there are thousands of people, ready to communicate, from all over the world. It is a high time to start choosing who to communicate with. We have to return value to communication up to that primitive level when each contact could teach a man something new, something useful and even helpful to survive.

"10 Friends" Experiment

Social and technological progress have devaluated communication, and now responsibility for raising its quality is exclusively on the personality.

Let's hold an experiment which is called "10 friends". The core of it is that you are allowed to communicate with only 10 people within the next week. You can't get in contact with others. You are forbidden to answer calls and to have any conversations . . . 10 people are not so few. It is not 3after all!

You should select 10 people for communication in the next 7 days.

Write them down straight here.

1. ________________
2. ________________
3. ________________
4. ________________
5. ________________
6. ________________
7. ________________
8. ________________
9. ________________
10. ________________

Let us guess:

1. Husband/wife
2. Mother/father

3. Brother/sister
4. Daughter/son
5. Friend
6. Boss
7. Colleague 1
8. Colleague 2
9. Colleague 3
10. Any guy in reserve, just in case.

Bet you had to rack your brains on the last 2–3 lines.

Now there is one more request. Opposite to everyone lower than the 4-th point write down an answer to the question:

What useful information might this person tell you?

I hope you will have an answer.

When we held this experiment in a lecture hall, a major half of the students did not cope with the task.

Now we suggest you close the book and return to reading with the results of the week. See you!

A week has passed and you have got the game results.

Obviously this is not true. You have continued reading, only a minute passed. And you have hardly dared to run the experiment.

Only the bravest ones are capable to pass the experiment of “10 friends”. Hope that you are among them. You have found the strength to overcome your unwillingness and have opened for yourself a new world overflowed with pleasure from communication.

A week with the 10 closest people is not such a great payment for that, is it?

Write to us at arsdallan@arsdallan.ru how your 7 days with “10 friends” passed and what you felt when the experiment was over.

"100 Phrases" Game

After you are through with the “10 friends”, you can play a new game—”100 phrases”. The rules become more complicated, the number of words which you can use is limited now. Not more than 100 sentences per week.

But you can communicate with anyone via Emails, SMS, Facebook, Skype and other communication channels also count.

Do you think 100 sentences are too few?

Go on and check, live one day with 14 phrases.

It is not that difficult.

Having learned to communicate with those who are important to you and for what is necessary, 14 phrases is quite enough not to feel embarrassed.

After these experiments, it becomes clear how we are using the most valuable of gifts—the word.

We are blowing it off.

It is not surprising that the pleasure from such a use becomes smaller and smaller. It is clear why the number of sociopaths is growing.[26]

It will be only worse further, unfortunately.

Without personal responsibility for pleasure, a person will not only be imprisoned by it, but also will start experiencing pleasures less and less often.

1.3.2 Game-mania

Invited experts:

Roman Mandrik, CEO, Active company—the company developing slot machines

Mikhail Safran, founder of Questomania, Israel

In the XX century games from the sphere of entertainment and training entered practically all areas of the public relations. With the advent of computers, games turned into a separate industry influencing mentality of people not less than movies and television[27].

If earlier video games involved only teenagers, now with the development of technology they became more interesting for adults to play as well. 30 percent of players of video games are in the age of 18–30 years.

Today the market of corporate games promptly grows[28]. Modern games have a set of new functions. For example, such companies as Skiliks help to determine an administrative potential of a manager. Many organizations use a Skiliks game as one of the interview stages. The candidate passes a 2–3 hour game with deep immersion in a real working environment with management tasks and situations of making administrative decisions.

Games, like Virtonomica allow to learn how to develop own business. In this game a user has an absolute freedom of choice. He receives an initial capital and is free to develop his company in any direction. Only he defines the purposes, strategy and tactics, there are no obligatory “scenarios”. The game process represents a series of administrative decisions. The game is conducted not only and not so much with the computer, as with thousands of other players—competitors and partners.

Something similar is done also by Storewars company, but it only has narrowed the segment to a retail. Players get used to a role of the director of a supermarket network and get deep understanding of interaction between the producer, retailer and consumer.

Games help in eliminating psychological difficulties and treating mental diseases. Thus, the scientists of the Cambridge University developed a computer game helping to improve the episodic memory of patients with schizophrenia. The game which received the name "Wizard" is to help the patients to cope with daily vital tasks and work. The first results of using such a method of treatment are published in the Philosophical Transactions of the Royal Society magazine.

Doctor Randy Kulman, from the "Learning Works for Kids" company specializing in developing games for children claims that the game Minecraft in which, as we know, it is required to construct buildings, helps children with autism to improve their ability to interact.

In recent years, a blast wave of quest games has rolled all over the world. In Russia, this market grew from 0 to 1.5 billion rubles in 2013–2014.

These are 200 companies, 950 various quest games, extra 450 new locations are under construction for input in 2015. Moscow has outrun the whole world by concentration of quest games. Earlier Budapest was considered the capital of quest games, but its 40 rooms for games performance is nothing against 600 Moscow sites.

Quest games have become more and more complicated and psychological. At the time of writing this book, plot quests or quests-reconstructions were gaining popularity in Moscow, Participants of these games reconstruct palace plots or arrangements of revolution. The moderator formulates a certain role task to each participant depending on the latter's psycho type. Performing this role the player acts as the gear starting the mechanism of a great plot which should finally lead to the end known only by the moderator.

Often scenarios of such quest games are written by professional psychologists, and professional theater actors or stuntmen are used to direct the actions to the necessary course.

Gamification is a growing trend.

We will learn more and more information playing. For example, already today it is possible to come across a game modeling family scenes called "Academy of parental sciences." A player performs a role of a parent and searches for correct behavior models in complicated family situations.

Among the game levels there are such as a dispute concerning who and how should admonish their teenage daughter and how to react to children's rudeness.

There are games which help to learn how to give first aid or, for example, training to drive safely. So the insurance company MSK released a simulator training drivers how to behave in twenty two situations which cause the lion's share of road accidents. It is interesting that in each of these situations a driver can find himself without breaking any traffic regulations.

In the future, games will be improved, and dependence on them will only increase. No wonder that gamification has seized the minds of marketing specialists. A case is known where a museum seeking to increase the number of visitors started a competition: it promised a tidy sum to the one who will be able to steal a picture of a famous artist costing them several millions. Can we say that after the announcement people flooded the museum halls?

There are theories appearing on how to create whole business structures with game mechanics. One of such advanced concepts is holocracy.

Holocracy is an arrangement of a company which denies a need of the long-held structure, especially the hierarchical one.

Instead of positions there are roles. Instead of departments there are circles. Decisions are made together during meetings. Everyone has a veto right. Both roles and circles often change so that people don't get used to their functions.

The concept gains popularity, despite its obvious minuses. The holocratic structure was already introduced by ZAPPOS online shop, by MEDIUM blogging platform and some other famous brands.

We won't stop for a long time on business gamification. It is an extensive subject to which a set of useful books is devoted. It is worth special studying which is expedient to begin with Kevin Werbach, professor of law and business ethics at the University of Pennsylvania, namely with his work " For the Win: How Game Thinking Can Revolutionize Your Business ".

What attracts us so much in games?

The point is that any game is set up on "a hook principle" based on neurophysiological peculiarities of information perception.

It is known that we perceive a game win as an encouragement.

Having won, a person achieves the objective, thereby receives his portion of pleasure. The brain encourages the player with a discharge of dopamine and oxytocin.

The desire to get more motivates a person to continue the game.

The more difficult the win was, i.e., the more effort it took, the more neuromediators are being discharged. After all, greater pleasure is required for "covering" the expenses.

Then why does not a man stop playing after a loss?

The matter is that our brain perceives a loss in a game as a training level.

It fixes the negative experience as a one more step towards knowledge. Having lost, a person considers that he had learned the incorrect course, deleted one from the list of unsuccessful strategies, thereby came closer to realization of a victorious one.

Thus, with each loss, the brain also encourages a person, stimulating memorization.

How is transition to a new level perceived?

The brain perceives it like training as well.

Transition to a new level is a positive support for storing the victorious strategy.

Progress from one level to another is estimated as improvement of skills.

Thus, in a game there is no element causing rejection. Everything in it—defeat, and progress, and a victory promise pleasure and force a person to continue playing.

The Reason of Dependence on Gambling.

They say that conviction of weaknesses is already half a victory. Therefore, let us consider why gambling causes a habit. All the point is in irregular confirmation.

The prize comes unexpectedly. Here is the entire secret.

Paradoxically, but scientists claim that less people would go to a casino if the prize was guaranteed, but its size would be smaller. The guaranteed lottery with a small prize which is hardly exceeding the ticket cost is obviously a failure. And to win 100, and even 1000 times more, than the bet—here is a real temptation, especially if one had been a witness of something like that already.

Changeable confirmation stimulates discharge of a large amount of dopamine which strengthens expectation of a prize.

We will have a simple mental experiment.

You have an appointment with a significant mister, say, the boss of your boss. How would your behavior differ if in the first case the big boss warns you of the appointment delay and in the second case when the time has come and he would not appear?

Most probably, in the second case, you will constantly look back, whether he had come into the cafe. You will peer into every car passing by.

Same with a prize, thanks to dopamine we expect it, anticipating pleasure every second.

A Prophylactic Role of Games

It is interesting that many people blame computer video games for abundance of violence and even declare that those very games become the reason behind the aggressive behavior of teenagers. Television demonstrates awful news on how a school student had rushed into a classroom and shot everyone he met on his way. And his camouflage precisely replicated the clothes of a game character. Now more details.

On April 26, 2002 Robert Steinhäuser killed 17 and wounded 7 people in Gutenberg-gymnasium, the city of Erfurt, Germany. Robert neglected schoolwork could not get on with teachers. 14 of 17 killed were teachers. After speaking with the witnesses it became clear in particular that the teenager had been playing in Counter-Strike. The authoritative newspaper Frankfurter Allgemeine Zeitung had published an article "Programs for a Slaughter" in which it was written: "the murderer was trained by computer games".

And you won't find Quake III, for example, in any shop in Germany. Such games are forbidden by the law.

In 2004 it was reported in Great Britain that a 14-year-old teenager Stefan Pakeerah was cruelly killed by his friend, a 17-year-old Warren Leblanc in February of that year in the city of Leicester. Leblanc had enticed Pakeerah into a local park where he brutally beat and killed the latter. In court the accused guy declared that he was "zonked" by the game Manhunt. Although the court of the city of Leicester considered that Leblanc had committed murder for the purpose of a robbery, the mother of the killed teenager, Gizel Pakeerah, believes that computer games were the reason for that.

Multiple charges of games in stimulation of cruel behavior make game developers curtail their releases. Such hits as Mortal Combat and GTA are forbidden in many countries.

However, the data from a recent research of Professor Talmadge Wright and his colleague Paul Breidenbach from Loyola's university in Chicago refute this opinion. On the contrary, he believes that games help to build up relations in the usual life and teach effective team work. Tough computer games rather discharge the mental energy which is saved up during the aggressive self-affirmation of teenagers in the usual life. Thus the violent scenes in the games do not influence upon the subsequent cruel behavior of teenagers.

Playing video games can even increase children's learning ability, strengthen their mental health and improve their social skills, as it is written in a survey research about the positive effect of video games; this research is published by the American psychological association. The great majority of the playing teenagers do not show any cruelty, and even, on the contrary, their behavior becomes more reserved in comparison with the previous years, deprived of virtual violence.

Scientists explain that there is a thirst for cruelty in any person thus we like horror films, we cannot turn away our head from a car accident although we are trying not to look there with all our strengths. A need for cruelty is one of the primitive instincts. Observing acts of cruelty on a ring or in a game activates mirror neurons in our brain, which are responsible for experience of sensual emotions. In other words, a person himself does not live through this moment, but, observing others' emotions, he feels the same.

For example, a soccer fan for certain, feels pain in the same place, probably even touches it, when he sees where the ball released by the real cannon—Roberto Carlos, for instance, hits a player standing in the wall.

He is wincing, feeling similar emotions, like the player in the ball park.

So, scientists have proved that the opportunity to satisfy the need for cruelty by computer games does not increase aggression in teenagers, it even reduces it.

How Not to Get into the Game Dependence

The role of games grows in our life, and its growth will proceed.

Therefore, it is important to remind ourselves of what makes us continue the game.

In any game, our desire to play is caused not by the prize, but by the expectation of pleasure from it.

In order not to get into a game loop, it is necessary to define at once the rule for yourself: the prize has no value if you do not gain any useful skills or knowledge for yourself during the game.

The prize might attract to itself like a diamond at the sunset, might promise a great benefit and intimate secrets of being, but it is not worth a pin if you didn't surpass yourself for a jot on the way to it.

In such a context a super prize in a "useful" game does not exist. One should choose only those games in which encouragement is spread by a thin coat all over the game field.

By encouragement we mean not the game pleasure, but a part of that purpose which the player moves to.

Choose those games which are more similar to reading a book. As a result of the victory you will read the entire book up to the end. But if the game stops on the halfway, you will learn only a half of the book.

Avoid those games which are like a soccer championship, where each new level gives an illusion of approaching towards a super cup which can be obtained only by winning the final match. If you are eliminated earlier you get nothing, nil.

Such games use kluges of the physiological brain, forcing one to get into a pleasure loop.

The brain mistakenly takes progressing to a new level for real training and stimulates a person by a desire.

It is important to distinguish between what does not allow us to stop playing: an illusion of training or acquisition of a really important skill.

To Use Games for Benefit

Knowing the mechanism by which games take us on a hook, it is possible to create our own games. We mean not programming, but self-development.

Imagine a typical situation: in a company of friends it seems to the spouse that his wife pays more attention to one of his friends, than to him. He starts getting angry and pokes the poor thing on every occasion.

Is it familiar to you? If yes, then I am sorry, but do not be upset, a game will help to save your relations.

Try to perceive each of such meetings as the next level, which you can pass only if the number of your gibes is no more than three for the whole evening. Take a clicker with you—a remarkable mechanical thing allowing you to count anything. One press on a lever is one point. But no, you will not count the gibes which were said, believe me, your soul mate will do that for you. You will count those gibes which were kept in your mouth.

Stake on. Let's say today I will keep 34 acrid comments to myself, my bet—I will buy a present for myself.

If the bet had played—my congratulations!

Levels can be complicated, figures and criteria of measurements can be changed, but one point has to be stable—honesty. If you really want to change yourself, you cannot lie to yourself. Just in case I remind that half-lie and concealment are lies too.

Therefore write about the rules on a paper beforehand and try not to break them.

After all nobody except you really needs that.

Games can teach. But games can also suppress, promising the easy and available pleasure.

One of our students admitted once: "Games do not make me empty, they fill the emptiness". It was a terrible confession.

Games were not created as the main occupation of a person, nor should they take any place in his spiritual space. But unfortunately, weakness for easy pleasure leads the situation to the opposite. We speak not only about computer games, but also about social ones. In this regard Johan Huizinga's work "Homo Ludens or Man the player" is interesting. He represents all human culture as a game giving pleasure to a man[29].

The people who got used to the game mechanics introduce it to other aspects of life as well. Thus for the last decade a game-playing relation to information has formed when from one update to another people live in anticipation of unconscious pleasure. We will talk right about pleasure from information in the following chapter.

1.3.3 The Growing Informational Dependence on Social Networks

A Life in the Phone

An average modern manager, say, a department head in a large company, surely, reads books with his phone in hands (or directly in the phone) so that, God forbids, not to miss an important message, an E-mail, a post, oil rates, dollar exchange rates or news from different parts of the globe. He is constantly in an expectation state of a message from his girlfriend, a friend, family . . . [30].

The Body Is Melting

A lot is written about absorption of modern people into their phones and into their info stream. However, we would like to emphasize that not only our mentality but also our bodies are being transformed due to that. They are degrading, becoming less and less adapted for the life in the ambient environment. It is a fact. Employees of large corporations answering mails and SMSs, rustling with papers and puffing over "Power Point" become weaker and weaker. For many people an iPad is already heavy, an iPad mini is required.

We began to live longer—it is true, but our hands have become thinner, shoulders have narrowed, the breast is disappearing at all while sides and hips, on the contrary, confidently present themselves.

An average man weighs 80–90 kg, but his strength will hardly be enough to hang on his hand for more than two seconds. A human body is obviously weakening.

If this trend proceeds, people will become so fragile that any street dog will be able to bite in half a foot of an adult man. Many people have heard of Charla Nash's tragedy which happened in February, 2009 in Stamford, Connecticut. Charla had arrived to help her friend Sandra Herold, who couldn't force Travis, a chimpanzee belonging to her, into the house. The animal fell into fury, attacked Charla and tore off her nose, lips, eyes and hands.

Is physical weakness of a modern man a defect of genetics or a result of the social adaptation? It is known that ancient people were not so coddled as residents of the modern metropolis. And Spartans would hardly allow a monkey to tear off their noses. The environment does not require physical strength from a man today. Just like the animals which had gone to live in caves, began to give blind offspring, people ceased to give genetically the physical strength and endurance, which seemingly became not necessary, to their children.

It is not a secret that we live in the world built only for people. The unprecedented urbanization can even cause disappearance of a human need for walking in the future. Already today an average man passes no more than 1 km a day[31]. And as it is known: if there is no need, the ability vanishes. This is the law of nature.

The environment of human inhabitation turns more and more from natural into informational. Today, if a citizen wants to find out about the weather, he would rather look for the forecast in his phone, than out of the window. Perhaps, it is a natural tendency of the Homo sapiens development: to fall into stress on the fourth minute without his phone, but to overcome calmly 20 thousand km from one end of the planet to another; feeling no discomfort, getting into a plane in Moscow and leaving it in Los-Angeles. It means that our planet is no longer that blue ball which Yu. Gagarin was so delighted at. Our planet is terabytes of information. It is the space of sounds, pictures, texts encoded into media. Very soon people will learn to encode both smells and tactile feelings; bio implants capable to deliver true emotions will be developed.

Press a button and it becomes funny for a person, click and he becomes afraid.

All this is going to take place. People are informational beings and information is our habitat.

The authors of innocent commercials which promote digital detox elicit a kind smile. Do you remember those sentimental shots of a young couple lying in a bed on their backs with their faces burrowed in their smart phones? Yes, everything is like that. It is an evolution trend.

People condemning the technical-informational progress remind those who are panting for their long gone childhood. Certainly, the informational world will further reconstruct the real one, though "real" is an improper word, after all, the new world is not less real, it would be correct to say "natural".

Today, the true pleasure can be obtained by a person not so much from communication with a friend, as from the sight of the latter's avatar in the phone, the avatar which has turned into a symbol of pleasure which was previously obtained from their hot correspondence in social nets. The pleasure which used to be many times greater, than a personal meeting could provide. Pleasure from a date of lovers is not an exception, although, apparently, it should be the last to pass from the natural world into the informational one.

Temptation of Information

What bribes a person so much in this information world?

Besides the ease of access, it is its infinity.

People constantly find something that they have not seen before.

Scrolling the newsfeed in Facebook, they constantly see the updated posts: something new, again something new and so on endlessly. People are getting hooked on the strongest dopamine diet.

In fact, they don't consume anything else, but a huge desire to learn what is there else left.

An excellent aphorism about a man clicking channels is known.

"It is not important to a man to know what is on TV, it is important to him to know what else is on TV".

More and a little bit more again, and each time people think that they will finally find what they are looking for. But we are not looking for anything, we are just eager to continue searching.

Having invented the infinite tape, Stewart Batterfild and Caterina Fake, authors of the Flickr project, hit the jack pot.

But we should pay tribute to those who had really introduced it first.

The brothers Lumiere did. It was them who had invented the changing pictures and put billions of people in front of a box in hope that in a second they would see something interesting.

While their consciousness was being deceived by an illusion of something interesting, the brain was deriving pleasure from something new. And pictures kept on changing. New, and new, and new.

1.3.4 Codependence

We, frankly speaking, have no dependence on information; we have dependence on news.

To live a week out of the information stream—this is the real torture.

This is the real journey.

You can stay in the same apartment and even not rise from a sofa but if you leave your information stream—you will start a journey that very hour.

And vice versa, you can go to a world cruise but if the regime of the Internet visits is kept—you remain on your sofa.

We are like turtles—our lodge is always with us. Only it is not a shell on the back, but a set of gigabytes in our pocket.

We derive pleasure from news because we consider it useful.

For millions of years of evolution the brain got used to consider that all new is useful. It is such naivety today. Even investment managers, who really need to be aware of all news, try to check news according to a special schedule—not oftener than once a day. Nassim Taleb in his well-known book “the Black Swan” confessed that after the purchase of an investment portfolio didn’t open news reports about the company within half a year, it helped him to protect himself from premature decisions.

We easily confuse a need to receive news (including messages in Facebook and emails) with expectation of pleasure. It seems to us that if we do not check information now, we won’t get benefits and thus pleasures—and therefore we will suffer.

In this case the loss is not the action; on the contrary it is inaction.

It concerns everything where the itch from lack of action appears—smoking, having meals after six, and checking news in particular. It seems to people that the efforts made for overcoming the desire to check mails won’t be reimbursed since something very important will be missed.

The people who decided to reduce the time for consumption of useless information can follow only one advice: before reaching out your phone, write on a paper—WHY you want to check it. WHAT exactly you want to find there.

If you have no answer, it is better to put the phone aside and to concentrate on current things. You only have to put up with the fact that you will have to live one more hour in the world which has not been updated.

Marketing and News

Marketing specialists are well aware about the dependence of people on news. They also perfectly know the channels of obtaining information by users. Therefore, having covered their commercial interests with a mask of humanity, they go to the grass roots. If it is an insurance company, it is enough for it to announce about the strangest and most ridiculous insurance policy, and probably even sell fan (waste) insurance policies via Facebook. Like Alpha Insurance did, distributing insurance policies "from a doomsday" which more than 40 thousand people obtained by the way.

Banks can tell about interesting ceremonies in exotic countries where it is possible to go, having saved up miles by cards; food shops tempt with pictures of reduced prices; fashion brands don't hesitate to discuss dresses of celebrities and many other things.

All this is pleasant to consumers. But there are things from which they simply lose their heads.

Stories and Storytelling

People adore stories, like to listen to them, like to retell them. Having heard an interesting story we want to share it promptly and if a friend isn't nearby, we are itching. Like the blonde from the movie "Ivan Vasilievich Changes Profession" who was bragging of the trip to Gagra, we want at once to share with someone.

Neurobiologists reveal evolutionary roots of our love to stories. It is known that long time before the appearance of writing people conveyed information from mouth to mouth. Information acquired heroes, a plot and interesting details. For example, a message that dogberries were poisonous and could not be eaten could appear as a story about a forester who came once during fox hunting into a thicket where bushes similar to currant grew. They were bestrewed with beautiful bright red berries. And since he was unlucky to catch any fox for a week, he satisfied his hunger with the berries. He had gathered them and brought to the village. He treated his wife; she cooked a salad for kids with them. In the evening they all went to bed and in the morning none of them woke up. And so they remained lying in their bear-clothes, in the same pose in which they had lain down. Here is the terrible story. Don't eat dog berries!

Understanding the reason, the consequence and the life situation in which an action took place, our ancestors adopted information better. It is also difficult for modern people to remember incoherent facts, for example, statistical information. While an interesting story is remembered in every detail. All remember how the princess Diana died, but not everyone knows the number of people dying annually in road accidents all over the world. Moreover, from a narrated story people easily draw the arising conclusions, but aren't always capable to do so upon obtaining information in the form of a set of dry facts.

It is one more feature of human thinking which is successfully used in marketing. Scientists called it "distortion of a narrative". Kahneman, Ariely, and many other theorists of the behavioral economics many times attracted public attention to this property of the human brain. Marketing specialists created a new advertising discipline on its basis—storytelling, the most famous adherents of which include such authors as Annette Simmons, John Trub, and Robert McKee.

People easily draw conclusions from the private, but it isn't always possible to conclude from the general. It means that it is easier for us to draw an inductive conclusion rather than a deductive one. A heap of facts and statistical data tell us less, than one entertaining story from the life of a person like us.

All the matter is that people do not trust in sense, but do trust in feelings.

Looking at the facts, people do not feel anything and therefore cannot believe them. As Professor of neuroscience Antonio Damasio said: "A man is a feeling machine which is thinking".

When we hear a story, emotions, feelings arise in us. They literally push us to subsequent reflections and form our conclusions.

Of course, marketing specialists know it. Therefore more and more advertising is being based on stories. Celebrities or an invented hero might be telling them, it can be a fascinating legend or a reference of an honest client. But anyway, if a marketing specialist knows the science, it will be a narration complying with the laws of storytelling.

Born for Gossips

People are gossipers by their nature.

The human brain rewards a person for information transfer. This way of stimulating the development of social communications is the most important of the factors which had raised a man from a primitive step of development.

Until the era of excesses has set in, the ability to transfer information was being encouraged justifiably. Nevertheless a lot of things have changed with the growth of information amount. Not all the information is transferrable anymore. The public morals appeared. It constrained the unlimited need for pleasure, forcing out the excessive garrulity into the sin area. Gossips, rumors, discussing behind one's back—everything became unallowable in the decent society.

However, as we know, interdictions hardly withdraw pleasure; on the contrary they are more likely to increase it. A person, having carried the pleasure from stories including obscene ones, through all the history and having lived till today, has got into the most real information paradise. There is the Internet and social networks. It became possible to share stories, remaining in a mask of anonymity. And even more—to share it, to blow the trumpets all over the world! After all the number of listeners of an ordinary Muscovite in 2015 is more than population of an average village in the 19th century.

The morals have been transformed.

Today, it is unclear what is good, and what is bad if we speak about likes, reposts and podcasts. Thus, we are again left face to face with the pleasure from stories. How many of them are around! Unfortunately, the more rashly we give in to desire, the more often we feel disappointment instead of pleasure.

The world full of desires is likely to turn into the life full of guilt.

Information Ecology

Some time ago ancestors of people wandered in fields and meadows searching for the places suitable for life.

Now we have to search for our information environment, choosing megabytes of the most useful information stimulating our development. Environmental friendliness of our activity today consists in the care for the surrounding information environment. Unlike the natural world, oil or chemical plants, exhaust gases and other emissions poisoning air and the soil aren't frightful to us in the information ecology. No matter how people resist, participate in volunteer clean up days, throw out batteries in a special container and plant trees, all the same they feel a harmful effect of these giants. But in the information world everything is different. Here a man can fully control the environment. He can let in only the information which does not poison the climate and does not break the balance.

The quality of the information environment depends only on our ability to know what we really want, and ability to derive pleasure from the result of our actions. No matter whether these are fine landscapes in which information proceeding from us many times surpasses the arriving one, or it is a noisy dirtied turmoil, with garbage of earlier consumed information. Therefore it is important to be able to derive pleasure from information, the true pleasure from the result of consumption, and not to be conducted by a dopamine promise, consuming "information popcorn" in gigabytes.

As always, the right choice is the hardest. To form own information space, having refused a mainstream, means to go counter with the dominating idea of normality. Unfortunately, for nonconformists, neurophysiologists found out that they deprive themselves not only of public support, but even of encouragement from their own brain.

1.3.5 Usefulness as a Program of Encouragement

They say: "Let the one who can be himself be nobody else!" But only who can be himself now? Today to be and to remain yourself is a big luxury. It is not that everyone could do. There is a trend. That is, what you should be. 10–15% of elite representatives protect it and do not allow anybody to interfere. The remaining 85% of the society are passive followers of the trend who themselves provide its existence.

There are another 5% of the society members who do not give in to the trend—black sheep. They are divided into those who want, but can't get into the trend and those who simply do not want to be such principally, who can't go against their hearts.

What is happening in the soul of a person and why does he so easily forget about his "being good"? The answer to this question is given by neurobiologists. And again it is connected with pleasure.

Pleasure from Social Confirmation

It gives us pleasure to give pleasure to others.

A teenager with his deviant behavior wants to show how brave he is, how risky, so that to deserve respect from his equals, so that they like him. Girls turn into yes-girls because they want to be liked by guys. Eighty five percent majority wants to correspond to the trend because they like to be liked by others.

To bring pleasure to the society by means of the behavior appropriate in this society is one of the strongest sources of pleasure.

It is significant to notice a point of view of a young Libyan on nonconformists, i.e., about people who do not look like all, who put on provocatively extravagant clothes: wearing mohawks, color hair, piercing and so on.

When I buy a sweater and look at myself in the mirror in a fitting room,—he noticed,—then first of all I think whether it suits specifically me, my figure, my temperament and mood.

But then I surely imagine whether this sweater could break emotional comfort of the people around, whether it will annoy them. It is important to me that my clothes and appearance are pleasant to an eye of people and do not stress them. This is what every Libyan thinks".

In the eastern culture people feel the highest pleasure from social confirmation and approval. The centuries-old communal way of life is reflected even in a shopping manner.

In Russia there is no such worship to the surrounding, but nevertheless dependence on pleasure derived from compliance to public standards is huge.

Fashion, status, study, career, success—all these are manifestations of our aspiration to compliance.

Non-conformism as a Mistake

Trends can change, but the structure of the society remains unchangeable: a small part of people defines the trend, the majority supports it, and another small group falls out of the trend at all for various reasons.

From the neurophysiological side, to have an opinion different from the majority's one is almost the same as to be mistaken.

An interesting report on this subject was made by Vasily Klucharev, an associate professor of faculty of psychology at the University of Basel (Switzerland), a leading expert in the neurobiological bases of social influence and in neuroeconomics. He told about an experiment where participants were invited into a room with the people instigated in advance and there were three black cubes put on a table. The participants were asked of the cubes' color. All answered correctly—black.

Along with that the experiment conductors measured the brain activity by an electroencephalograph. At the moment when the participants were asked for the first time, the sensors showed that people were absolutely confident in their answer.

But as soon as the false participants had answered in chorus that the cubes were white, the sensor showed that the zone of the brain responsible for recognition of a mistake had become more active.

And although all the participants were standing on their own, nobody was so inspired as to start seeing black as white[32] . However a program recognizing a mistake was activated in the brain.

The brain remembered this experience as incorrect and did not encourage the organism by the dopamine discharge. In other words, when people go against the majority, their brain always perceives it as a mistake. No matter what it is, length of lines, color of figures or presidential elections for the next term.

Making a decision with social conformism, i.e., agreeing with the majority, people get a huge amount of dopamine, thus the brain lets them know that everything was made correctly. Even if a person has jumped off a bridge[33].

Conformism as a Way of Survival

People are conformists on the biological level. Since the times of saber-toothed tigers it became a custom: the one survives who is in the herd. But the situation has changed radically. People are dying in multitudes nowadays.

Up to 70 thousand drug addicts die annually in Russia[34].

It is the highest rate in the world, higher than in Africa, Afghanistan and elsewhere.

In road accidents which traditionally hold the first place of mortality, 20–30 thousand people die annually in Russia.

4800 soldiers died in Iraq, 14 453 people—in Afghanistan, 25 000—in Chechnya.

According to the UN office on drugs and crime, the vast majority among drug addicts is the youth: 20% are school students, 60% are young people from 16 to 30 years old, 20%—people older than 30;

When the reason for the use of drugs is concerned, the pleasure pales into insignificance. People wouldn't use drugs if it was denied by their circle of contacts.

In psychology two forms of conformism are known—informational and normative. In the first case people concede to the opinion of others, groups, and in the second case they obey the majority because they want to be pleasant to them, to be exact, don't want to be derelicts.

However, exactly because of drugs those become derelicts by the age of 25 who in their 13–15 years were the life and soul of the party and romantic school revolutionaries.

Pleasure Dualism

The pleasure can play a dirty trick with people; being an unstable nuclear combination it is both capable to give energy for life and to destroy.

The pleasure was given to a man for learning and surviving during the era when he, seemingly, had no chances in fighting with the wild nature.

But now it takes away the learning opportunity, leads to degradation and extinction in the conditions when people should have started living most effectively.

All primary threats have been removed: a man fell out of the food chain, practically does not depend on climate conditions, is not subject to epidemics (at least to the former ones, killing whole cities), is free, he does not have to work 20 hours per day to earn his living (the workaholics who are sitting up in offices until late at night do it voluntarily).

The pleasure like a werewolf, helps us to live under the rays of the sun, and kills us under the light of the moon.

None of the world wars, repressions, or weapon took so many lives, like this time bomb did being wound up inside of a man.

Therefore it is important to emphasize that the ability to neutralize it in time and to use energy in the "peaceful" purposes is a way which will give freedom to everyone in particular and will give hope to all together.

The main thing is not to lose faith in goodness and not to exchange the pain of being oneself with the pleasure from being a part of a crowd.

The dopamine devil can take many guises, sometimes even hiding behind such, seemingly, a noble desire as to be useful to people around.

Pleasure from Being Useful. Help Cures

Hybrid engines, assistance to a colleague, paper packages, certificates of honor, charity—what is common for all these?

All of them give a person the pleasure from understanding that he is useful. To bring benefit is in our blood.

We like to help and be useful!

To help an old woman to cross the road—it is excellent!

To get a kitten from a tree—it is easy!

To help a girl in tight jeans to change a wheel on a highway—surely!

After rendering assistance we feel better, we are cheering up.

Scientists held an experiment, they invited people in dejectedness. For purity of the experiment they had strengthened the bad mood of the participants by showing a three hour long depressive movie to them. And then they divided the participants into two groups.

One group was suggested to get rid of their depressive mood by their own habitual methods. And the other was sent to hospital to help serving patients.

Representatives of the first group were getting out of the bad mood like they got used to—some went to a bar with friends, some brought home a bottle of wine, some ate too much chocolate, some decided to sport, and the majority, of course, settled on a sofa and got into the Internet.

Scientists were not surprised. Their hypothesis had worked out, those participants who they sent to do seemingly depressing work—to take care of patients and moreover to do that free of charge, the next day described with inspiration their feelings. They said they had been filled with power, and their mood if had not become fine, had considerably increased.

It was impossible to tell the same about the second group which resorted to self-treatment. Their mood remained suppressed, the motivating force was weak, optimism and smiles were completely absent.

How did it happen that interaction with patients which should have caused only increasing depression, since the examinees observed how other people suffered, had led to a reverse effect?

All the matter is that the participants of the experiment saw grateful eyes of the patients. They were realizing their help to people in enduring pain or in coping with a difficult situation.

Mute gratitude, and at times just a simple understanding that a person makes a good deed, starts the program of encouragement. And the person is fed with dopamine and literally comes to life.

It is similar to charging. Physical exercises are not especially important to do when you are full of energy and vital forces, no. Exercises should be done when it seems to a person that he is unable to lift a pencil, when feet give way and the body, as if being magnetized, is attracted by a sofa. Exercises should be done, when you are worn out—for this reason it is also called in some languages as "charging". Like for a phone. From physical exercises which, apparently, take away strength, people are charging just like a phone from a charger.

The same way the brain improves our state after acts of kindness. There is no easier way to get out of bad mood, than to help someone with your active work and to feel his gratitude. By the way, during the era of an economic crisis help is the cheapest way to be out of doldrums. After all to carry a heavy bag of an old woman is much cheaper, than to buy a bottle of Chivas or Macallan.

A Desire to Help Is in Our Blood

To help others is such an important component of a human life that the brain has made it a separate program and encourages a person every time he is inspired to help a neighbor.

Altruism is a natural feature peculiar not only to humans, but also to the majority of social animals. It is proved that altruism is not a result of self-consciousness, but rather an instinct of survival in groups.

For many years a world famous biologist Frans de Waal studied the life of chimpanzees and bonobo monkeys. In the course of his research he has revealed obvious rudiments of ethical behavior in the community of primates. According to the author, the morals are not a strictly human feature, and its sources should be searched for in animals. Empathy and other manifestations of some kind of morals are peculiar to monkeys, and dogs, and elephants, and even to reptiles.

Deviation Towards the Norm

Often a sophisticated mind plays mean jokes with people. A case when a person realizes the benefit provided by him is just one of such.

What feeling does he have after making something good, not even just good, but something outstanding?

Let's say today he spent twice less money, than usually, which means he saved much. What will he do tomorrow?

Or he has bought a hybrid car, and now, each time taking the wheel, he realizes that he saves the planet.

How will he behave on the road surrounded by drivers of six liter Touaregs and Chryslers which pollute the atmosphere with the exhaust gases?

Or, he ate nothing, strictly keeping to a diet, even missed a usual lunch, having replaced it with a liter of kefir. What will he eat tomorrow? Obviously, it will not be kefir.

If today the day was lived better, than usually, what will be tomorrow? Right—there will be an indulgence.

Tomorrow he will spend more, will be more intolerant while driving, and during his lunch he will eat the meals that didn't allow himself earlier.

A person can afford to be worse only because yesterday he lived a day slightly better. People are inclined to help others, however after that many become more demanding to people around.

Indulgences: More Often, More Numerous

To make something good which is incommensurable with the soul size is a big test for the personality.

Say, an ordinary man—drunkard, lazy, envious, boastful, somehow, someway saved children sinking in a river where their excursion bus fell into.

He made a heroic deed, but did not become a hero out of that.

He remained the same lazy being.

Will his life change after that?

Will he become a rescuer; will he turn this accident into the norm? Will he bring virtue to people after that case? It is unlikely.

An interesting experiment proving weakness of human self-checking for indulgences was carried out by Princeton psychologists Benoit Monin and Dale Miller. The respondents were offered to agree or disagree with a thesis before making a decision on hiring a woman or a black candidate.

One group got the thesis " it is better for most women to stay at home and to take care of children, rather than to work".

The other got the following "it is better for some women to stay at home and to take care of children, than to work.

Those respondents who firmly disproved the first thesis with higher probability were showing sexist behavior upon making a decision on hiring candidates, than those who reluctantly agreed to the second thesis.

McGonigal explains this paradox this way: the respondents, who rejected the obviously sexist statement, felt that they had executed the moral duty. They proved to themselves that they were not sexists, but it prepared them in its turn to what psychologists call the moral indulgence. Having made a good deed, a person, as a rule, is satisfied with himself. And thus trusts his impulses more, including "bad" ones as well.

Moral indulgences allow us not only to act badly, but also to refuse from good deeds. For example, people who were asked at first about their former generosity, donated for charity 60 percent less than those who were not reminded of their previous kind acts. In a business game directors of plants were less eager to buy expensive cleaning facilities if they remembered their former ethical actions.

Returning to our "hero" who rescued children, we will notice that a great kind act can make him even worse. It can give a reason to become proud, opening a door to a set of awful indulgences which on the whole can eclipse that good thing, once committed by him. Therefore the good acts made by a person should be proportional to his personality.

To Surpass the Pleasure from Help

It is possible to find strength inside, and to determine upon an outstanding act. And it is possible to learn not to notice own kind acts, or, at least, not to attach much importance to them. Yes, it steals the pleasure from help, but, on the other hand, removes the risk of indulgences and mute boasting.

Own unnoticed good act opens space for greater goodness in soul. Without any conceit and indulgences. And, on the contrary, self-condemnation for committed evil can help us sometimes to make further great good acts.

Here Goethe was precisely right, calling Mephistopheles a part of the force which endlessly creates good, wishing evil to everything.

Sense of guilt, even for a small offense, can force a person to redeem it for many years. It will pacify arrogance, will shorten the tongue and will direct attention to how to satisfy this pain.

In understanding of fault there is huge power because it is pain. And as we know, any pain demands pleasure. The pleasure for removal of an itch from the fault is atonement. And this is a way of goodness. L. N. Tolstoy was able to show this thought in the novel “Resurrection” better than anyone.

Dark Side of Fault

You should not blame yourself and revel in remorse. It is known that it can lead to an absolutely reversed effect.

In search of anesthetics, a person starts indulging his vices. It can help, but only for a short time and then the fault comes back with new strength.

No matter how good a person considers himself, there are always people suffering from him. As F.M. Dostoyevsky was speaking with an aged man Zosimus’s lips in the novel “Brothers Karamazov”: “Everyone is guilty to all”.

A man is a pain source since the first second of his birth. Therefore there is always a reason to seek to redeem guilt in righteous behavior. It sounds very religious. Perhaps, it is strange for a book dedicated to pleasure. But it is natural for a research directed on identification of ways of pleasure management.

Pleasure is only a means, like a windmill. Of course, it is pleasant if the wind helps us to pound life grains but it is impossible to count on it. The wind is changeable.

Ignoring pleasure from committed goodness, a man opens for himself an opportunity to create greater goodness.

Only active understanding and will, will help a person not to notice those good things that he does, allowing to do it not for the sake of personal pleasure, but for the sake of a result.

Exempting himself from indulgences in the future, a person exempts himself from aspiration to recognition. Thus good acts bring good not only to those who are being helped, but also make better those who help. And it means that each following kind act will be much easier for a person to take.

Who knows, maybe once the destiny will give you a chance to save the country?

You don't want to become the one from whom the Planet should be rescued afterwards, do you?

Having considered the main pleasures of the XXI century and ways to surpass them, we closely approached the main subject of our research—the Ultimatum of Pleasure.

What it consists of and how it is shown, what are its bases, why we call it the most important challenge of the modern civilization, and the most important thing: whether it is possible to respond to the ultimatum—the following chapter "The ultimatum of pleasure: Consumer capitalism VS Humanistic culture" is devoted to it.

1.4 TECHNOLOGICAL EXPLOSION AND SHIFT OF THE CIVILIZATIONAL DEVELOPMENT VECTOR

The technological change of the world which has been observed since the era of Modern times has entered today into a new, bifurcate phase of development when technological explosion starts to change the nature of a man. Kevin Kelly in his book " The Inevitable: Understanding the 12 Technological Forces That Will Shape Our Future " has outlined the directions of future mutual transformation of the world and a man. We have shown earlier that the pursuit of pleasure generates new desires which in turn stimulate emergence of new technologies and new things accordingly. If earlier a man didn't want to perform hard physical activity and invented technical means for this purpose, today we already don't want to overwork ourselves intellectually. We have created artificial intelligence, having given non-creative work to it so far. Perhaps the next step is not far off. In any case the computer already wins in chess even over the great grand masters, not to mention mere mortals. In 2011 the robot named Watson was invented which is perfectly making diagnoses, helping to develop drugs and making individual recommendations for patients on the basis of the collected data.

Today robotics can perform many activities much better than a man. Therefore some professions already consign to the past, but naturally the new ones appear, which provide a person with pleasures from creativity. The tendency, in our opinion, is that the pleasure "filters" professions, leaving only those that will give pleasure to a person. It will be creative professions, although non-creative professions don't exist in our opinion. It is all about the attitude. So the attitude of a person towards reality and towards himself will be changing. Ability to creative self-realization, so-called "self design", will be considered as the highest blessing.

Perception of time and space is changing. The computer accelerates many processes, payment of bills, purchase of goods. The latest news today means those events that occur right now. Valuable goods become those which it is impossible to copy — for example, trust. Recommendations of the respectable companies will be highly appreciated in the market. It multiplies the value of human qualities and first of all humanity. The pleasure will be delivered by trust, decency, responsibility, loyalty and other human qualities. That is, the main pleasure for a man will be the pleasure to remain a man. Therefore ambivalence is present in development of high technologies as well as everywhere else. On the one hand a threat of the loss of humanity is increasing; on the other hand, by contrast the value of human qualities is growing.

In the future we expect change of the brain activities. Already today people obtain information generally from screens, which promotes development of utilitarian, associative thinking. In the future access to products will be more important, than possessing them. Already today it is possible to watch movies, to listen to music, to read books online, without purchasing them. Ownership fades into the background, having given the first place to access. Further it will cause the increasing decentralization and dematerialization. Thanks to continuous copying things become general, it means no one's. This tendency will be amplified, washing away a concept of property. Thus the pleasure of the future is transformed from the pleasure of possession to the pleasure from use. It can lead to reduction of social inequality—an old dream of mankind.

Some time ago cooperation took away a man from the animal world. Today it helps to become a new man. The Internet generates new forms of cooperation, uniting people and teaching them the principles of interaction. By means of new technologies people begin to participate in a process of creating things, and not just in consumption of an end product. The border between reality and virtual reality gradually disappears. All devices will become virtual ones soon, and communication with the computer will be mental. People will be ready to constant openness. Anonymity in the Internet will consign to the past. Everything will become transparent. It will change the nature of a man, will transform his existential experiences, for example fear, suspiciousness, greed, envy and others.

Today there are quite daring attempts to predict how the future will change by years. So, one of the most famous techno futurologists and specialists in the field of artificial intelligence, the technical director of Google Ray Kurzweil thinks that in 2019—wires will consign to the past, in 2020—computers will reach the capacity, comparable with the human brain, in 2025—the mass market of gadgets-implants will appear, in 2028—the solar energy will satisfy all energy needs of mankind, in 2030—there will be the golden age of nanotechnologies in the industry which will lead to cost reduction of all goods production, in 2031—3D-printers will be used in all hospitals to print out human organs, in 2042—there will be the first potential implementation of immortality, in 2044—the artificial intelligence will become billions times more reasonable, than human, in 2045—there will come the era of technological singularity. The earth will turn into one huge computer, in 2099—the process of technological singularity will extend over the Universe.

It is an ungrateful thing to describe the future by years. We can hardly tell what is waiting for us tomorrow. But, nevertheless we are obliged to foresee things in order to adapt to the future changes. How will a man change and what measures should we undertake already today?

A famous scientist, director of the Institute of biophysical chemistry after Max Planck, Professor Patrick Kramer, considers that we should speak not about the Internet of Things already, but about the Internet of Us. Within 10 years implants in the brain will appear, and people will be directly connected to the Internet. Today there are already known examples of inserting implants into the brain of people having these or those diseases. In the future brain activities of people will be connected to each other. People with the inserted implants will work one hundred times more productively and quicker, than now. Our brain will become more powerful. And it will change everything completely. They say that connection to the Internet with the use of implants will enter the mass market within two years. And, it won't cost much because the main goal is to make these developments available. Thus, before our eyes a man turns into a cyborg which can be controlled from the outside.

Moreover, the whole world gradually turns into Skinner's box. And all this thanks to pleasure! Now we will give you a bit more details about this. In 1930 a psychologist from Harvard named B. F. Skinner made a box and put a hungry rat there. There was a lever on one side of the box. When the rat was moving in the box and was touching the lever, some food fell inside. After several accidental pressings of the lever the rat learned to go straight to it and to press purposefully: the award provoked the corresponding behavior. Skinner presumed that this principle is applicable also to a human. He called his invention "an operant conditioning chamber" known under the name "Skinner's box".

The main principle of behaviorism is that human behavior can be considered as a function of incentives and awards. If we understand the principles of stimulation, we will understand the principles of behavior then. Having designed the correct box, we will be able to control behavior.

The principles of behaviorism are realized in the applied discipline—"behavioral design", used by companies and state organizations to control daily decisions of people: from purchase in a shop to political elections. "Interactive technologies" become an important part of the life of people and are used for accounting, training, and caring about health.

B.J.Fogg—the founder of "behavioral design" showed experimentally that people were spending more time working on the computer if this computer already had helped them earlier with the solution of some task. That is, the relations between a man and the computer submitted to the same "rule of reciprocity" which psychologists apply to social life. Fogg's experiment confirmed that the principles of psychology can be applied while developing computer programs to force people to do what they wouldn't do, meaning to control them. He called the new science which is on the cross of informatics and psychology "Captology" (from English: Computers as Persuasive Technologies—"computers as technologies of influence"). Subsequently captology developed into behavioral design. E-mails forcing people to buy something at once; applications and games which take attention; online forms which compass people to choose one option instead of others—all this was specially developed to use instincts, peculiarities and weaknesses of human behavior to get the required result.

According to Fogg's theory of controlling behavior three things are required for a person to make some action: a desire, an opportunity and a stimulating push. The trigger—a hint on making an action– will be effective, only if a person is extremely interested in it and it is very simple to make this action. The more sudden and more intensive the emotional response of a person during the first experience is, the more pleasure he feels during it, the more probability is that this service will become the basic choice of the person. A correctly made (or "hot") trigger is offered at the moment when a person is most motivated to action. The motto of behavioral design, by Fogg's avowal, is "Set up hot triggers on the way of motivated people" and one more—"Give superpower to people!"

One of Fogg's students, Mike Krieger, co-founder of Instagram, developed a project under the name "Send the Sunshine" which would allow to send emotions via mobile phones to lighten a friend's mood. Today there are hundreds of millions users sharing dawns, sunsets and selfies.

In response to social interactions, even to their most low-quality imitations, the human brain emits substances which give us pleasure and form habits, and other people act as the most active triggers. A book of Nir Eyal—one of Fogg's students is called this way—"Hooked: How to Build Habit-Forming Products ."

Thus, new technologies turn people into sort of experimental rats. Fogg himself repeatedly pointed out the ethical aspect of such manipulations, while all-mighty manipulators only indulgently smiled at this.

N. Eyal slightly modified Fogg's model of behavior control, having shown that triggers aren't external factors, and are located inside of people. An application becomes popular if it satisfies basic emotional needs of the user even before he realizes them. These are existential feelings of people: boredom, curiosity, loneliness. And, of course, the strongest one of them is expectation of pleasure. By arousing psychological dependence in them, people are actively manipulated, for the sake of commercial benefit, trying to attract and keep their attention by all available methods, the attention which is sold for money afterwards.

One of Harris's principles sounds like this: "The one who controls the menu controls the choice as well". The more influence on behavior such technological products receive, the less people can control themselves. It is known that a person checks his phone 150 times a day on average. It is similar to a drug addiction. It isn't accidental that the industry of gambling became the leader of behavioral design.

The anthropologist Natasha Dow Schull in her book "Addiction by Design" calls gaming machines Skinner's boxes for people. They use the principle of various awards. A player, pulling the lever, doesn't know what he will get for that and thus plays again and again. A person can lose everything and all the same can feel pleasure. If he is close to "a painful point", an offer of a free dinner in a steak house turns this pain into pleasure, and a person again has a motivation to continue.

However technologies are capable to help in developing useful habits as well. There is just a fundamental conflict between needs of people and needs of business. So it is required to manage the ethical aspect of business. It is necessary to close the box from the outside. To cease being a hostage to captology, it is required just to learn to control pleasure.

Indeed the ways of evolution are inscrutable. If a man of the past giving in to the pursuit of pleasure was losing control over himself and was closer to the animal world, than the community of Homo sapiens, then the development of modern technologies turned this dependence on the thirst for pleasures into the means of manipulating people. On the one hand a man moves away from his human essence again, more and more turning into a cyborg, and on the other hand,—into a manipulated herdlike being.

Thus, pleasure makes its ultimatum again—"Overcome or degrade!" However during the era of high technologies and techno civilization it will be already different degradation. Towards the cyborg operated from the outside.

Meanwhile we teach animals to control robots. You don't believe, do you?

A group of scientists from the Center of advanced science and technologies at the Tokyo University designed a robot, sensitive to smells, capable to move in the direction of the smell source. The most interesting fact in this design is that a butterfly of a silkworm which sits on the top of the mobile sphere looking like the trackball of a computer mouse acts as "a driver". Having scented a smell, the butterfly begins to move on the sphere surface in the direction of the smell source, and optical sensors follow the sphere translocation and move a mini-car robot to the relevant direction. The point is that the butterfly of a silkworm has sensitive organs catching certain smells — pheromones. During the tests 7 different butterflies showed a 100% positive result, having passed precisely along the offered route.

This is a vivid demonstration of efficiency of the bio-robotic system, showing that live organisms can interact well with robotic systems for making new types of devices. In the future specialists of the Tokyo university plan to create a more maneuverable and powerful car, which gene-modified butterflies of a silkworm will be able to steer. Gene modification will give butterflies a chance to be guided not only by the smell of pheromones, but also by other smells which sources might be, for example, a smell of smoke or other dangerous smells. So the techno civilization moves in the two-way direction. And if you see an animal on a motorcycle on the street, don't rush to a psychiatrist. Probably the future is already here.

Changes of the nature and essence of living beings due to the technological explosion is only one of the expected manifestations of the new era. Its much more serious consequence is spatiotemporal transformations of the world. Albert Einstein predicted gravitational waves, spatiotemporal distortions due to gravitation shift more than hundred years ago. Today, in our opinion, it is already possible to speak about spatiotemporal transformations due to technological penetration of a man into the micro and mega worlds.

Change of the spatiotemporal metrics of the world.

The modern stage of development of the human tragicomedy is marked by approaching of people to the cherished, long ago predicted, as much desired as much cursedly frightening, two-way line of the virtual "Hell-Heaven". On the one hand, a man has approached as close as never before the border behind which he loses his dignified title. The cruelty with which some people treat each other, treat the surrounding flora and fauna, would strike the most aggressive predators. On the other hand, despite this, a man remains the most reasonable and noble being on the planet, the creator of not only the "secondary" world of the technique, but also of the "primary", natural one. The fact that today wild animals, having got sick, come out to people and ask for help demonstrates eloquently that a man has risen in his progress up to understanding himself as the being capable and obliged to create something and help his smaller brothers.

Since the most ancient times a man as it has been shown, as well as all living beings though, is on the dopamine addiction. The pursuit of pleasures still fulfills the role of an evolutionary factor. Energy from pleasure allows to overcome the physical difficulties of development. Today however new technologies practically change the evolution vector, allowing a man to do without any physical and even intellectual activities. In a pursuit of pleasures a man creates virtual reality which will submit already to specific regularities.

The ambivalence typical to the human nature has reached today the culmination exactly by making the unprecedented artificial means of grandiose creation and destruction. The technosphere, having reached the scale exceeding the usual human idea of own nature, distorting spatiotemporal existence of a man as a species, threatens transformation of his essence. It allows many researchers to say that an era of the post-human is coming.

A lot is written about the modern mankind having entered a new phase of its development. We would like to stop briefly on those features with which the new step of the techno civilization development is connected.

One of the peculiarities of the modern stage of science and technology progress is that they have allowed the mankind to get into the matter depths, in nanoworlds, making amendments there which sometimes complicate the processes of the natural self-organization. Total differentiation and fragmentation of the modern world multiplied by people gaining greater speeds, has led to transformation of the spatiotemporal metrics of the world. Not only perception of space and time by a man has changed, but also the spatiotemporal characteristics of the world included into the sphere of human interaction were transformed. It can lead to a shift of the human development vector. The pursuit of pleasures can once again lead a person to "drug addiction", but not from chemical things this time, but from technical ones.

The great message of Albert Einstein to mankind consisting of the special theory of relativity, about dependence of spatiotemporal parameters of an object on the speed of its movement, should be "environmentalized", i.e. expanded over all things existent. Each being in the Universe has not just its own spatiotemporal characteristics which depend on the speed of its movement. Movement speed, of course, depending on the specifics of the object, its contents and structure, and on peculiarities of the environment in which it moves, changes not only the spatiotemporal characteristics of objects, but also the essence of both the objects and the environments of their existence. So, a man, by means of the unprecedented speed of intellectual progress, creating artificial vehicles, gains more and more powerful speeds, changing the environment of his existence, and turns himself practically into another being. That is, the mankind today acts as means of "mutation" of not only its own oikos, but also of its own nature. New beings are forming a new planet and vice versa. There is some kind of mutual transformation. The environment has generated a being intended for its own amendment. The same happened to a man who invented the technique which changed the vector of civilizational development. And the reason for that, strangely enough, is the uncontrollable, unconscious pursuit of pleasure. Having realized that, the mankind must change the attitude to pleasure.

Once in the infancy of mankind these mutual changes were reciprocally useful, whereas the same can't be said for the modern transformations. It is enough to see information broadcasts about the changes of the ecological situation in the world to be once again convinced of that. At his time Karl Marx noted that invention of the steam engine had promoted transformation of the feudal society into the capitalistic one. Today we can state that satellites, spaceships and devices, the Internet, high information and nanotechnologies have changed the spatiotemporal characteristics of our planet. Apparently, nearby is the time when the image of the Earth will change significantly as well. Therefore, in our opinion, the time has come to add Einstein's theory of relativity with "the principle of correlation"—the dependence of properties and even the essence of objects and their oikos on the speed and vector of movement. A man moving in the micro and mega-worlds is already absolutely different being, than the previously known to us Homo sapiens.

The environment is being changed also by means of its getting learned, and not only physically, but also by amending of human perception. The most powerful microscopes and telescopes change the essence of a man as a perceiving being. Thereof the way of perception of the world changes and consequently, the world does.

Recession into the microworld, an opportunity to act in the space where a man doesn't exist and can't exist in principle, transforms not only its scale, but also the essence. For the nanoworld a man turns into a super-being. Not the attitude towards moral standards is the criterion of a modern super-being as Friedrich Nietzsche considered, but the speed, means, character and the scale of impact on the external environment are. Thus, a super-being is a relative and dynamic concept. In one metrics it is a usual, normal being, and in another—"a super" one. It is important to emphasize that the word "super" in this case doesn't carry any moral coloring; it can be with both marks—"plus" and "minus".

They usually say that practice is the source and criterion of the knowledge progress, but write little about the fact that science, while developing, changes the world as well. Progress of science changes not only thinking of people, it changes the world on physical, biological, mental, socio-economic and socio-political levels. Evolution of science leads eventually to the fact that it is considered as a certain solution for social and economic problems, meanwhile the science today turns into the noospheric force forming a new world. Scientists, despite the attempts of the "movers and shakers" to constantly point them to "where they belong", turn into the power of "the collective demiurge"[35].

The feedback effect of society on science is obvious. Totalitarian society stimulates development of the defense industry while there is not enough attention paid to consumer goods in such society. In the Soviet Union it was passed over. Today it is "on the programme" in Northern Korea, Iran and other countries. In R. Merton's monograph "Social theory and social structure" four types of communications between the social structure and progress of science are revealed, tension points between institutional norms of science and political dictatorship are traced[36] . Understanding of these facts sometimes forms hostile attitude of people towards science which is accused of creating mechanisms of civilization destruction . . . .

Usually many people don't see that the responsibility for the negative impact on the world lays not so much on the science as on the society generating a civilizational paradigm, determining such development of it. In order to develop the science should find a support in the society values, scientists are also people liable to public consciousness, public psychology and ideology. Science depends on the cultural values cultivated in the society. Therefore successful progress of science assumes, first of all, forming of the positive attitude of the society towards scientists because the destiny of the country and all mankind depends on their activities. The monograph authors on the example of fascist Germany show how a political regime can deprive science of autonomy, forcing to deal with certain problems. We, in turn, can add that sometimes they try to turn science into the means of pleasure search, including the one from the feeling of own superiority over others.

Another civilizational challenge from modern scientific technologies is no less important—a possibility of parallel existence of a man in many worlds. A man can do this today thanks to his consciousness. To get into the hierarchy of a material world by means of the ideal one, by consciousnesses, having found life on different levels of matter, to learn to control space and time by changing the sizes of objects thanks to modern technologies (super-micro and telescopes, etc.)—a prerogative of a super-material being. But the real face of this being can be shown only thanks to the vector of its activities, nature of impact on these worlds. Will he feel pleasure from his superhuman capabilities or will aim to promote natural self-organization?

However there is more to come. Due to his uniqueness a man can perceive also the objects of the ideal world. The science has not entered into the "terra incognito" of the spiritual world so far, therefore it can't provide the genuine material verifying or falsifying this thesis. In order to prove that it is enough to provide the facts of intuitive vision of some regularities, discoveries by instinct to be convinced that Goethe's expression: "I see the ideas" should be taken literally. And Platon's vision of "eidos" is far from being the result of his philosophical speculative activities as sometimes short-sighted and at times even completely blind compilers write. Therefore the uncontrollable techno humanization can certainly lead to impoverishment of human nature and, perhaps, to destruction of the human essence.

Thus, acquirement of the unnatural for humans speed of motion in space, multiplied by creating artificial means of changing the scales of space, changes the world metrics which is being subjectified thanks to transformation of own capabilities by a man.

The third component of a technological challenge to human development which is closely connected with the two previous ones is energy, more precisely, the level of its mastering. Discovering more and more powerful energy sources, a man gradually comes off from his terrestrial roots, forming centrifugal force of a universal being. All this is still realities of today. What is waiting for us in the future? Already today scientists speak about possible shift in time, transformation of fields, including gravitational ones, and about many other still improbable phenomena.

Not only a man and his natural environment change, but also the social environment does, as well as the society and the laws of existence in it. One of peculiarities of the modern society is total mimicry. A sign, as postmodernists note, replaces the meaning, a phenomenon—the essence, visibility and simulacrum—the object. It is easy to illustrate this thesis, resorting to money. A check replaces a banknote which replaces the money which has replaced the objective actual value. Money acts as a universal equivalent of potential energy of the subject possessing it. However we should note, that the "possession", and not earning this money symbolizes the power of a person in society, allowing legality of its unlawful obtainment. It transforms the system of moral values, replacing honor and dignity of a person with his "efficiency", and happiness—with "being successful". Everybody writes how to become successful, but very few people say how to remain a man in this world and just to be happy.

Exponential, unreasonable and unsupported growth of bank notes generates new, unreasonable things which main "advantage" is their high price. Therefore we are surrounded by the most absurd and absolutely useless things. The former world of a radiant dream has turned into the swamp of self-interests in which the purest ideas sink. Platon's brilliant ideal world, completely swallowed by the practical world of K. Marx and sexually anxious world of S. Freud, has generated F. Kafka's and A. Camus's absurd world. This is the price for the pursuit of material pleasures.

The following step of existence mimicry is uncontrollable development of computer technologies and, in particular, virtual reality of the Internet. The reality removed to "the box" in order that all living "go home in a box". Not the God dies, as F. Nietzsche noted, but the one who should have carried Him in the heart—a man. Resuscitation functions remained with philosophy and religion which had received a powerful blow by the absurdly mad society of mass consumption which had idolized a banknote as a certificate of power of its owner.

The vulgar materialism, thus, has destroyed "tomorrow", belief in tomorrow, having removed, therefore, the ground from under both religion, with its focus on the Kingdom of Heaven, and philosophy with its reflection over eternal sense problems. All advertizing is oriented to momentary consumption of goods: "Only today—there are discounts! Tomorrow will be late!" Aggressive inflation: "Your money will burn down tomorrow! Spend it today! Tomorrow may not come!" And even more, soon the doomsday will come! Note, the idea of the doomsday is profitable to those who are interested in quick withdrawal of money from people. In this way they are similar to criminals robbing the population with only one difference: money is given to them voluntarily in exchange on not completely necessary, and sometimes on completely unnecessary, but well advertized goods.

Similar moods are supported by mass media, constantly exaggerating information about murders, diseases, catastrophic crashes, natural disasters etc. The Doomsday is not only expected, but also is highly propagandized and welcomed. Even, as everyone knows, a certain date is being announced; however, periodically it is being adjusted. As soon as the doomsday expected by everyone doesn't come, "friends of mankind" offer another no less heartily welcomed date of general death, which is greeted nearly as an international holiday.

Even the concept "society of mass consumption" changes its sense, now meaning not the mass consumption of absolutely useless mass goods, but "consumption" of masses by mass media. It means that already not masses consume but rather they are consumed by those who hold mass media and other levers of manipulation. Interestingly, both derive pleasure from that. Almost like in love relations. Goebbels's words are recalled: "Give me the mass media, and in a while I will turn people into pigs!" It is interesting that there was not found a more suitable word for people, rather than "mass" which is purely physical word, for example: body mass, curd mass, etc. although the words "population" or "people" are not much better, meaning what is populating or what was born. However these are not physical, but biological terms meaning nonetheless a living being unlike "mass", though not yet absolutely worth respecting. The word "society" is perceived more neutral ethically.

Impetuous obtaining of the superspeed and building-up technical means of existence lead to the fact that a man himself becomes more and more artificial, if not in his essence yet, then in his existence for sure. Quite a lot is written about life turning into absurd existence. Brilliant works of A. Camus, J. P. Sartre, M. Heidegger, K. Jaspers, F. Kafka and other great philosophers remove the need of the detailed argumentation of this thesis. Much fewer researches are devoted to socio-cultural and spatiotemporal specifics of this existence. Besides we are interested in the conditions of origin and establishment of the so-called "false" existence which has entirely seized the modern social all-levels subjects deriving pleasure from that.

Under the conditions of the increasing speed of the true values depreciation and declaration of the false ones, the social mimicry forces out authentic life. Formalism as a method of "false existence" is established. People turn into "counterfeiters", creators of absurd, invalid values, robbing not only others, but also themselves. They derive similar perverted pleasure from that. Millions of the smartest and worthiest people all day long are engaged in the bureaucratic fuss imposed from above. This way the system switches off the brains of the elements which still keep a capability of creative thinking and true pleasure from self-realization. Capital punishment is replaced with bureaucratic shutdown of the wakeful consciousness. Thus people are turned into meek zombies.

It is interesting that the Russian words "steal" and "lie" have much in common. They are also connected existentially. At first one should start to lie and, first of all to oneself, then to others, and then there is one step left to theft. Not accidentally the public opinion about honest people is formed as about the losers incapable to exist successfully in the modern society. Hence is the success as the main category of consumer pseudo-existence. This way the "thieves' consciousness" is formed. It isn't important what, how and at what price—it is important that it was made in time. This is what is called happiness as manifestation of the highest pleasure.

Let's try to look into the socio-cultural determinants of false existence. The modern mode of being which has idolized money first turned everything into commodities, and then actually replaced the true values with a constantly devaluating piece of paper. Moreover, joint-stock capitalism, having performed a double pirouette of depreciation, replaced money with shares which already are roughly connected with these or those values. They are just pieces of paper on which it is written that their owner possesses something. Invention of the electronic exchanges entirely virtualizes the value, putting the owner of electronic shares away from reality, including human feelings. It is known that a man parts with electronic money much easier, than with paper one and doesn't feel any displeasure when parting.

It leads to virtualization of reality, establishment and domination of the values which don't exist or don't work in fact, to the use of words which meaning is not known even to a person using them. The society of mass consumption turns into a mimicking society imitating the use of simulacra, the so-called society of mass somnambulism or illusion. By the way, the word "circus" comes from Greek "circus"—"circle". Locking ourselves in a circle of senseless existence, we get to a circus where all things play absurd roles—a bear rides a bicycle, and a lion jumps through a hoop and ramps! Own madness is not enough for a man; he also brings animals to a nervous breakdown, persistently pushing his head to their mouth! That is done not only to get particular pleasure, but also to sell it profitably!

Grandiose invention of mankind is a bureaucratic apparatus which created an algorithm of the reality absurdization which is taking away any sense to distances, which are remote and inaccessible to human mind. The form which was announced a self-goal and which is torn off from the content turns into the punishing sword of a bureaucrat hating the sense which can disclose his empty essence. Nakedness of the king can't be noticed in the conditions of a strictly formalized game. And only a child who is out of the game is capable to see the absence of not only the king's clothes, but also the king himself. Clowns in royal attires come forth to a proscenium. Pawns know that "it's all for fun", the kings are hyped-up, and the armor is phony. But it is the nomenclature brotherhood which runs the show and which is not only to indoctrinate everybody of its importance and establish its rights, but also to force the true heirs of the royal throne to feel own negligibility in front of the new rules of the most difficult formalized game. The bureaucrat's language is not only difficult, but is also senseless which puts a professional who is eternally trying to understand everything into the dead-end of a helpless status. Right here the triumphing dullness and lack of talent recoup on the master, who is timidly looking down and confusedly acknowledging own wrongness. No wonder that a lot of such bureaucrats are capable to perversely feel pleasure from ordinary human joys.

In attempt of forming a classless society, a public, and in fact, a state pattern of ownership a powerful official class was built which, in turn, was complicatedly structured. One of peculiarities of this class is that it itself develops both the rules of the game, and the exposition language, incomprehensible to the uninitiated. This is some kind of modern hieratic priesthood which is torn off from all segments of the population. If antagonistic classes can't live without each other, mutually being "a friend- a foe", then the bureaucrat is self-sufficient, he needs an apparatus and some process. And, the more absurd the process, the better it is for the bureaucrat. An optimal thing, if not to say the perfect one, is the endless, formalized, dressed in absolute nonsense circle run, emasculating the remaining brain from people involved in the process which participants have no idea of its purpose.

What is the society which has generated such a monster? It appears that the name of it is "the state totalitarianism" or just state totalism. What was called socialism for a long time, in fact, turned out to have nothing in common with it. Instead of public property on means of production they managed to form only state and official property after all. But it is also paradoxical that capitalism which is being formed in totalitarian societies today, also has nothing in common with it.

It is interesting that the Russian word " government", coming from the word "governor", represents his possessions, and the governor himself is identified with the God, and the entire territory which is the country, and not at all the government, is named ownership, property of the governor. And should we be surprised if its ordinary citizens are living uncomfortably there? It is the Government by definition.

But all is not as simple as it may seem at first sight. Absurdization of reality began from the first days of existence of a man. Already a primitive man, mythologizing the reality, began to put the life sense outside the brackets of own existence. He began to give sense to things and the elements which he himself had invented. And people who were inventing sometimes laughed at those who believed in it and subordinated their life to absurd fantasies. It was not always done for the purpose of the power usurpation. Much oftener "creative producers" were simply self-realizing and self-asserting by means of their fantasies. But others, the so-called "strongmen", the predators, who lacked this creative abilities, understood how it was possible to use the already thought up. They fixed the absurdity in mass consciousness and made it a tool of own eminence. Their existence began to go on in another, nicer role for them—in the status of terrestrial gods. Everyone was getting pleasure from what was closer to his psychotype. And artificial means (tools) were universally giving pleasure from the feeling of own superiority.

Already then the symbols representing nonexistent and at times even ridiculous qualities of their bearers were created. Those were idols—statues, different amulets, body signs, tattoos. "Masters" were so skillfully deceiving masses, that themselves began to believe in miraculousness of own fictions. And they derived incredible pleasure from that. This is already top class.

Still in slaveholding society an accurate structure assigning reality absurdization to people as their profession was formed. During feudalism the religion role in this process of sense creation repeatedly increased. However the most interesting and inconceivable thing happened during capitalism. The ideal and absolute simulacrum—money was idolized. Money was invented much earlier, of course, but it turned into the absolute means of "the sense killer" during formation of capitalism. A receipt has not only replaced a thing, but also became the sense of human life. People sometimes can't even answer what they need money for. It is necessary and that's all. Exactly checks, receipts, but not real things. Dead things not only enslaved, but also killed all live. Indeed: "People die for a piece of metal!" And once again derive pleasure from it!

The next act of moving away from the sense was a brilliant invention which was checks for checks. Instead of money as checks, you were given a piece of paper according to which you became the owner of a part of the entity and could apply for its profit. If, of course, it will be shown officially. That is, you give terribly earned money, a part of your labor and time to get a piece of paper which grants illusion of its growth. Most likely, you will never sell these shares. After all it is the long-term capital which can be given to your children and grandchildren if by then the entity doesn't go bankrupt, and its manager won't leave for . . . London. For now you are getting pleasure from owning . . . shares.

But that is not all. With the development of modern computer technologies there was virtualization of existing in general, money and shares in particular. But since money and moreover, shares, are already only simulacra, symbols, paper checks, then the third round of the sense removal from the object led to greater absurdization of reality.

In Russia the above stated realities are multiplied by the ideology of "false mirrors" of the former Soviet Union, causing epidemics of the "social schizophrenia" which is blowing the mind of ordinary fair toilers. Bifurcation and "tri-furcation" of reality and sense lead to formation of empty, distant from sense, non-established persons about whom existentialists wrote. The only way of survival and furthermore, successful functioning of a person in such society, is "existential mimicry".

The schizoid pursuit of pleasure from money possession has closed the circle by the aspiration to pleasure from power, from the mad thirst for it. Although both money and power, especially power, are not a panacea at all, but rather are contraindicated to many ones. Power is an opportunity to control another one's will. But if a person has weak will and can't control even himself how can he control another one's will? The paradox is that the people having weak will often aspire to power, compensating their will weakness by official parameters, scooping it from the outside. Then they "will-deprive" those who they control. Freedom-loving people, having strong will by nature are especially hated by the officials. Autonomy of will, about which I. Kant spoke, is impossible for the bureaucracy which is zealously trying to destroy it. But, according to Kant, right the autonomy of the will is the basis of moral and ethical behavior of a person. It means that excessive bureaucratization of society promotes devaluation of morals in it.

Not incidentally total automation and technicalization leading to the automating conformism, according to E. Fromm, generates in people mass psychosis of a pursuit of power which makes an illusion of receiving pleasure in helpless and lost people. This illusion of pleasure by means of force, power and wealth as an eidos controls the modern world, making people unhappy.

On the other hand, development of individualism and freedom inevitably leads not only to autonomism, but also atomization of a person. Material welfare and individual freedom of a person of the techno civilization is followed by his increasing alienation from other people, generating an illusion of pleasure from personal self-sufficiency. However on this background the number of diseases connected with absence of normal human communication among people is growing. The quality of communication significantly influences the quality of life among various age groups of people. Especially elderly people are suffering from it[37]. Researches show that chronic loneliness leads to depression, alcoholism and drug addiction which in turn leads to loss of the normal circle of contacts and health. It is no secret that one of the reasons of divorces, diseases which quite often end up with a lethal result is termination of communication between the spouses.[38]

For some 20–30 years people have changed, the nature of communication has changed. Consumerism more and more parts people, turning them into alien, impersonal consumers of mass production goods. It is interesting that not only commodities, but also people have turned into the goods of mass production and consumption. Earlier we only read in books about this mass, atomic person (H. Marcuse, J. Habermas, E. Fromm, etc.).

One of the crisis manifestations of the modern techno civilization is, certainly, destruction of the family. The fact that classics of Marxism absolutely unfairly and short-sightedly connected the family with a private property, the fact that the Bolsheviks tried to destroy the family, breaking not only all religious, but also human foundations, having proclaimed "generality of wives and freedom of relations", led to an unprecedented sabbath of depressive singles who are vainly rushing about between Don Juan, Hamlet and lady Macbeth of the Mtsensk County.

Insufficient attention in special literature is still paid to a problem of the family which is facelessly called "a cell of society". The family is not a cell, it is the core of society. The family is not presence of parents and children, it is certain relations and values, it is the core of culture which is created and collapses right in the family. Let's remember Confucius's words: "Each villain and criminal started with becoming a bad son". Unfortunately, absolutization of the basic values of the mass consumption society—pleasures, money, power, improperly understood freedom—leads to destruction of the family.

Freedom is an unconditional social value, but when it is hypertrophied, then like everything else, submitting to dialectics, turns into its opposite. When a woman both doesn't want to be in charge of housekeeping, and it is, certainly, her personal matter, and refuses to give birth to children, suggesting her husband to do that, it is too much in our opinion. We remember the words of wise Socrates who answered the question: "What is the most important thing in life?"—in one word—"Moderation". And on the question: "And what is the most difficult?"—he answered in two words: "Be moderate".

In the conditions of such realities the question of the human life sense is very actual, a lot of literature is devoted to it. One of the most respected authors by us remains Victor Frankl who perfectly showed all complexity and importance of the problem in his work "Man's search for meaning".

However, perhaps, the most grandiose challenge to modern civilizations is the process of culture globalization which, transforming the culture of mankind in general, changes local national cultures as well[39]. Both the nature and direction of these changes often don't coincide, and on the contrary, sometimes contradict the general direction of globalization. What happens to the culture of mankind in general and to the cultures of separately taken ethnoses today? What is the response to these challenges?

A serious political and economic consequence of globalization is the fact that the underdeveloped countries historically having traditional culture can be left not only without modern technologies, but also without own national culture in general. The modern technologies invented, as a rule, in well-developed countries for pleasure of consumers in less developed countries can result in the opposite effect. Possession of them only by a rich part of the population can lead to serious escalation of class contradictions.

Georges Bataille in his book "The Accursed Share" emphasizes that economically developed countries think up thousands of methods of "ritual consumption", uselessly destroying own resources, directing them to the sphere of artificially invented entertainments, but don't redistribute them to economically backward countries for the purpose of their support.[40] That is, the cruel law of the jungle takes also the form of absurd time destruction. Resources, Money and Time get into one food chain. Not accidental is an absolutely absurd expression "Time is money".

As it is known, one of creators and at the same time creations of globalization are transnational corporations (TNC) which act as the main players of the world economic and political arena today. Development of transnational forms of activities, intensification of commodity and financial flows through the borders becoming more and more transparent lead to rapid growth of number and sizes of TNC which capital exceeds budgets of many countries of the world today. They count more than two thousand TNC today, each one of which extends the sphere of its influence on more than dozens of countries. They easily cross state borders and manage activity of the population of the less developed countries.

TNC today not only plan the development of economy of certain sovereign states, which branches of economy these countries shall develop, but also influence the development of needs of these countries population. They control the process of getting pleasure by them. So, the producers of Pepsi Cola are forming the need for this drink among the inhabitants of the whole world. Forming the needs, they are forming the required mode of behavior as well. It means that control of pleasure, eventually, results in control of people's behavior.

We should note that one of the positive consequences of globalization is increase in the general level of living of the underdeveloped countries population. So, twenty years ago an average resident of Malaysia received 350 dollars a year, and today he gets more than 5000 dollars a year. Entering into the single world economic market assumes a certain equalization of the material capital of players.[41] Universal computerization and telephone installation are going on increasing the level of technical literacy of the world population. In 2000 yet more than a half of people on the Earth didn't make any phone call, and already by 2010 3 billion people had the Internet, and almost everybody had the telephone communication. Today almost everyone has the Internet connection.

Representatives of original cultures understand that the technological, economic, political and legal universalization will be followed by changes in their traditions and the way of life. But it will happen afterwards, for now pleasures and processes of their obtainment are being universalized.

As an example of influence of the globalization process on spiritual culture it is especially interesting to consider the religion which being more static and conservative, continues to remain one of the low-changing culture pillars. Meanwhile the religion not only grants great pleasure from love to God, humility and service, but also promises eternal life as the most possible blessing.

Total rationalization, commodification, technicalization, virtualization force religions to reinterpret own strategy, to become more tolerant to each other, to be ready for a dialogue with other faiths as with the like-minded, as with people of spirit recognizing the priority of the inner world over the material one.

Religions resist to all perishable, momentary, "mercenary". Therefore the religion role doesn't decrease in the modern time, but rather grows. Firstly, development of new technologies facilitated communication between representatives of different faiths. Various teleconferences, the Internet, satellite communication and many other things allow them to communicate, being located in their regions, to watch various ceremonies and rituals of different religions and to see their unitary sense in many cases.

Secondly, representatives of various faiths unite in the face of the total growth of soullessness and mercantilism. Thirdly, one of the responses to the modern civilizational challenges is rapid growth of new, unconventional religions some of which have an obvious extremist nature. One of the features of these organizations is their amazing "turnover" also because of rigidity of their requirements.

Another peculiar feature of many of these new unconventional religious movements is their pagan nature. Perhaps there is nothing terrible in it, but it alarms that, as a rule, extremism of various sense acts as reaction of pagan religious movements to civilizational challenges. It is necessary to differentiate global and local religious projects. Local are associations which influence, extending in one or two regions, doesn't go out of a separately taken country. Global ones extend worldwide as it was already shown. They slightly differ from retail chains, using methods of the network marketing well-known worldwide. They widely carry out their advertizing campaigns, presentations, seminars, have periodicals. They promise their members, "brothers", not only health, success in career, wellbeing of family life, warmth of communication between the like-minded, mystical experiences and supernatural abilities, but often the eternal life as well. New information and communication technologies and promises of eternal pleasure help them to involve more and more people in their ranks.

The majority of traditional religions give the weighed assessment to civilizational challenges. On the one hand, the arisen threat of cultural identity of ethnoses, their ecological and demographic stability is noted, and on the other—the benefits are specified which globalization grants—development of new technologies, growth of international contacts in various spheres, positive influence on the economy of underdeveloped countries. In these conditions religious organizations could promote achievement of mutual understanding of people with different values. After all the tolerance, liberality which is much spoken about recently is the fundamental value of almost all religions. A dialogue of cultures, the need of which is constantly noted shall begin with the dialogue of religions and religious organizations, for the purpose of overcoming the misunderstanding leading many people to confrontation. It must lead to formation of tolerant relations between representatives of different faiths, religious movements and organizations.

Technicalization couldn't avoid being reflected also in such a form of public consciousness as art. Not only the content and form of works of art change. The general utilitarization and pragmatization of life change even their goal and purpose. The art being more and more guided by pleasures of consumers turns into the means of business, into commodity. Technicalization of culture leads to prevalence of the form over the content, the sign separation from the meaning about which J. Baudrillard was speaking. Let's remember the sculptures of J.Paik, the machine-like sculptures of J.Epstein and others. Mass character of the modern art practically leads to its death because the individual and personal initiative which is the substantive characteristic of art is lost.

On the other hand, the art is that powerful force which forms that national identity about which they write so much today among the representatives of both own and foreign culture. Here, however, as well as everywhere, the main thing is not to go into extremes. Acknowledgement and study of own things must not lead to ignoring of the rest.

Jeremy Paxman in his work "The English: A Portrait of a People" writes: "It seems simple to be an Englishman. They were always the most easily recognizable nation detected by the language, manners, clothes, the mere fact of tea drinking. Now everything is much more difficult. When accidentally we meet someone, with a typical upper lip, well-groomed footwear or clothes or a manner to identify himself with an Englishman, we suddenly are excessively surprised– the convention which used to identify the English, are dead, and singers or writers act more as messengers of the country, than politicians and diplomats"[42]. Many scientists explain the cultural originality of the English with the island location of England which, as well as for the Japanese, acted as the Iron Curtain for other cultures earlier. During the globalization era these geographical barriers disappear. The cultural values remain which have taken deep roots in the national consciousness.

Along with unification there is also the culture fragmentization observed today. "On a personal level,—A. Toffler writes,—we are besieged and blinded by contradictory and not relating to us fragments of a figurative row, which cut the ground from under the feet of our old ideas and fire on us with torn off and deprived of sense "clips", instant snaps. In fact, we live in "the clip culture"[43]. The same is noted by Jeffrey Woolf concerning fiction and by Daniel Laskin—concerning documentary prose. "The idea of any exhaustive synthesis,—writes the latter,—seems insolvent. An alternative decision is to assemble the world at random, especially its most amusing crocks"[44]. Splitting the figurative row of a person into tiny crocks isn't limited to literature, it is even more shown in the mass media and electronic means of communication. A. Toffler emphasizes that a modern person already almost forgot to perceive the whole system information. He feels well enough under the bombing of blitz: one and a half minute clip with news, a half-minute commercial, a fragment of a song or a poem, a heading, an animated cartoon, a collage, a piece of news, computer graphics. Not only the mentality of the modern person has changed, the way of perception of information and reality has changed as well.

Such changes dictate the need to change also the way of people interaction with the social and social-natural systems. For this purpose it is necessary to obtain new methods of integration and conversion of information. "The more diverse the civilization, the more differentiated its technology, its energy forms, the more information shall pass between its parts to have an opportunity to connect them together, especially in the face of global changes"[45].

Not only the ways of interaction of social subjects change, but the environment changes as well. Today it is already impossible to speak irrevocably about purely the environment. Our environment "is being more and more intellectualized" and computerized. There is no need to remember science-fiction works to illustrate that any more. It is enough to look at the technical achievements, capabilities of already existing robots, functioning of "smart homes" doing some homework for the owner, ordering products for the owner in supermarkets, to be convinced that the habitat of the modern person has become intellectually mechanized. In means that along with the new techno, info and social spheres "a new ecosphere" has been created today. It is not quite the same what Pierre Teilhard de Chardin and V. I. Vernadsky called a noosphere, but, probably, the term "noosphere" can have such a meaning as well. Perhaps, in the near future the machines will call the human society "the surrounding".

Absolutization of relativism characteristic of present postmodernism, deconstruction, de-universalism, unfortunately, affects also the morals. The borders between good and evil, decent and dishonorable are erased. And the word "honor" sounds already almost like an anachronism. Today the behavior of the youth is unified which allows to speak about a global youth subculture. Movies, celebrities of the show business form the patterns of behavior for the youth all over the world. Even the youth slang is unified so that today the young people of all countries can clearly understand each other without knowing foreign languages at enough level. The "glamorous" way of life often including drugs consumption is being established. We have broken through the wall of inviolability of frontiers, and there is no way back",—A. Toffler emphasizes.

All these socio-cultural transformations of mankind can't but affect also the personal level. In a global "supermarket" a person becomes not just a consumer, but also a lonely, indifferent, passionless, nervous, aggressive and afraid of everything mass consumer. A. Zinovyev calls the XX century perhaps the last human century. "To replace it,—he writes,—there approaches a bulk of centuries of superhuman or post-human history, history without hopes and without despair, without illusions and enlightenments, without seductions and disappointment, without joy and without grief, without love and without hatred . . . "[46]. In other words, development of the techno civilization leads to robotization of a man (let's remember A. Camus's works "The Stranger" or F. Kafka "The Trial", etc.). The main characters of these works almost forgot to feel human emotions. And really, in the society where everything becomes techno commodities, a person has almost put up with the fact that he had turned into a robot. And what does robot need feelings for?

All this became possible thanks to the established rational vulgar-materialist scientific paradigm.

Chapter Two

Pleasure as a Catalyst for Development of Society

2.1 THE PLACE AND ROLE OF PLEASURE IN THE ECONOMIC DEVELOPMENT

Under the expert redaction of professor of behavioral economists Alexey Belyanin, High Scholl of Economics, Russia

Modern economy is a science focused on decision making. It studies the decisions that society takes for the purposes of resource allocation. Resources fall into non-renewable and limited, such as raw materials, labor, buildings and constructions, and unlimited, such as human needs. Thus human needs can be thought of as falling into the categories of vital (indispensable to life), prestige-ritual and spiritual ones. The first needs are determined by the biosocial human nature, the second ones—by the society's character, its culture and existing ways of socio-mental realization, and the third ones—by the individual level of human development. Marketing began with studying the market and tried to manage it, than it passed to the formation of consumer needs and today it can manage the dependence of humans on their needs, i.e. dependence from pleasure. Marketing has become a means of getting people hooked on "the needle" of pleasure, namely, on yet more ephemeral phenomenon—waiting for this pleasure. But first things first.

Analyze all your today's decisions and you will realize that during the decision-making process, among numerous options each time you have chosen the one that had smaller and fewer labor inputs (I) needed to carry out the decision than the expected utility (U) from the decision. It constitutes the formula for pleasure achievement.

Using this formula, today you were choosing whether to drink some tea or coffee in the morning, put on a blue or white shirt, go to work by car or subway.

What are the inputs:

Often the labor inputs are expressed not in the efforts we make for doing actions, but take shape of unpleasant emotions, for example the feeling of guilt.

For instance, let's take a skipping exercise. Going to the gym requires more energy inputs than staying at home, but that very feeling of guilt to which you expose yourself would cause considerably stronger mental anguish than the physical efforts and time.

In its turn, pleasure can be experienced not immediately (short-term pleasure), but can be delayed over time (long-term, or lasting pleasure). Such decisions we often call "a duty" or "a must," mistakenly believing that they are fulfilled without any hesitation, not thought of as pleasure. However, if we are honest with ourselves, we must admit that each of us at least once has felt pleasure from performing the duty. In the subchapter "Pleasure from Duty" we will elaborate on this.

Pleasure surrounds us everywhere, sometimes the two types of pleasure (short- and long-term) are mixed, confusing us and forcing us to choose between them.

For instance, after awaking, you feel you are torn between two pleasures:

1. immediate, short-term—to have more sleep and to indulge yourself in bed.

Figure 2.1. The formula for pleasure achievement.

2. delayed, long-term—to go to work and avoid a reprimand from your boss.

If you are a boss to yourself, your delayed pleasure would be avoiding the feeling of guilt over being lazy.

No matter how difficult the choice is, one thing remains constant: humans choose the option in which the difference between pleasure and inputs is the biggest.

The pleasure expected at the moment of decision-making is the key parameter defining your choice. Humans make decisions based not on the real pleasure's factual value, but the predicted one. Herein lies the reason of a great number of mistakes and disappointments, because the human brain quite frequently distorts future feelings. There is about 70 forms of cognitive biases one of the most commonly used ones is temporal discounting, or diminishing the significance of events and feelings when they are expected to take place in the future. We will elaborate on this when we analyze the market examples, in which a consumer makes a decision with the long-term pleasure in mind, for instance buying insurance.

Overestimation of the present or underestimation of the future often results into disappointment. In fact, in such cases the difference between pleasure (P) and inputs (I) is negative. We avoid this, having experienced a mistake we learn and adjust our behavior correspondingly.

Formula here: $P—I \leq 0$

A mistake in the inputs estimation: Situation: you take a decision to have a sleep for an hour or so being sure that it would cost you just your boss' look of verjuice. But it turns out that he decides to dismiss you. (perish the thought)

Expectation: $P—I > 0$

Reality: $P1—I1 < 0$

P—Expected pleasure—morning delight.

P1—Real pleasure—morning delight.

$P = P1$

Estimated inputs (I): your boss' look of verjuice.

Real inputs: ($I1 = I \times 2$): dismissal.

$I2 = I \times 2$

Result: feeling of guilt.

Consequence: you keep in mind this experience as a mistake and change your behavior. At your new job (far better previous one) you come to the office on the dot.

A mistake in the estimation of short pleasure: Situation: you take a decision to have a sleep for an hour or so being sure that it would cost you just your boss' look of verjuice. But the drill—you neighbor gets started the bacchanalia.

Expectation: P—I > 0
Reality: P1—I1 < 0
P—Estimated pleasure—morning delight.
P1—Real pleasure—a song of your neighbor's drill.
P1 = P/2 I—Estimated inputs—your boss' look of verjuice.
I1—Real inputs—your boss' look of verjuice.
I1 = I

Consequence: you keep in mind this experience as a mistake and change your behavior. Now you aren't tempted by lying for a single hour in your bed. A mistake in the estimation of long pleasure: Situation: you make your mind to come to work in time to merit reward from your boss. But it occurs your boss is on a business trip and a half of the office come at 11.00.

Expectation: P—I > 0
Reality: P1—I1 < 0
P—Estimated pleasure—merit reward from your boss.
P1—Real pleasure—there's no.
P1—P*0
I—Estimated inputs—to force yourself to get up.
I1—Real inputs—to force yourself to get up.
I1 = I

Consequence: you keep in mind this experience as a mistake and change your behavior. Now you are frequently late.

There can be a lot of combinations but pleasure and inputs (including emotional) always lie on two scales. People always make such a decision, in which pleasure, according to their current evaluation, outweigh inputs.

An individual makes millions of decisions, routine and fatal, according to this principle.

Living conditions can be changed, even the person can change, and those things which used to bring you pleasure would fade, while those ones that used to make no difference would start giving you pleasure. For example, your smoking and morning run habits can change, but your desire to receive pleasure from them will remain unchangeable.

We analyze the decision-making process and the role pleasure plays in it. But we did not stop here. We have gone further and looked into the future. What we have seen has made our blood turn and moved us to write this book.

2.2 PLEASURE AND ADVENT OF NEW ELITE

Recently, evolution has both accelerated and become complicated. This, of course, is not a secret for anyone. Everyone understands that technologies allowed a human to take a huge leap in development.

However, previously nobody noticed or simply refused to notice that not everyone takes part in evolution. At some moment, humans divided into two groups: those who have been thrown into the new evolution's cycle, and those who have been left behind. Definitely, the first one is in the minority. During the last century they have concentrated the most capital in their hands, and with it the science, i.e. all the technologies which have turned their owners into Overman, whose aim is to speed up their own development and to protect it from the majority that was left at the previous stage.

The evolution's wheel is spun up and it is shining with the progress' spokes. But the human majority cannot catch up with it. We are living in the world built by the people of tomorrow for people of the past. One of the most important criteria for the differentiation is the personal degree of creativity.

Has it occurred according to someone's brilliant plan or due to evolution—the question is of no importance. It's important that today we are living in the world where the development is not only discouraged, but also suppressed. The question of whether this process has specific secret beneficiaries is not so important, as the question of what should those billions do who are thrown overboard of the development. In search for the answer, we are facing the pleasure phenomenon again. Hence we start referring to it with a capital letter, as it turns out that it is the Pleasure that has become the main tool for keeping humans at bay on the evolution path.

2.2.1 Pleasure Became a Commodity, and Marketing Enslaved People

It all started with the development of market capitalism. At the beginning nothing boded ill.

On the contrary, capitalism brought prosperity and freedom of self-expression for people. In other words, it created ideal conditions for the development. However, the more prosperity was accumulated, the more appetite was developed. The market was growing at a galloping speed. In the end, consumption had far exceeded the needs and spilled to the pleasure field.

Supply no longer satisfied the demand. Pleasure began to provide it. This thin line signified the emergence of modern marketing, different from its predecessor, as it was no longer the art of rhetoric focusing on product advantages, but the skill of manipulating the behavior at the decision making level.

Ever since the marketers found out what drives every personal decision, the world has changed once and for all. A new product—Pleasure—has entered the global market. Trillions of dollars have flown into the accounts of companies selling 'Pleasure.' As neuroscience is developing and neuro-marketing is coming of age, we can conclude that this process is as irreversible as accelerating. Pleasure will never cease generating money. On the contrary, it hides an unlimited potential for wealth. It is obvious that in the future the mechanisms making a person run to a store to buy pleasure will only improve and become more sophisticated. Today, it has turned into an itch caused by the perceived disparity between self and the desired image, often constructed in the person's mind with the help of advertisers, mass-media, movies and pop-culture. Today, the desire to get rid of the itch is a powerful driver for billions of human lives. What will tomorrow bring?—We don't know yet.

However, we can claim with certainty that if humans continue relinquishing to corporations the complete control over pleasure, the main driver for all human actions, there will be no chance for development. Evolution cannot stand still. If there is no propulsion, then there will be regression and degradation. The world will be flooded by the creatures, which deserve no more than to be called economic erythrocytes. In other words, they would become particles whose function in the huge economic organism will be just to transfer the capital from one system to another and whose potency will be evaluated through the purchasing power. Can we even refer to them as "humans," when as the subjects of economic activity they have characteristics close to those of a plastic credit card? It is worth noting that boded marketers have coined the term "consumer," having literally downgraded the Homo sapiens to a simple function.

2.2.2 The Ultimatum of Pleasure

"To rise above the pleasure principle and to develop oneself further, or surrender to it and fall out of the evolution ship's board"—states "The Ultimatum of Pleasure." In the 21st century, a great responsibility has fallen upon the majority—to choose its own path. This opportunity may never come up again. Today, the majority has a chance to return the right for development by snatching the fate's leading strings out of hands of the minority.

To further evolution, the majority must overcome the principle of pleasure. Pleasure cannot dictate humans what to choose, humans must derive pleasure from what they choose. Lusts and desires that drive us to act, promising but not delivering Pleasure, make humans an easy target for the dictatorship of marketing.

The motivation system, designed to satisfy the pleasure expectation itch, forces a human to grasp any chance that would make that itch disappear. In our age of consumer capitalism, almost all such opportunities are equated with a purchase.

The majority must learn how to want something consciously and intelligently, rather than want to satisfy desire as quickly as possible, which will ultimately bring discomfort. This means pleasure should begin when we receive the object of desire, not end with this, simply taking the itch away.

To wish for more all the time, having no awareness of why you need something and lose interest immediately after you receive the object of your desire. To live in anguish resulted from the unconscious needs, to suffer from dissatisfaction of the expected pleasure, and after having received it, being unable to fully enjoy it, immediately start suffering from a new pain—this is the vicious cycle that must be broken.

2.2.3 Can Humans Resolve the Ultimatum of Pleasure

Authors often make a disclaimer that their books do not have answers to the questions they themselves raise and only present reflections on the subject. However, these authors consciously deprive themselves of the pleasure of irresponsibility. Moreover, we welcome critical remarks as we share with the reader our vision that each of us can change the polarity of our force of attraction. We must start attracting pleasures rather than being attracted by them.

We have a reason to believe that humans have enough vigor and resilience to change their nature and learn to reward themselves with pleasure.

In fact, all human history is a story of success in rising above and overcoming the human nature. Judge for yourself, today we are living incommensurably more time in the handmade world than in the natural one. According to the "Experimental Investigation of Purification Function of Air Conditioner Research", we spend about 80–90 per cent of our lives in the air-conditioned environment.

In other words, if tomorrow we are forced to live at a space station with landscapes painted on the windows, we would hardly notice any difference. Business-centers, apartments, cars, supermarkets, the Internet, gadgets—they are our natural environments. We have changed the nature!

Today, even "in childbirth" we face not the things we used to call the nature, we are greeted by sophisticated medical robots. In-vitro, where a woman is artificially inseminated, is a habitual thing of modernity. More and more we hear about surrogate mothers, who tomorrow will be substituted by robots. Next step is to synthesize sperm and eggs from biomaterials.

We have changed not only the environment, but also our bodies. Today, implants substitute our limbs and internal organs. Tomorrow, we may entirely consist of the artificial parts. Such markers as sex, age, and ethnicity will disappear altogether. We will not have to have a human body in order to be called a human being. Rising above nature is at the core of human existence.

So, can the majority de-monopolize evolution and break the vicious cycle of desires?—We believe the answer is "yes." Simply because, humans do not need to have social influence, money, or power to do so. Neither do they even need the modern technologies for this. In the struggle for freedom from enslaving pleasures, the mighty elites of this world and ordinary citizens are equal. It is an internal struggle with ourselves, with our "driver" that we inherited from our ancient common ancestors—cavemen.

2.2.4 What to Expect If We Succeed

Imagine how the world would change when humans stop chasing after pleasure, and start feeling it on their own based on their conscious choice. The terms "failure" and "disappointment" will disappear from people's vocabulary. Guilt and fear of the unknown will also disappear. Everyone in the world will breathe freely, having rid themselves of the marketing shackles and the feeling of dissatisfaction with oneself imposed by the marketers.

Every human being will release the energy to know one's true essence, thus opening the way to becoming a God-Man.

It is worth pointing out that by admitting each individual into the next cycle of evolution, the humankind will remove the risk of emergence of the Nietzsche's Man-God. This is the very risk that today is unequivocally embraced by the elites, who have moved far ahead in their development by using advantage and superiority for the exploitation and suppression of the majority. We'll talk about this in more detail in the chapter on Pleasure Traps.

2.3 THREATS OF THE PLEASURE PARADIGM

Pleasure can destroy a person not only when it openly seduces him like, for example, it does with drugs or alcohol but also when it remains unconscious. Sometimes people think that they act excluding all pleasures, being guided by cold mind, sometimes even intentionally avoiding pleasure, but even then it is a hidden motivator of their actions. The phenomena, which seems absolutely far from pleasure, such as submission, jealousy, and even sufferings all the same conceal it in themselves.

Without realizing unconscious thirst for pleasure, people move towards it, sacrificing what could make them happy.

We call it a pleasure trap, i.e, a situation in which the aspiration to unconscious pleasure deprives human life of "forming happiness" elements. The word "trap" is used because at that moment more and more pleasure is required to a person, and he aggravates the situation.

Unfortunately, having got into such a trap, it is very difficult to get out of it by oneself and, as a rule, the end is really tragic. Therefore, we would like to tell you about these most widespread traps.

2.3.1 Suffering

The feeling opposite to pleasure is suffering.

In chapter 4.5 "Train willpower" it was noted that pain may contribute to the emergence of pleasure. When a person doesn't derive pleasure from action, he can feel pain from inaction. Then, avoiding pain from inaction, he will automatically derive pleasure from action.

This mechanism isn't new, but unlike its conscious use, people throughout centuries were using it, without understanding that they hurt themselves only to receive a portion of pleasure, having removed the pain. Unfortunately, with such an approach the suffering exceeds the derived pleasure. As a result the unconscious aspiration to pleasure fills the life with pain. However the short-term pleasure doesn't compensate the long-term suffering.

This is the first and, in our opinion, the main trap of pleasure—Unconscious search of sufferings in order to derive pleasure from removing them.

There are many examples how a man dooms himself to suffering for the sake of the prime target. We ourselves saw the dark and crude hole where, deeply underground, the father Gregory, founder of Gregorianity was put. The tsar Trdat, the Great ordered to imprison him for preaching Christianity in the yet pagan world. The father Gregory courageously stood all the burdens and deprivations of the cruel imprisonment, understanding that he suffered for a good cause. One day the Tsar fell seriously ill. Even the well-known doctors were powerless. He addressed to Gregory then. The latter without a shadow of vindictive gloat, with humility inherent in Christians helped his executioner, having healed him of an incurable illness. After his wonderful recovery the tsar Trdat himself believed in Christ and contributed to christening of his country—Armenia. So the Christianity for the first time became the state religion. And the father Gregory was canonized.

Many people have been to Jerusalem and seen Golgotha—the place of Jesus' crucifixion.

However, such self-sacrifice was made not only because of religion. Let's remember Socrates or Giordano Bruno who voluntarily chose execution. To be oneself, despite any tortures, and therefore to go to eternity is the highest blessing and pleasure for the great people.

Unfortunately, the usual life is full of other examples when a person is guided not by the highest ideas, but simply gets into psycho-physiological traps of his feelings.

An example is the life of a woman who lives with her husband, who always beats her. What keeps her from a divorce? Maybe the tyrant possesses the unique charisma, the willpower which attracts her so much? However, most often ordinary drunkards happen to be such husbands.

And maybe the matter is not in him, but in her? After all she doesn't leave, she can't make the decision. She can't because the pleasure which she derives from living with him is stronger than the pleasure from living alone or with another man.

Every time during a scandal her pain was reaching its peak. It became unbearable for her to live. However, with the help of relatives, she was removing this pain afterwards.

What did she feel when the pain had gone? Correct, pleasure! Unconsciously, without admitting to herself, but all the same she felt pleasure. If there was no pain—there would be no pleasure. Not all, but many people have it happening like this.

It is a disgusting and improper, but still a pleasure formula.

People can strive for sufferings and derive pleasure from them also because of a guilt complex. Unforgiving themselves these or those acts, some people consider that they aren't worthy a happy life, and only sufferings can recoup their sins. Experiencing deprivations and pain, they still derive pleasure from the justice triumph and they will manage to get rid of the sense of guilt. Psychological researches confirm it with facts. One patient of a psychiatrist constantly sought to hurt himself, doomed himself to the deprivations and sufferings invented by him, although he couldn't himself explain why he did that. After long examinations psychiatrists found out that such unusual behavior was connected with the work of the patient. He worked as a butcher and was constantly cutting beef hulks. Apparently his unconscious was keeping the unpleasant feelings which had been arising in him upon cutting off different parts of animal bodies. Therefore, he unconsciously aspired to pain and suffering as he considered it fair for the sufferings of animals.

We witnessed the sufferings of one rather good dentist-surgeon, who was angrily calling himself a bad person because he had to extract teeth of patients. "Who allowed me to take away a part of a human organism? I won't get away with that!" When people tried to object that he does that with the aim to keep the health of people, he was waving his hand and tipping another shot. Although he perfectly knew that doctors had forbidden him to drink...

Wilhelm Reich in his book "Character Analysis" gives a lot of examples from his practice confirming the thought that many people intentionally strive for sufferings and pain to derive pleasure. He explains it by the fact that in the course of life they have got psychological traumas which formed kind of "a muscular carapace", "a rigid shell from which both blows of the outside world, and internal inquiries were jumping off ".

"This shell, W. Reich emphasizes,—makes an individual less sensitive to displeasure, however it also reduces his libido and aggressive needs and thus his capability to get pleasure and achieve the desired".[1]

Pleasure from sufferings is familiar to everyone.

It is not that only women are able to derive pleasure from pain. This ability was developed evolutionarily in all people irrespective of the sex. It rather looks like perversion of the true human nature though.

But still many people derive pleasure from pain. Such deviation of some people reaches a clinical level. It is already pathology.

However, let's remember a bath-house, this extremely hard ordeal which for all rational reasons should bring the real suffering. People are sitting in a closed, badly aired room heated up to 70 degrees, sometimes even to 100 degrees, sweating, losing moisture, and then the most heartless one puts on steam, and the room turns into a boiling caldron. It is impossible to breathe, heartbeat is accelerated, the nasopharynx burns. And the "executioner" starts beating his friends calmly with the branches collected in a bunch. He whips with all his might, having pre-dipped the besom into the boiling water. It rather looks like a medieval torture, than a procedure which many people rush to, anticipating pleasure.

To derive pleasure from the removal of pain is a physiological property of humans and the majority of mammals. However, to aspire to pain for the sake of a possibility, to remove it, and thus to derive pleasure is a feature of human mentality. We call it a pleasure trap. Unfortunately, it is not the only one. There are a lot of traps. We are disclosing only the most important of them, which are presented most widely in usual life.

In the following chapter, we will discuss another trap, not less widespread, than a trap of "sufferings" and its name is pleasure from isolation.

2.3.2 Loneliness

Isolation entices people with a promise of pleasure. However, if isolation doesn't serve to a productive purpose, it turns into a trap since there will be less pleasure, than suffering, and with a high probability it will force a person to aggravate his loneliness, by exploiting the model of obtaining pleasure through pain.

Some people decide to take extreme measures while seeking freedom from pleasure.

Demonizing the society with its maniac aspiration to excesses, they doom themselves to seclusion.

Often when we watch how another sociopath locks himself in the apartment, we feel pity for him, considering that he has lost all the pleasures in life.

Is it really as it is?

Can a man feel pleasure from what was created for suffering by the nature? No gregarious being can derive pleasure from loneliness. Can we say the same about humans?

It is known that the priests and monks who are living in ascetic life, not knowing material pleasures, experience true ecstasy. They wouldn't exchange their solitude and a quiet prayer by a candle into anything on earth. They do not care about parties, young ladies and idle splendor of life. There is no pleasure for them at all in that. But there is abundant pleasure in self-denial, in the knees worn out with prayers and even in hunger—people hold the great Lent with pleasure.

What is a curse for any gregarious animal, what was scaring us for millions of years—renunciation of our tribesmen—becomes pleasure for people who have learned to replace public life with the service to the highest ideas. They choose the ascesis. Not as punishment, but for the sake of pleasure.

Impossibility of solitude—is what brings suffering to such people.

Let's shift to hot spaces of Ancient India and fling ourselves into the philosophy of the Indians. In 563BC, the "axial" age according to K. Jaspers, when the mankind everywhere was approaching the understanding of truth, universal for its existence, in a family of an Indian maharaja (in our language, the prince) a boy was born who was called Siddhartha, a full name—Siddhartha Gautama Shakyamuni. His father was foretold that the destiny of his son would be to become either the governor plunged into pleasures and delights who would unite many Indian principalities, or the eremite and founder of own doctrine if he faced sufferings, diseases and death. The maharaja wanted to see a happy successor and governor in his son, thus he ordered to protect his son from sufferings and injustice.

But once, during a ritual a white elephant on which Siddhartha was sitting, had enraged and broke the gates and found itself outside of the princely palace. There it was when Siddhartha got acquainted with realities of life, with beggars, starving, suffering and ill people. He understood that life was full of sufferings. He could not return to his magnificent life full of pleasures, having decided to learn, what the reason of sufferings was. He became an ascetic, he wandered for a long time, meditated, until he had got the truth and became Buddha (enlightened, awakened). He had formulated the four truths of the Buddhism:

1. Life is suffering.
2. There is a reason of sufferings. It is the desire (greed of pleasures)
3. It is possible to stop suffering, by eliminating desires (to cease pursuing pleasures)
4. This is possible by means of an octal way of clarification, (ennobling desires).

Thus, Buddha, having understood that desires can't be completely eliminated, suggests to clean them, to ennoble. This self-improvement lies on the way of transformation of the thoughts, speech, intentions, actions, will and meditation into the correct ones. Desires remain, but they change and turn from the life purpose into its means. First of all, it is necessary to begin with the correct thoughts, to leave in the consciousness only the ideas promoting self-improvement of the personality, the correct vision of its essence, mission. Having learned the scenario of his life, a man strengthens his will and corrects his further life through meditation, communicating with the supreme intelligence.

Is it possible to say, that loneliness granted pleasure to Siddhartha? After all he felt shock, he suffered, suffered from the fact that he didn't know how to help people, how to eliminate the reason of their tortures! And maybe he was guided by anticipation of pleasure from an opportunity to solve their problems?

Pleasure from isolation is possible. But why do we call it a trap? If a person is happy, being alone, why not to recognize his right to enjoy the loneliness?

The matter is that isolation as an end in itself, as a way of searching pleasure, will start bringing sufferings sooner or later. As a rule, it acts as a condition of achieving the goal, the highest idea in which a person believes with all his heart.

Serving to the purpose gives him pleasure, but not isolation by itself.

Sociopaths, who had preferred the Internet at home to healthy communications, aren't capable to derive pleasures which are given by serving to ideals. Isolation by itself keeps inside a lot of sufferings since it isn't eco-friendly by its nature. Having rashly decided to be limited to the company of himself, a person risks to increase his pain so that to enjoy the pleasure from the pain removal. In aspiration to get rid of it, he will begin to plunge himself deeper and deeper into loneliness, trying to be sated with that insignificant pleasure which he will be able to find in it. This is exactly how the pleasure traps work: a man unconsciously produces pain to enjoy the pleasure which is given by removing it.

However, traps are called traps because the pain in them exceeds the pleasure and in a pursuit of its larger amount, a person continues to reproduce the pain.

One of the most artful traps is "the pleasure from belonging" when a person feels pleasure from understanding of his belonging. It can be a woman bearing jealousy of a man, it can be a teenager seeking to be a part of subculture or a soldier in barracks considering himself the homeland tool.

2.3.3 Dependence

Probably, it is the trap containing danger for women more than for men.

Desire to belong is a pronounced female need which sometimes gets its followers into the wilds full of sufferings.

Many women, at least once in their life derived pleasure from jealousy of the partner. They like to be under his wing and to know that he will take care of them. Of course, such feelings were formed for thousand years of evolution. Over time the society was complicating, and similar relations had gone, however its rudiments are met even in our days; sometimes in the most non-constructive form.

We are talking about jealousy, more correctly, about the fact how some women seek to be the object of jealousy for the beloved man. It leads to unconscious provocations and, as a rule, to fast destruction of the relations.

The pleasure from jealousy forcing to turn life into a real nightmare is a widespread trap that which many people get into.

Without going deep into psychoanalysis, it is possible to conclude that some girls get pleasure when they feel the right of a man to possess them. They like to feel the power thanks to which men declare their proprietary claims.

Thus some girls make sure that the heart of the beloved man is not indifferent to them.

Some women find a man especially attractive at the moment when he swears and curses. They intentionally enrage partners, giving reasons for jealousy.

Feeling aggression directed on them, they get pleasure.

During a visit to a psychotherapist one patient confessed: "It is a pity, I didn't know about this feature before, I would understand the behavior of my former wife then. She did everything for her pleasure. While I was nearing a heart attack, she was nearing... an orgasm".

The trap from belonging forces girls to look for pleasure in the destructive sides of the relations.

Instead of avoiding a conflict somehow, they subconsciously seek to bring it to apogee to enjoy the proprietary impulses of a man. Often it destroys the relations, and sometimes lives.

It is much more difficult to feel the necessity without destructive motives.

It assumes soul closeness.

It is hard to accept the thought that a person can't be someone's. One should suppress the image imparted by the nature that a woman has to belong to a man. For higher relations it is necessary to learn to derive pleasure from other forms of demonstration belonging deprived of egocentric ambitions. They might be care, self-sacrifice, or involvement in co-creation.

2.3.4 Interrelation of Domination and Subordination

Once upon a time there was a small village in Ancient China nearby the Himalayas. Peasants were peacefully living there.

But a disaster had struck once—the village was attacked by a Golden Dragon. Every year it took the most beautiful girl, suppressing the resistance by ruthless fire. So it happened year after year. One day a courageous young man dared to challenge the dragon. Despite the overall fear and pleas to give up and not to enrage the monster, he jumped on a horse and went to the dragon's den. The young man was brave and believed that he would be able to win. And so it happened, after a long fight the dragon fell.

The hero remained in its castle so that all people remembered who had killed the monster.

The man was respected, people started to fear and obey him. After a while the killer of the dragon began to rule the settlement. He started collecting tributes. He was judging people. His desires were growing over time. And one day he decided to marry: "bring the most beautiful of your daughters to me" he told the elders.

Three years had not passed from the day of the dragon's death and the brave young man had himself turned into a dragon.

The trap is not only in the pleasure from domination, but also from submission.

The parable is old, but it shows the influence of power on a person better than many others. The power rarely reveals the best qualities in anyone, but despite that millions of people seek for domination over others. It is not surprising, since the power conceals huge pleasure in itself.

Not for nothing they say:

"Who possesses the power, is obsessed with it".

However, we are interested not so much in domination as in its consequence—submission.

Surprisingly, but submission also brings pleasure.

There are undoubtedly many times more people deriving pleasure from submission than those who look for it in domination.

The aspiration to dominate is conscious, as a rule, and an individual, in a varying degree, is ready to face the metamorphosis which he will be subjected to by the pleasure from domination. Pleasure from submission is different, it is imperceptible like gas, fills the whole being, and if a person is ever able to realize it, most likely it would happen when it is too late to change anything.

The invisibility makes pleasure from submission the real trap surpassing the trap of "pleasure from domination" by sad consequences.

The competition for leadership is biologically input into a man. The aspiration to domination is provided by active discharge of dopamine. It is natural, since the aspiration to be better is the means to keep and develop the species.

The nature created the adaptation mechanism of gregarious animals by means of submission to a stronger individual, i.e., to a leader. In extreme situations the survival of a pack depends on ability of its leader to mobilize everyone to solve the problem. It is interesting that the leader wolf of the pack becomes "a democrat" in the summer, showing loyalty to some troublemakers, and in the winter, in conditions of cold and hunger becomes a dictator, cruelly punishing for disobedience.

A man by nature has the ability both to dominate and to submit since it is required for the species survival.

Domination is a possibility and ability to impose one's will, to influence activity and behavior of other people, even despite their resistance[2].

By means of domination a man realizes a potentiality input by the nature to expand his influence over the habitat. He is not just a manager now, but a branch head, a department head, a deputy CEO.

Showing domination, a person turns from an independent single being into the head of a more powerful being, into the Leviathan.[3]

Interesting facts are provided by the psychological researches of Theodor Adorno described in his book "the Authoritarian Personality"[4]. In the section "Authoritarian Syndrome" the author reveals the reasons of emergence of the pleasure which an individual derives from authoritarian behavior.

"Question: What you are happy with?

An answer of an examinee: "Well, I am the first man—the foreman of the shift, we work on shifts . . . (the interviewee emphasizes his "leading" position)—five people in each shift—it satisfies me personally . . . five people work for me, they come to me, ask for my advice in matters concerning our production, and the final decision depends on me. The fact that the final decision depends on me, and I make it, and I understand that I make it correctly, gives me personal satisfaction. What I earn for my living, doesn't give me satisfaction. Those things which I mentioned give satisfaction, and also the understanding that I please my chiefs satisfies me too".

Adorno notes that double satisfaction: to rule others and at the same time to please one's chief—is quite natural to a man".[5]

On the one hand, nothing gives as much pleasure as freedom does. However there is also the other side. The world is contradictory, and the law of unity and struggle of opposites is universal. Any object, any phenomenon comprises its opposite. An acquaintance of mine confessed once: "I have never been as happy as then, stepping in the military array among equal comrades". In response to the interlocutor's bewilderment, he said that it was not required to decide anything, it wasn't required to doubt anything, to care for anything, to feel responsibility for anything. His words sank down into my soul; perhaps, professional military people are a classic example of deriving pleasure by a person from submission to another one's will.

The process of decision-making causes tension of a person. We repeatedly noted that exactly tension a person feels as displeasure and seeks for relaxation which is giving pleasure. Tension can be not only mental, but also moral and ethical. A classical example is the life of "a henpecked", unfortunately, well-known to all our compatriots not only from fiction, but also from life. A husband shifts all responsibility for decision-making to his wife, making, according to E. Fromm, an escape from freedom. He derives pleasure from the fact that not he strains himself, but another person does, even if loved strongly by him. However he doesn't understand that this temporary short pleasure which Epicurus warned about will result in long displeasure and his wife will start treating him worse. He will have to look for relaxation not in communication with his wife then, but in the company of drinking companions. Sometimes it ends even more tragically. Let's remember Tihon from "The Storm" by A. N. Ostrovsky's. He removed himself, pitting his mother against his wife. Katerina's choice is known to us, she like Aesop preferred death to slavery. Do you remember the last words of Aesop: "Where is the abyss for free people here?"

In order to make a person start to derive pleasure from submission it is necessary to make him feel a possibility of choice in his behavior.

Whether he will use it or not—isn't important, but illusion of free will, of a possibility to take everything into own hands—is the secret ingredient turning the suffering from another one's will into pleasure. A soldier waits until he becomes a general, and together with it he will be free from total submission. A henpecked is convinced that he is the chief in the family and at any time can terminate the oppression of his wife. An electorate is convinced that submits to a president who itself had chosen and can change him etc.

Illusion of freedom turns submission into pleasure therefore a man runs from freedom.

Nothing is that simple and unambiguous with a submission phenomenon. Submission can be not only destructive for an individual, besides both for the subject, and for the object of submission, but can be constructive as well. We will give an example. For certain, many have observed more than once how a father, playing, fights with his children, gives in to his son, saying: "Oh, how strong you are! You are my hero!" And the son, taking the praise at its face value, strains muscles and with a proud face shows all the might of a warrior. It is constructive submission. Both parties derive pleasure. The son derives it from the fact that he is growing and becomes stronger and he is told about that, and the father—from the fact that he contributes to the growth and development of his son. This applies not only to physical competitions. "I understood,—one of our students confessed,—that my father almost always gave in to me, playing chess, when unintentionally I saw how he won against the person to whom I always lost"." Giveaway chess" deprives a pupil of the growth possibility, but, on the other hand, eternal defeats can kill the desire of a child to play chess at all. Like everywhere else it is important to know where to stop.

Constructive submission can promote mutual growth. One becomes stronger, the other—becomes kinder and wiser.

Another example is when spouses give in to each other, wishing to support the second half. Usually a woman gives in. Firstly, she is more often wiser, more intuitive, and secondly because men's activities of competition are expressed more brightly. Women more often compete concerning their appearance, and men compete functionally. Remember the movie “Kuban Cossacks” in which the main character, the role played by Marina Ladynina, competes with the chairman of the neighboring collective farm in the races and winning, slowed down the horse to keep the dignity of the man she wasn’t indifferent to. Everyone derived pleasure from such submission. As a result a new couple appeared, and more importantly, it was a happy couple.

2.3.5 Escape from Freedom and Decision Making

In aspiration to remain in a comfort zone, many decisions, especially difficult ones are postponed which leads to loss of pleasure. However pain continues to be saved which can lead to the polarity change and the comfort zone may turn into a zone of sufferings.

We run away from decisions—we save pain.

People are often afraid to leave a zone of comfort and to lose pleasure from stability. This is a trap. Because behind the calmness there is sometimes a life deprived of pleasure from decisions. Once the bowl with pain is overflowed, it will become impossible to suffer any longer, and the imaginary zone of comfort will turn into the real hell. Everything that used to calm down earlier will start irritating. All postponed decisions will declare of themselves. Much strength will be required to overcome the pain.

As an illustration it is possible to give an example with postponing a visit to the doctor. It hurts, but not much really—it is possible to bear. And we bear it! We save the pain, until it hurts so much that we rush to the doctor, forgetting everything in the world.

The postponed decisions produce pain. And once it becomes so much of it that a person can be tempted with the most forbidden pleasure—the pleasure from escape from life. We mean a suicide. More than 1000 000 people[6] per year find in it riddance from sufferings worldwide.

Paradoxically, but it often happens that sufferings appear only because a person admits a thought of a suicide. Realizing that the death could be under control, a person loses fear of it, and then the aspiration to pleasure which it gives—disposal of any pain—gets stronger. An individual can subconsciously strive for sufferings, since the heavier his current state is, the stronger the pleasure will be from their removal.

Thus, some suicides are themselves responsible for, apparently, the objective tragic situations, preceding their self-willed leave.

Lev Tolstoy in his novel “Anna Karenina” ingeniously told about the trap of the pleasure from escape.

The pleasure had thrown Anna into young Vronsky’s embraces, and the pleasure pushed her under the train.

The pleasure had formed the mental tension, which was beyond the strength of Karenina to bear. So she got rid of the pain. And she made this act not because of the sense of guilt or social shame, but owing to a psychological break, disappointment in Vronsky, in her love for the sake of which she had sacrificed everything. If there was no love, she should not live too.

Thus, once again we face various levels of the personal dissonance—physiological, mental and social.

It might be an escape from oneself, from own physiological needs. Anna Karenina made it, having married an elderly person who she did not love.

It might be an escape at the social level when she, having ignored the public norms of decency, left her husband for a young loved man.

And, finally, the last escape . . . into the embraces of the train—leaving from the mental pain, from the hated life which had given her such strong disappointment in love only for the sake of which, in her opinion, it was worth living.

Suicides often imagine how it will be. Our acquaintance was not an exception. He dreamed: there will be no routine everyday life, no eternal headache, only the feeling of a free fall.

Stop the tortures with one move. To destroy the shell preventing to live! A suicide bears in itself riddance from suffering.

The trap is that sometimes a suicide himself looks for that intolerable pain, which he will be unable to bear, and then he will be able to present himself the long-awaited pleasure.

The destructive is preferred to the constructive.

This ill-fated shell can be also destroyed by positive methods though. For example, by creative activity or communication with the beloved person who understands you.

2.3.6 Sense of Guilt

People with the guilt complex consider that they deserved punishment. Excessive religiousness, moralism, ostentatious correctness may be indicators of unconscious sense of guilt. A person, getting used to such behavior, starts feeling pleasure from it. Even failures and punishments can be perceived with pleasure as he considers that he deserved them.

Why don't people with the guilt complex dare to be happy?

Because they feel pleasure from it.

During a visit to a psychotherapist an elderly client remembers his schoolmate with whom he used to have sincere youthful friendship. The girl was very good and answered him with the same pure feeling. No adult relations—just Platonic feelings. Although they had no talk on future life, they were somehow sure that they would get married, would have a lot of children and would live long and happily. But life as always had introduced its amendments. They parted, entered Universities in different cities. Absolutely different life began. And in a couple of years the guy got married. But all his life he was tormented by the sense of guilt towards his first girl. He considered that he had broken her heart. She believed in him, and he betrayed her. In a year she got married, and everything was fine in her life. But the sense of guilt all the same haunted the guy. He couldn't concentrate on his own life and receive pleasure from it. And, when finally the relations with his wife were destroyed, they divorced, he considered it fair and deserved.

What was it, conscience or mental pathology?

Some psychologists consider that guilt belongs to social-cultural regulators of human behavior. It means a person has the sense of guilt if he doesn't follow social norms. In particular, such a position is taken by I. S. Kon. Others connect guilt with a split of "I". When one of "I"'s of a person which is the reason of an act contradicts the central "I" of a person. It is interesting that F.M. Dostoyevsky grasped this side of guilt, having called his main character Rodion Raskolnikov[7].

The guilt is first of all a feeling of regret for the inconvenience, something negative, pain given to another person.

That very Raskolnikov had the sense of guilt, conscience torments for the murder of an old woman. Although rationally he acquitted himself with his theory, his soul which was not spoiled by fashionable book information presented a bill from the positions of eternal truth and values. He was so exhausted with the sense of guilt that considered it pleasure to confess in everything and to go to penal servitude. The same is with the main character of the novel "Resurrection" by Tolstoy. When he recognizes in a defendant the girl with whom once behaved dishonorably, he quits everything and goes to penal servitude with her.

The guilt appears when an act of a person contradicts his essence. Not always a person comes back to his own essence as a result of the sense of guilt. Very often he continues to go away from it, making similar acts and even starts feeling pleasure from this contradiction. For example, an unfaithful wife can come home with the pressing sense of guilt and at the same time with a sweet feeling that she had, at last, revenged this "villain". One of her multi-personalities (according to Assagioli) resists another one and feels satisfaction from the fact that another one feels bad. Like an envious friend who feels bad, when her friend has perfect relations with her beloved man.

It is known that S. Freud considered guilt as the reaction of "I" to the requirements of "Super I". So the guilt appears in case of discrepancy between the behavior of a person and the norms and establishments of the society.

M. Klein for example, considers that guilt results from the conflict between love and hatred to the same being.

The understanding of the sense of guilt is rather interesting in existential psychology which admits the presence of guilt in existence, and not just in the mentality of a person, in other words, considers it as ontological essence.

Rollo May's thoughts are interesting, in our opinion. He considers guilt as a contradiction between the real and ideal personality, that is, the idea of a person of what he should be like.

According to May, guilt is a consequence of the loss of communication with the Absolute. So, guilt is the result of the break with oneself "real".

In our opinion this is the more thorough understanding of guilt. A person can feel pleasure from guilt, at least because he realizes the need of this communication with the Absolute, it exists in his consciousness, although is temporarily broken off. "I am not like I should be. I feel guilty, but at the same time it also gives pleasure to me because I know that I am not like I should be. It means that someday I will be like I should be."

"In transpersonal psychology,—Arina Skibinskaya writes,—it is considered that "the right for pleasure" is one of the matrixes input at birth. In the eastern philosophies this right is referred to the second chakra. And very many people consider that they are "undeserving" pleasures. They want an expensive beautiful dress, but why, I would rather buy a new phone for my son, it is more useful. To learn to allow oneself to feel pleasure without the sense of guilt, to live a free life filled with joy is a big problem for such people ".

A monument to the betrayal is set on a pedestal of guilt.

The pleasure from guilt is a trap since it provokes a person to repeat the action which is giving rise to guilt in him. The guilt plunges the mentality of a person into stress and as McGonigal writes: " shame can work as a preventive measure but when everything is done, the guilt would force more to sabotage, than to self-check ". It is connected with the fact that in a stressful situation created by the guilt, we are inclined to address to the easiest and simplest pleasure, and exactly it, in a consequence causes guilt. Thus, a person gets into a vicious circle.

Every time punishing himself and feeling guilt, a person considers that he redeems his deviant behavior. However, it is obvious that the sense of guilt doesn't bear in itself a piece of constructive action and can't change the objective reality. As well as the resentment which is opposite to guilt, in its essence, is a bodiless ghost.

Feelings live only in the mentality of a person. Therefore, it is so important to activate those which help to make the right decisions.

It is much easier to many people to derive pleasure from guilt, than to forgive themselves and to feel a keen desire of a new, earlier unknown source of pleasure—productive work.

Neither guilt, nor another feeling can be a motive for actions—this role is assigned to pleasure.

The best deal in a case when a person is "tormented" by guilt might become its exchange to anticipation of pleasure from correcting the situation. Unfortunately, for many people it can be very difficult, since pleasure from self-flagellation is present here and now, and atonement demands to refuse it in favor of illusive pleasure from productive work which can be felt only in the future.

However, the human happiness in many aspects depends on the ability to trust in oneself and to show patience waiting for the pleasure postponed in time.

Of course, there are much more traps of pleasure. We tried to describe the most widespread of them. The traps are artful not only because a person doesn't notice how he gets into them, but also because they force to plunge deeper into pain and suffering, motivating by easy and short-term pleasure.

In order not to get into the traps of pleasure, we should not try to learn them all. It is enough to remember that in any action we pursue pleasure consciously or unconsciously.

If life circumstances seem overflowed with suffering, it is necessary to analyze which pleasure a person aspires to in the long run. Probably, having spent several hours, he will be able to find that very drop of pleasure in the sea of sufferings, which has led to the current state of things. In such case, having changed the pleasure to which the desire aspires, it is possible to get rid of all pain.

Having learned to control his pleasure, a man moves to a new level of evolutionary development where his will starts playing the defining role. The future of the entire global human community will depend on whether his will would be directed on the power and domination or on the overall cooperation and productive creativity.

Chapter Three

Civilizational Threats of the Pleasure Paradigm

3.1 THE CONCEPT OF "CIVILIZATIONAL PARADIGM"

One of the peculiar features of the modern era is the increasing dependence of social reality on the dominating in the world, or at least in the leading developed countries, understanding of the backbone purposes, meanings, values, priorities of social development. Today the term "civilizational paradigm" which meaning disclosure is a necessary prerequisite of our further research was firmly fixed in special literature. The word "paradigm" translated from Greek means an example, a model, a sample, is often treated as set of establishments, perceptions, concepts, meanings, a way of vision of the world. With a helping hand of an American scientist Thomas Kuhn the concept "scientific paradigm" was widely adopted, and started to be understood as the theory dominating in science, a model of the reality description[1]. The paradigm describes a set of problems which have the sense and decision, including also the methods to solve these problems.

The paradigm not only promotes this or that description of the world, but also sets the world by means of its symbols and elements. Literally translated as "superlook", the paradigm makes a setting for this or that understanding of reality. It is based on some knowledge, conviction, but most often on the belief in this or that state of things which, in turn, are naturally determined by other phenomena which essence needs to be disclosed for their adequate understanding.

Some researchers call a model of the dominating mentality, a mental model of the world and the world order based on the commonly accepted ideas and concepts in this society determining its behavior and the attitude towards the world and themselves a paradigm. However the word "mentality", although it is extremely fashionable today, is a little ambiguous. Not individual, but social or public mentality, of ethnos for example, is meant of course. But nevertheless mentality is connected with the rational-conscious component of mind. Is it possible to include the unconscious, in our case the collective, into the contents of the concept "mentality"? Then perhaps will it be better to call the way of spiritual attitude to the world a paradigm? In any case the concept "paradigm" is close to the concept "outlook" including both world view, and attitude, and world perception together with its unconscious component.

Some authors call the paradigm of this or that culture its nature, others prefer to consider it the main idea of culture. However such attempts are very conditional since they don't reflect the real interrelation between the concepts "paradigm" and "culture". Besides the concept "idea" is often confused to the content of Plato's concept "Eidos". A paradigm appears as a result of functioning and developing of a certain culture, particularly the historical way of the attitude to the world around, and the eidos of culture represents that spiritual image which lies in its basis, i.e. it itself initiates this culture.

There are also various definitions of a civilization. Without deepening into theoretical analysis or as it is fashionable today to say "discourse", we will note that we will understand a certain stage of cultural development as a civilization. At least because the word "civilius" means urban. That is, at the stage of emergence of the cities and related to them realities there comes the era of transformation of culture into a civilization. The second concept as we see is considerably narrower than the first one by the extent. However if we address again the remarkable book of Oswald Spengler, we will see then that as a civilization he understands not only a stage, but also a certain nature of culture, namely technogenic and aggressive-expansive ones. "A civilization,—he writes, are those extreme and artificial conditions which the highest type of people is capable to perform. They are completion, they follow as what has become after formation, as death after life, as immovability after development, as intellectual anility and a fossilated world city after a village and heart-felt childhood shown over lorica and gothic. They are the inevitable end, and, nevertheless, with internal need they were always reached"[2]. We can't disagree with it. But, probably, a certain stage of development is connected also with the nature of culture. Moreover, we suggest also to distinguish the natures of civilizations. In our opinion, the cornerstone of identifying this nature should be the values of civilization determined by the values of people's way of life, the way of their activities or the way of adaptation.

By the word "civilization" they understand a certain concrete historical stage of culture, i.e. specific time frames of cultural development. And this cultural development isn't necessarily connected with a city and techniques as some researchers think. It is more important in this case to emphasize the nature of culture because during different periods of cultural development, this development had specific features. For example, "the axial age", as K. Jaspers called the 6-5th century B.C. during which there was a formation of the main civilizational strategies, can hardly be compared with the usual time of the mankind development. But the concept "civilization" is treated also in a different way. Sometimes it is contrasted with barbarity and wildness, sometimes it is used as a synonym of culture, more precisely, for designation of cultural and historical types (A. Toynbee). Sometimes they understand completion, death, cultural decadence as a civilization. Exactly this way O. Spengler understood a civilization. We won't focus attention on negative shades of the word "civilization".

We are interested in a civilization as a certain stage in cultural development, character of this civilization as a way of adaptation to the world. How did the principle of aspiration to pleasure favor the survival of a man? What type of behavior was chosen depending on the character of a civilization? The western civilization after some hesitations "placed its bets" onto force, on the external conquest. Nietzsche sounded out the bible of Modern times, the superman Zarathustra's precept to people, this percept safely leads us to the society of mass consumption. Today this Bible is called techtury, nectury (from the words techniques, necro—death, etc.).

The litmus paper defining the character of the civilization was the attitude of a man towards pleasure as a criterion of the civilization direction programming the brain on this or that condition: to be a servant or the master of pleasures, and generally speaking of his own destiny. Dependence of the person on the surrounding nature in the primitive society was changed by slavery from people during the slaveholding era, then it turned into slavery from the hypertrophied religion, then—into slavery from science and technology during the Modern times and, finally, during the era of capitalism has resulted in slavery from money. Pleasure indulged it because it, and to be exact, the dependence of the human brain on pleasure, was the reason of this slavery. The pleasure not only from material possession, but also from understanding of the domination over other people, animals and even the nature in general, pushed a man toward the following round of development of the technogenic civilization. Nietzsche said: "the God has died". Pleasure, having fondly believed that, began to pretend to take His place.

Sometime there must come the era of the domination of a man over his pleasures, the era which we call the era of New humanism, the era of a free creative person. Really a brilliant prophecy of Goethe is Faust's victory over Mephistopheles. This is the sense of the new humanism—to subordinate individual pleasure to happiness of people assuming understanding of a man as an eternal being, not limited by the frames of only his biological time.

Summarizing, we will emphasize that a civilizational paradigm represents a certain outlook, world perception and world description determining by itself the way of activity, the attitude to the world and the problems arising in it, the way of adaptation and adapting the environment, the way of understanding and solution of vital problems. In a civilizational paradigm they single out a set of special ways and methods of solving the vital paradoxes worked out by the society for a long period, the paradoxes which are passed over from father to son by means of traditions and imitations.

As it was already emphasized, in a civilizational paradigm it is important to consider not only conscious and rational, but also unconscious and irrational components. For example, besides the values and super values of a cultural era it is important to reveal and research dominative in a certain historical time settings and attitudes (social establishments) which determined the direction of civilizational development.

O. Spengler's emphasis on distinction of civilizations depending on the attitude to such basic concepts of culture as "formation" and "formed", "friendly" and "alien", "soul" and "body", "possibility" and "reality", "me" and "not me", "life" and "death" is interesting. He connects the concept "life" with formation process while everything which was formed is associated by him with death. All sensual he calls alien which came from the outside, and "me" is friendly, own. Particularly important for him is the concept "direction" of formation, amendments which he associates with the concept "time". "If,—he writes,—simultaneously giving prevalence of the unconscious over the conscious, to designate the soul as a possibility, and, on the contrary, the world as the reality, expressions about which the internal feeling doesn't leave any doubt—then life will be the image in which realization of the possible is performed. Based on the directional feature the possible is called the future, the realized is called the past. The realization, the center and sense of life we call the present. "The soul is what is subject to realization, "world"—the realized, "life"—the realization".[3].

He divides the world pictures depending on what determines a certain culture—formation or the formed, direction or length, time or space. Proceeding from that, O. Spengler divides culture into possible (i.e. culture as an idea of existence) and real culture (as the body of this idea). He considers that culture represents the embodiment of the soul, the main idea of human existence, but his words are possible to be understood another way. "The soul,—he writes,—aims to realize itself in the image of the world around . . . ". That is, the world around, including the natural one, is reflection of the soul of the people inhabiting it. Actually, in our opinion, quite the opposite, the soul is reflection of the surrounding natural and socio-cultural world. In this case the environmental law of concentration formulated by us also works: an element is the concentrated expression of energy of the system. If culture and soul of the people mutually determine their contents, then the character of the natural environment already has different regularities. The cultivated nature, of course, bears the impress of the people creating it. If the main content of the human soul is aspiration to pleasures, then the nature turns into the means of bringing this pleasure.

Spengler notes that just like the ancient Greeks had no word for designation of space, they had no feeling of the landscape, the horizon, the distance, and also the fatherland extending to great space and covering a big nation. It was a consequence of the way of life of Greeks and the nature of their polis civilization. The internal and the external mutually determine each other. But the development goes from the outside to the inside, from the system to an element, and not vice versa. This is the essence of our law of concentration, or the fundamental law of environmentalism according to which an element is a result of "condensation" of the environment, of the system. The system creates an element by means of concentration and interiorization of the external into the internal. Our pleasure is created by the system in which we are included. An animal derives pleasure from those products which surround it. The body interiorizes "tastes" of the environment.

Therefore the cities look shall be created taking into account its impact on the body and soul of a man. Expectation of pleasure can turn today into the means of "psycho engineering" creating a certain type of civilization. Meanwhile the modern city planning is guided by a paradigm of pleasure from conquest and subordination of space which reflects the dominating paradigm of the modern techno civilization.

3.2 TERRORISM AS A THREAT OF THE PLEASURE PARADIGM

The twentieth century which entered the history of mankind as a century of unprecedented weapon and bloody wars was replaced by the century of terrorism, unprecedented by its scales. In fact, only the form of manifestation of money hegemony in the world has changed. If in the first half of the twentieth century money, hiding behind the high, and at times even the low nationalist ideas, unleashed the world wars, then today the terror of money dominates everywhere in the world forming new reality as if with the wave of a magic wand. Does it give the grounds to claim that terrorism has turned into one of the civilizational paradigms of the present? Or does it represent only a modification of a paradigm of the Roman civilization based on force and violence? Is terrorism caused by the sufferings of the unfairly oppressed people or is it generated by aspiration to the highest pleasure—eternal life? Indeed, these are terrible questions, answers to which stipulate for the sociocultural and social-psychological analysis of the terrorism phenomenon.

It is enough that one person would hate another,—and hatred, passing from neighbor to neighbor, infects all mankind—Jean Paul Sartre warned. Total rationalization, technicalization, commercialization and virtualization of the world have led to extreme separation of social subjects from each other. Instead of a constructive dialogue the cultivated ethno-egoism generates the socio-cultural narcissism which is pushing together the foreheads of various civilizations. Social deafness of one people, dumbness and helplessness of others are shown in desperate attempts to frighten the opponent even at the price of own death. Terrorism has turned into a specific deviant means of modern communication based on fear, hatred, ignorance, despair and pleasure from . . . death, which diagnostics shall help to restore the constructive dialogue.

"Terror" is translated from Latin as fear, horror. According to the Big encyclopedic dictionary, terror is "violent acts for the purpose of deterrence, suppression of political opponents, competitors, imposing a certain line of behavior".[4] Terror is a system of actions aiming to frighten the political enemy, to seed horror in its ranks. Usually under the term terror they understand threat of physical violence, violent acts for the purpose of frightening, of suppressing political opponents, competitors. Anyway, terrorist actions always represent a message from sometimes deceived, sometimes fanatically believing in own mission, but almost always weak and desperate people. But getting great pleasure from awareness of own correctness and justice in return.

The synonyms of the word "terror" are the words "violence", "intimidation", "deterrence". The complexity of understanding of terror today is that it has ideological reasons based not only on the belief in own correctness and on religious conviction in the higher justice of righteous indignation of the oppressed, but also on aspiration to the highest pleasure from the promised eternal life. Anyway terror acts as a means to gain particular purposes although its true motives, as a rule, aren't realized by terrorists. They are buried deeply in the unconscious as always.

Why do people resort to terror? Why do they, risking their life, sow death around, spill the rivers of blood and cause tears? What pushes young people to such extreme measures? Is it commitment to an idea? Fanaticism? Hatred? Confidence that force might be opposed only with force and violence? Fear and ignorance? Or perhaps, strangely enough, thirst of pleasure? These questions aren't as simple as they can seem at first sight. It would be the easiest way to give in to a temptation and following many researchers to announce terrorism just one of the ways to solve political problems by spreading fear and horror. However such understanding would be very naive.

A psychological basis of terrorism is fear as a rule, a desire to remove this fear out of limits of own essence, that is, to transcend it to the environment. According to the second law of thermodynamics the system is kept by means of constant removal of entropy out of its limits. So the system keeps the negentropy, i.e. the order in itself. This phenomenon is observed also while forming the whole modern industry of Fear.

Let's address to the Explanatory dictionary of V. Dahl—"fear, dread, shyness—a strong anxiety, disturbing state of mind from a fright, from a threatening or imagined disaster . . . "[5]. Arthur Reber in the Big explanatory psychological dictionary treats fear as " emotional state arising in the presence or anticipation of a dangerous or harmful incentive. Fear is usually characterized as internal subjective experience of very strong excitement, desire to run or attack and a number of sympathetic reactions[6]. Physiologists consider fear a manifestation of a natural reflex, passive—defensive reaction with slight braking of the cerebral cortex. Fear is always connected with death and pain, loss, misfortune and is opposed to life, wellbeing, health.

Fear unlike intimidation is almost always pathologic. An intimidated person always knows what exactly he is afraid of and can explain why. Whereas fear is irrational and can be unconscious. According to psychoanalytic researches the reasons of maniacally cruel behavior often root in the early childhood and aren't realized. In these cases fear and hatred merge in the unconscious of a person.

According to S.Kierkegaard Fear is generated by Nothing. "Fear,—he writes, is a definition of the dreaming spirit . . . . Fear is the reality for freedom as an opportunity for a possibility".[7] That is, fear generates an opportunity for implementation of other possibilities. And it is very important for its understanding. Fear acts at the same time as means of generation and implementation of sets of other opportunities. This is its potential force as the strongest human feeling. A lot of human achievements including great ones are determined by fear. That is why many people love fear, get very much pleasure from it. Both when they experience fear and when they overcome it.

It is completely confirmed in the speech because they say: sweet fear, sweet intimidation, surprising fear, timid fear and so on. According to S. Kierkegaard "fear is the desire of what we fear, it is sympathetic antipathy; fear is an alien force which captures an individual, and yet he can't get free from it,—he doesn't want actually because he fears, but he fears what he desires. Fear makes an individual powerless, and the first sin always occurs in weakness; therefore it happens apparently as if unconsciously, but such absence of consciousness is the real trap"[8]. He compares fear with greedy aspiration to adventures, to something awful, mysterious, emphasizing that this fear is inherent in all people where childishness has remained as "spirit dreams". As it was already noted, in traditional societies in which strict upbringing from the father's side based on fearing him is kept, there is the highest probability of forming aggressive and destructive in the future persons.[9] In such case traditionally reproduced fear brings to life aggression as a response. Terror of the tradition of suppression generates the tradition of terror of resistance. At the same time the tradition of submission causes fear of freedom and even hatred to it. Let's remember "Escape from freedom" by Erich Fromm.

According to M. Heidegger fear is person's intimidation of himself owing to unforeseen freedom of nondeterministic character, i.e. freedom to which the subject "hasn't grown up" yet. Fear opens in front of "existence" its last opportunity—death. Psychoanalysis treats fear as a result of not actualized vital aspirations, suppression of unrealized desires. In neofreudism fear contacts with the absurd and irrational nature of the modern capitalistic society which leads to total neurosis, it means that fear in that case acts as a consequence of social existence.

Fear is directly connected with a phenomenon of threat which emergence requires its expectation. If there is no expectation of threat, a person is not afraid of anything. Even if something happens, he won't be frightened. And on the contrary, if a person has a threat expectation, he will be afraid of everything, even of his own shadow. Therefore the main idea of terrorism is hypertrophy of threats, and modern mass-media produce people who are afraid of everyone and everything. As a matter of fact, all our life turns into a reflection of the threat which is hanging over us. We have got accustomed to derive pleasure from expectation of fear. It is interesting that those who have accustomed us derive pleasure from it too.

The society of mass consumption in general represents a total industry of fear. The best buyer is the one who is afraid of everything. Is afraid of inflation, is afraid that he won't manage to purchase necessary goods, is afraid that they will be purchased by others, etc. paraphrasing the known expression, one may say, if the fear wasn't present in the nature, it should be invented. Power, especially the power of money, is impossible without fear. Unfortunately, terrorists, without understanding that, play into the hands of those whom they hate most of all, endangering and killing people similar to them, and, generally speaking, themselves. Thus, terrorism is a peculiar type of necrophilia, suicide because of fear of life, its challenges and love to death.

Fear as an emotional state arising in the presence or anticipation of danger, being characterized by subjective experience of strong excitement, is often connected with pain, loss, misfortune, death. It is always contrasted with life, wellbeing, health. Almost always the fear comes from the childhood. The fears imposed by adults tend to remain and grow throughout the whole life, and the habit to trust adults remains and develops into maniacal aspiration to fear an invisible threat. It is an example of the so-called being infected with fear.

Anxiety is above fear. Sometimes fear is the means of the anxiety outgo. Anxiety—fear—dread—this is the scheme of concretizing. Differentiate real, neurotic and free fear. The neurotic fear is aimless fear of neurotics, "a consequence of libido derivation from normal application". The free fear is general uncertain timidity ready to become attached for some time to any appearing opportunity and is expressed by being in a "timid expectation", the fear is pointless, not connected with any object. The pathology of fear is determined by its inexplicability, lack of control of consciousness over it, violation of adaptability of a person, growth of social tension in his life.

A person can put his fear in such value that there will be a need to share it with others. Therefore it is no wonder how people enjoy fear, watching horror films, turning them even into physiological value. Today TV commercials convince us that the best fight against excess weight is fear when watching horror films. "If you want to get rid of excess calories—watch the movie "Fear!"—such words can be heard almost on every television channel. Is not it a crime against people, against small children whose mentality is only at the forming stage? The fear industry is a constant source of income. And fear, as we know, destroys the human personality, no matter if we want it or not. A personality loses its integrity, and it means loss of viability of the society. Thus, act of terror is an attempt of infecting people with a mental disease.

Fear arises as a reaction of a person to understanding of the mismatch of the world, discrepancy of the desirable and real. "The world of enlightenment gives rise to catalepsy". That is, a person at some point realizes the real situation and his place in it. Fear arises at the moment of correlation of the subject and the objective situation. Although the fear itself, as well as a man in general, is bio—psycho-social phenomenon. Its nature, as we can see, is very complicated, and the structure is multilevel, but in this case we speak about the fear as a mental phenomenon.

Fear is closely connected with the will because it is also directed to the future, i.e. fear is first of all the fear of the unknown, what exists or doesn't exist in the future. For this reason fear also paralyzes the will, as it is an ideal reaction to the future. If this reaction is negative, and it is negative as a rule, because otherwise it would not be fear any more, then an ideal emotional and negative anticipation of the result blocks the energy of its embodiment. Fear is some kind of "Cassandra's brand—an eschato-embryo" of the negative will.

We can hardly agree with the authors considering that the fear of death is the cornerstone of fear. Rather the will of a person is affected most of all by the fear of life, of the unknown.

Judging by the importance which was given to fear in antiquity, it ranked high in social life. If such a courageous and educated for his time person as Alexander of Macedon, made sacrifices to the demon of fear, it is possible to imagine how seriously the ordinary mortals was treating fear. In our opinion, it is possible to speak about the culture of the attitude to fear in various societies. And in this sense the modern civilization has once again missed an opportunity to control the phenomenon, having appeared to be under its influence. And probably on purpose has turned fear into the profitable goods generating pleasure.

Fear is closely connected with freedom of choice, a possibility of alternative behavior. If there is no choice—then the conscious fear is inappropriate. Then its place is taken by the unconscious horror which, unlike fear, can unexpectedly affect the will, to be exact the willfulness, having repeatedly increased its power base.

The correlation of fear, information and entropy is interesting. As a rule fear, in our opinion, is connected with a lack of self-reflected information and excess of energy. Therefore the will as negentropy essence (potentiality) of spirit, is inversely proportional to fear. Larger deficiency of information takes place when a person feels anxiety. In this case he is not only unaware how to act, but sometimes he doesn't even know the source of the anxiety as the non-self-reflected existential state. A great Danish philosopher Soeren Kierkegaard has perfectly pointed to this distinction between fear and anxiety, having removed thereby the need of vast discussions on that.

Fundamentality of the role of fear in the mental life of a person was noted also by many modern writers (K. Jaspers, M. Heidegger, J. P. Sartre, A. Camus and others). Each one of them considers fear at an angle of the problems concerning him. As for the nature of the will, along with the concepts of information and entropy, it would be very fruitful to correlate the concept of fear to the concept of "self-organization". Namely, to consider it as "a signal" of the need of self-organization because a long stay in the embraces of this feeling threatens with the loss of a self-organizational potentiality. Full lack of this feeling would lead to atrophy of the instinct of self-preservation. Let's remember Aristotle claiming that courage is the middle between cowardice and fearlessness. Thus, fear "is ambivalent". The same is its impact on the will, of course with overwhelming prevalence of the paralyzing effect.

Some people aim for fear as for enjoyment. S. Freud and his followers see the reason of that in subconscious penchant for death and, at the same time, in the resistance to it. Such condition might generate depression—oppression of the will, and on the contrary might initiate activity.

We will note that depression occurs in case of spiritual dissatisfaction of a personality when the thought way and the way of life of a person don't match, and at times even contradict his "I". As E. Fromm notes, implementation failure of creative potentialities is transformed to the destructive force of aggression which, by remarkable words of Scheler, most often is manifestation of the powerlessness which is stewed in its own juice.

An appeal to fear as to the means of influence on a social subject is usually an indicator of backwardness of the frightener. A small child "terrorizing" his parents with crying; a leader in the primitive society imposing fear to his tribe people, showing force and cruelty as necessary means of his power. The more backward the society, the tougher the "terror" of the leader is. Indeed: "Each people are worthy their governor". Violence almost always generates a response—aggression and hatred, but they can develop into active actions only in the presence of the required social conditions, the major one among which is social inequality. Otherwise the response actions of the dissatisfied would have open character. Terror is always veiled, hidden, always stealthy.

Terror is possible only in case of social hierarchy as a desperate attempt of a weak to answer a strong. "It is better to die from extremes, than from despair"—these words of J. Baudrillard illustrate the mood of a rebellious person trying to find the sense in this mad world, at least at the cost of own life. It is sad that such a suicide which itself is already an unconditional sin is followed by a murder of absolutely innocent people. Probably, it is frightful to die alone! It is even more terrible to die senselessly, probably, more terribly, than to live senselessly. Therefore terror is always kept ideologically dark.

In order not to die from despair, a terrorist splashes out all his discontent, hatred, and aggression on people around. Let's remember Breivik who shot dozens of people only because they had arrived to his country. Or those people from the Maidan in Kiev who were shooting at everybody randomly: both insurgents and the police officers. What is it—manifestation of individual psychopathology or features of the modern civilization? In the work "The Transparency of evil" J. Baudrillard, analyzing the nature of the modern civilization, classifies social values, singling out a market stage when value acts as a means of exchanging, a structural stage when there is a value-symbol, a simulacrum and a stage of fragmentation when value is exposed to diffusion, like a virus spreading in all directions[10]. It is impossible to call it the value any more since its ideological essence disappears.

The modern capitalist civilization, as J. Baudrillard considers, leads to disappearance of spirituality, absorption of it by material mercantilism. The idea of progress has disappeared, but the progress continues, the idea of wealth which assumes production has disappeared, but production continues. Also the idea of policy disappears, but the political process continues, and even intensively gains steam. The policy turns into a game, and politicians—into indifferent players making their bets. "All things existent,—he writes,—continue to function, whereas the existence sense disappeared long ago. They continue to function with absolute indifference to own content. The paradox is that such functioning doesn't suffer from it at all, and on the opposite, becomes more and more perfect"[11]. Just like the existentialists warned, the essence came off from the existence which gained the unprecedented speed and power. The existence by means of mad speed overcame the gravitation of the essence. In fact, it is a formula of bureaucratization, formalization, but already of the universe scale. Indifference becomes a human god.

Terrorism today has also turned into a phantom which lost its idea on the way. Sounds absurdly, but terrorism, having been formalized, having turned into a structure, has lost its substantial basis. More and clearer we can see "the wood" of huge money behind "the trees" of the acts of terror. Quicker and quicker the trace of the Idea freezes and bloody trails of the Lie and Money reveal. Social inequality, poverty of one people and richness of others is the fruitful soil for deployment of this acting. The terrorist idea, speaking with Susan Sontag's words concerning cancer, reminds us "devil pregnancy". And the devil, as we know, likes to dress in noble attires. It isn't accidental that terrorism is mainly developed in traditional societies where, at least nominally, traditional values remained. However, as we know, the modern world economy is transnational, isolated economies practically do not exist. Therefore the traditional societies are also eaten by corrosion of simulacra. What was earlier determined by the Idea is called business today. "Nothing personal!"—is the favorite saying of modern "business people"—can be modified: "Everything is depersonalized!" Money requires its executors and puppets. And the more ideological and faceted the executor, the less money will be required to hire him. So an ideological terrorist as cheap goods is very popular. He doesn't only requires money "for work", but derives pleasure from implementation of "own mission". In Russia, unfortunately, it is well known by own history.

An important role in the growth of terrorism is played also by such a social factor as unemployment. When a jobless person has nothing to eat, money plays more significant role in his motivation to terrorist actions. There comes the era of global terror of Money. The golden calf turns into "the engine of external combustion"! Are modern media so actively propagandizing violence, cruelty, crime because all this brings money, strengthens social hierarchy, confirms domination of one over others? The mass-media continue to enslave people, feeding them with illusions of the virtual world. "Violence,—J. Baudrillard writes,—potentially exists in emptiness of the screen thanks to a hole into the mental space which it opens. To such an extent that it is better not to stay in the public place where the television is on because of a high probability of a violent event which the TV induces with its presence"[12]. And, really, the television as if provokes terrorists, advertizes them, amuses their vanity, calling them "guerillas", "fighters for the idea", etc. I.e. it consciously gives them pleasure as if encouraging on feats.

One of the social and psychological determinants of terrorism is frustration owing to the stress caused by the above-mentioned factors of the modern society. Unemployment, and social inequality, and aggressive policy of mass-media, and total technicalization, and automation of life, generating stress in modern people and thereof frustration, fix aggression in the mentality, as well as embitterment, envy, and sometimes even the inferiority complex, disbelief in themselves and lack of the will. By the way, the latter ones can also be a consequence of artificially formed, fantastically high claims which, without being implemented, generate hatred in a person both to himself, and to the whole world, the desire to finish with everything at once.

However most often " violence in its basis, as well as terrorism, is not an event, but rather the lack of an event taking the form of the explosion directed inside: political emptiness blows up (and not the rage of this or that group of people), silence of history (and not psychological suppression of individuals), indifference and stillness".[13] Terrorism as "a transpolitical mirror of the Evil", transforming today to various virus forms pursuing us, accelerates and gets multiplied in the political and moral emptiness. "Devilish energy of the outcast", "rage of the damned"—these epithets j. Baudrillard awards a terrorist with, calling modern western society too coddled to resist to terrorism.

Freedom and democracy in parallel as side effect release the Evil as the unused energy and as an alternative way of behavior—violence, crime, terror. The unconscious desire to live forever also pushes to terrorism, therefore they often resort to terror for religious reasons, previously having lost themselves, their natural existence. Having turned into the mechanism in "the clockwork city", the "former" human feels indifference, emptiness and almost metaphysical thirst for death, both his and people around. Thus, terrorism and violence almost always have the environmental nature.

Along with the idea of martyrdom and fanaticism they single out such phenomenon as social activism among the social factors of terrorism. There is an opinion that a terrorist is a lone fanatic, socially indifferent person trying to attract people's attention by his protest, i.e. the act of terror. However such a point of view is confuted by many facts. The quiet life of the whole society depends on how the social activity of people dissatisfied with life will be shown. The main question for any society is how, where, by whom and in what way the social activity and aggression are being directed, modeled and controlled.

There shall be socio-political conditions of self-realization of socially active people in the society. There shall be opportunities for a citizen to influence the progress of the society, to optimize the existence of the country, the state where he lives and works. "If there is no discharge of the collected tension aimed at the achievement of the socially important purposes (and the tension as well as the need for its removal, remains), then unsatisfied requirements are easily marginalized and take other forms—up to pathological manifestations in the form of narrow national ideological unity or aggression and fanaticism of small (not that small though) groups or even protests of singles".[14]

In the opposition of ideas, let them be misunderstood, even ephemeral, to money and power, servility, self-interest, the ideas almost always win because they are imperishable! Therefore terrorism needs to be opposed not with threats and force, but first of all, with an Idea. It needs to be shown the incorrectness and incorrect understanding of their own ideas by potential terrorists. Therefore development of civil society, its spiritual enhancement is prevention of acts of terror. And it is very important to offer them other alternative ways to get pleasure.

While analyzing the terrorism reasons, it should be noted that differentiation of the terror by the form, content, subject, object shall be one of the important methodological principles of the analysis. It is necessary to reveal not only common things in them, something that unites all forms of terrorism, but also their differences. The common thing is almost always a protest. This is what we should get deeply into understanding separately each case. A suicide bomber is not only inconceivable cruelty and barbarity. It is also a message which we should understand. Any dialogue is better than unilateral aggression and misunderstanding. The information war existing in the modern media space for a lot of years already, as well as any other war, isn't productive, moreover, it is destructive. It destructively affects mentality of people not to mention that it attracts unhealthy interest in a terror phenomenon among young people. Forbidden fruit is sweet, as we know. Therefore a priority task of anti-terrorist activities is to restore the dialogue between various social subjects.

Terror as a desperate attempt to intimidate the hated opponent represents repeated confession of a terrorist in own powerlessness. Firstly, he emphasizes senselessness and even absurdity of not only his own, but also life in general. Secondly, he confesses of the mere act of terror, confesses that he hates the opponent, and this is already confession of own weakness. Hatred as destructive emotion is always a consequence of inability of the subject to constructively influence changes of the situation. Thirdly, terror as a desire "to bite painfully" the opponent (imperceptibly if possible)—almost always is the evidence of not only fear, but also, as a rule, of fanaticism which is quite often representing a type of mental deviation, a paranoia.

However the most serious reason of terror is ignorance. Many people may disagree, having contrasted this thesis with the high percentage of educated people among terrorists. Let's notice that, firstly, having a diploma and formal presence of education aren't the evidence of education. And secondly, education doesn't solve, and sometimes even aggravates the problems of the present mental anomalies of a person. In this case we mean Socratic, but not Aristotelian understanding of knowledge. Socratic knowledge is the basis of virtue: "Who knows, won't do evil!" implies the true knowledge, but not availability of information. It is the knowledge which turns a person into the nobility. After all a reverse situation is possible when a person seems to be aware of what he is doing, but still "doesn't know what he does". Therefore ignorance is really a universal reason of the Evil. Darkness in the soul is being projected outside, setting darkness around. Indeed: " Send a fool to the market and a fool he will return again" (the exact translation from Russian: Force a fool to pray, and he will ram his forehead!") We should say, not only his forehead . . .

Thirdly, exactly this ignorance—the unawareness determines transformation of a potential aggressor-destroyer, a sower of darkness into a puppet which most often is unconsciously serving to implementation of other people goals. No wonder that many acts of terror happen at the deposit places of hydrocarbons (oil and gas). A terrorist without his consent is turned into a means to control oil and gas price.

Fourthly, in the basis of terrorist actions almost always there is such a destructive feeling as offense. It is the offense with unfair policy, offense for the people, the country, religion, oneself at last. And offense, as psychology convincingly shows, being a reason and a consequence of numerous complexes, destroys both a person and everything around him. A person gradually begins to hate life and everything that he used to love, unconsciously aiming at death. It was perfectly shown by F. M. Dostoyevsky through R. Raskolnikov. Exactly the split in mentality, in consciousness, in the value system, loss of personal integrity had lead Raskolnikov to the split of life (by "splitting" . . . the skulls of an old woman-moneylender). Raskolnikov's trouble is that he had got confused, contrasting Nietzschean will to power with the Christian will to Love and Freedom. "Let the one who can be himself be nobody else!" But who can be himself! Terrorists can't manage that. They aim at abnegation by denial of the world. It means that love to death, to eternal life exists in parallel with hatred to the world and to oneself.

And, fifthly, absolutely meanly and cowardly a terrorist strikes not only the one whom he hates and at the same time is afraid of (otherwise he would act openly), but also innocent, ordinary people, i.e. as unfortunate as himself. Those people who use trolleybuses and metro and can't response to him. And it is clear that they are not politicians and oligarchs, but old women- pensioners, school and university students.

Albert Camus in "The myth of Sisyphus" writes: "I see how many people die because, in their opinion, life is not worth living. Also I know those who, strangely enough, are ready to commit suicides for the sake of ideas or illusions forming the basis of their lives (what is called a reason for life, at the same time appears to be an excellent reason for death) "[15]. He connects suicide with thinking peculiarities of a person. "Suicide is being prepared in silence of heart, similar to the Great Act of alchemists"[16]. "The worm sits in the heart of a man; there it should be searched for. It is necessary to understand the deadly game which leads from clarity concerning own existence to escape from this world".[17] That is, in the consciousness of a person the program of self-destruction is started most often from the outside. An ideal mechanism of such start of the program for self-destruction is the idea of eternal life, life after death, death for the great idea. For this reason suicide is one of the greatest sins in all religions. The idea of eternal life in religion shall serve to spiritual purification and growth of a man, to give him strength to live in this world.

An act of terror assumes, on the one hand, recognition of the life senselessness (what is the sense in life of "a trembling creature "?), and on the other—the desire to self-realize, at least at the cost of own life, to give it sense by damaging the enemy. A Goliath is drawn in the consciousness of a terrorist, to whom he, like David, resists, risking his life. A. Camus illustrates discrepancy of consciousness of a suicide bomber. On the one hand, the belief in absurdity of existence is the guide to action for him, on the other,—suicides are often sure that life makes sense. But this sense is given to their lives from the outside, but isn't a result of the independent philosophical reflection.

A huge role in emergence of aspiration to Death is played by boredom which, being a result of mechanical life sets consciousness in motion. The disgust caused by brutality of a man himself, an abyss in which he is overthrown, having looked at himself, it is "nausea". Disgust for himself and nausea, causing loath of life, push a person to suicide. Therefore most often suicides including acts of terror are committed by marginal persons, i.e. by people who are in the borderline state. Those people who had left (not without some assistance) the "old shore", and are not stuck to a new one. That is why regaining of the lost sense, the real, own personal sense, and not the substitute imposed from the outside—is an important means of fight against such deviations.

The feeling of absurdity is born when comparing real life with the world lying outside this action. "Basically, absurdity is a split",—A. Camus writes.[18] It is interesting that the split in Raskolnikov happened after acquaintance with the theory dividing people into "having the right" and "the trembling creatures". It generated criminal dividing people into the free people and the slaves in his sick consciousness. The only criterion distinguishing the first from the second ones, according to Raskolnikov, was a capability to commit . . . a crime, acknowledgement of its correctness. It is a familiar philosophy, isn't it?

Nietzschean understanding of a superman as of the being crossing through the morals. The will to power—this is what, according to F. Nietzsche, distinguishes a superman from a man, i.e. the will to multiplication of own opportunities to influence others' behavior, the desire to control others. Nietzsche is absolutely right, saying that this desire isn't human, being super human's one. But what does "a superman" represent? In any case, it is not a man any more . . . And it is enough. Love moves a man, and not the desire to control others. After all not the one is strong who can force a person down to the knees with an only look, but the one who can raise him from the knees with an only smile! And it is taught by the philosophy of the Godman, unselfish loving man, and not the man-god selfishly dominating over the like.

Once during an interview to a TV reporter the metropolitan Kirill said that we live in the era when the sin is spread by the state and gets legislative support. And it is unimportant what state exactly. The sin industry is just a fixed source of income. And the sin, as we know, destroys the human personality, whether we want it or not. Where there is the sin, there is the death. A personality loses its integrity. It means loss of viability of the society.

What does hatred represent, this aggressive, strongly colored emotionally, extremely negative feeling? Why does it strike so much the soul of a person that he is ready to destroy himself only to do much harm to the hated person or a group of people?

We do not absolutely agree with the definition of hatred existing in modern scientific literature as "negative emotionally colored feeling". In our opinion, it is necessary to differentiate bio-physiological, biopsychic and socio-psychic components of hatred. In the socio-psychic component of this feeling an important role is played by ideas, social information which is often a myth and fiction.

So, the well-known hatred of the German fascists of the XX century to Jews, however, as well as all Nazis of different colors, is based on the mythical information, fiction which is dexterously manipulating big groups of people, and sometimes the whole people. Such mythologems become an excellent tool of destruction of personal nature of the feeling in hands of greedy manipulators, giving them mass character.

Let's note that a certain level of ignorance is necessary for the loss of identity. "When a vessel is empty, it is easy to fill it with any content!" It will be hard to infect a highly intellectual, educated person. The history, unfortunately, knows such examples. However we don't say that it is impossible, we only say that it is much more difficult.

But we in this case are interested not in every ignorant person, but in a person inclined to aggression and hatred. What happens to mentality of a person who is not moved by love, but by hatred? We proceed from the assumption that a man by his nature isn't kind, and isn't angry, he is ambivalent, and only a complex of external and internal factors activate one of the above-named programs in his mentality. Not only education and external circumstances, as educationists, K. Marx, his followers and other authors claimed, and not only internal predisposition (mental and even biophysiological) as Cesare Lombroso noted, but exactly their interaction. The fact that Taoists call Dao the way of formation and realization of the essence on which Dao as the essence no less depends.

The modern civilization as many experts of various areas of knowledge emphasize, unfortunately, favors the formation of a neurotic person whose mentality is full of unconscious anxiety and fears producing hatred and aggression. And reaction of a neurotic person all the time changes depending on the conditions of the socio-cultural environment. K. Horny in her work "The neurotic personality of our time" shows various criteria for evaluation of neuroticism of a personality depending not only on culture, epoch, but also on the sex of a person, and also his place in the social hierarchy. "Manifestation of superconcern and fear of the coming old age for a forty-year-old woman is "normal" while a man in a similar situation will be considered a neurotic".[19] Some interesting facts from anthropology are given by Sapir, showing how customs, traditions of various people influence understanding of "normality" of a person. Considering numerous factors diagnosing neurosis, K. Horny notices that a neurotic himself gets in his way, most often accusing the whole world of counteracting him. During a certain historical period, in our opinion, the whole nations, societies and even mankind in general can become neurotic. Is it possible to call terror a manifestation of social neurosis? Or is this all still a social manifestation of neurosis? The difference is great.

A general factor of emergence of neurosis Neo-Freudians call anxiety and those forms of protection which are built against it. "No matter how much confused the structure of neurosis is, anxiety is the engine which activates the neurotic process and supports its course!"—K. Horny writes[20]. These reactions aren't uniquely human. An animal which is frightened of something either runs away, or attacks. Aggression is often a sign of fear.

A neurotic not only shares the fears existing in his culture, but also inadequately reacts to them. Each culture, generating fears, generates also mechanisms of fight against them—traditions, customs, established forms of response to a standard situation, stereotypes. Not so much the fear exaggeration, as an inadequate reaction to it, "queer" behavior is characteristic of a neurotic. A neurotic always suffers more, than a normal man. He is a constantly suffering being and therefore almost always forces others to suffer, and often unconsciously. He blames others for own sufferings and does them harm, restoring justice. And sometimes his own imaginations can be the reason of such suffering. For example, a man suffering from pathological jealousy dreams of revenge to his wife. The matter can reach absolute absurdity—Othello who infinitely loves his wife kills absolutely innocent Desdemona.

Let's imagine for a minute that Shakespearean Othello wasn't that decisive and wouldn't possess such "hot" blood of a Moor. Let's imagine that the jealousy mechanism activated by Iago, would be tormenting Othello for years. It is unlikely that Othello would keep forces for a murder after a long "self-chastise". It would rather lead him to a suicide stretched in time, what we also observe in our ordinary life among millions of people: negative emotions, apathy, and aggression. No wonder that the number of suicides in modern most trouble-free megalopolises is much higher, than in other cities. It is known that one of the absolute leaders in this list is Paris.

Neuroticism of a future terrorist progressing under the pressure of the absurd functioning in a modern megalopolis turning a person into "an economic erythrocyte" which has lost the meaning of life makes a potential suicide from him. Victor Frankl in his psychological researches specifies the loss of the meaning of life by young successful people as one of the basic reasons of such a result. They don't work up a sweat to earn a piece of bread, i.e. they do not face the problem of physical survival. In the modern western and already in the eastern world, traditions also don't program a person as they used to. He doesn't do anything only because this is the way the things are done. He is searching for his own meaning of life. And often doesn't find it. Hence the high percentage of alcoholics, drug addicts, people breaking the law among young people.

As psychologists specify, one of the mechanisms activating neurosis is also the presence of the contradicting tendencies, most often unconscious ones. Let's remember once again R. Raskolnikov. Not for nothing Dostoyevsky chose such a surname for his hero. A split (raskol) is a bifurcation which can lead to schizophrenia in the long run. It is known that schizophrenia is diagnosed as a split of personality. In a neurotic personality this bifurcation has not reached a complete "split" on two or more personalities yet. In its mentality they live together as multidirectional vectors. K. Horny defines neurosis as mental disorder caused by fears and by protection measures against them, and also by the attempts to find compromise solutions of the conflict of multidirectional tendencies.

One of the mechanisms activating social neurosis is envy which quite often evolves into hatred and aggression. Unfortunately, envy is not always adequately understood in our culture. Many people confuse it to desire, calling the progress engine. For example, if one person has a luxurious car, and another one, "envying" him, wants to have a similar car and works without cease, in several years buys the car—this is, in our opinion, an example of not envy, but rather desire. Some people call such desire "light envy". "I envy you, but with light envy",—they say sometimes. Well, there is no "light" envy. Envy is always heavy.

We note that all objects and phenomena have eidetic substance and possess a color. The color of envy is always black. It is an all-absorbing and reflecting nothing color of low human emotions. Envy is a negative feeling to a person for the fact that he possesses something which the envying person does not have. Envy is expressed in wishing evil to another person, wishing failure, loss of the quality which is envied. Envy is always a manifestation of not only weaknesses and the inferiority complex, but also of meanness. And most often envy becomes the reason of neurosis and other diseases of the envying person. Not incidentally they say that happiness is equal to the number received as a result of division of one into envy, that is, a fraction which numerator is one, and the denominator is envy. And the less envy, the more happiness is. Therefore the envious person can't be happy a priori. So why does the culture of the modern society of mass consumption cultivate envy? It does so because it wants to cultivate the desire of the consumer and sometimes, seeing no difference, goes too far. Or perhaps it does it on purpose, sowing hatred between people so that it would be easier to control them. "Divide and rule!" –is as old as the world.

The question of the deformation level of a terrorist's personality due to neurosis is important. Often neurosis can be shown as a result of racial, national or religious discrimination. It can be expressed in inadequate and even aggressive behavior, desire to suppress, manipulate, and sometimes even to destroy another person. One of consequences of neurosis, to be exact of its basic component—anxiety—as hypertrophied unreasonable fear, is helplessness. A person is angry, tries to prove his consistence to himself and surrounding people, shows inadequate aggression. It is especially typical of a terrorist.

As a matter of fact, anxiety is the fear dictated by subjective factors, it is a feeling of powerful, inevitable danger in front of which a person is completely powerless. There are two factors in it—danger and vulnerability in front of it. Uneasiness and hostility can trade places as the cause and effect. As uneasiness can be the cause of hostility, so on the contrary, hostility can be the cause of uneasiness. And both of them act as the neurosis reason. Therefore when terrorists are represented in mass media as terrible, fearless bandits—it is an inexcusable mistake, we wish to think, an unintentional one. Since terrorist activities—are the result of unconscious and inexplicable fears and anxiety of a neurotic personality who, running away from them, extrapolates them to the outside. He frightens in order not to be afraid. They should not be killed, they should be treated! We should not be afraid of them, we should feel sorry for them! Poor blind "kittens" kill themselves to do much harm to others. The known words of Ben Laden: "death is more desired to us, than life is to them!"—are an illustration of necrophilia. But why should a young man feel pleasure from own death? Maybe he was already so much brainwashed? And it is a pity . . .

Pity to terrorists, broadcasted by mass-media, will lead to the fact that the sense of terrorist activities will disappear, because there is no sense to frighten if nobody is afraid, seeing your weakness, anxiety, fear and even helplessness. Such a position can look absurd since it is absolutely impossible to feel sorry for a coldblooded murderer. But in order to cure, it is required to diagnose first, and for this purpose it is necessary to understand.

Many mass-media themselves participate in terrorist activities, overblowing the threat and frightening the population which is, as a matter of fact, the purpose of terrorists-neurotics. And why not to make a psychological program "Aid to Terrorists" in which leading experts on psychology and psychiatry would conduct dialogues, discussions helping neurotics to come out from the "pre-terrorist" state? This way we at least would restore the dialogue!

As A. Camus emphasizes in his work "The rebel", terrorism in its basis often has a great idea. The idea can be really great, but what are the ways leading to its implementation? "Nothing on earth is worth gaining at the price of human blood",—fairly noticed J.J.Russo. F. M. Dostoyevsky will strengthen these words later, having added that nothing on earth is worth a child's teardrop.

"To determine the principle, owing to which the convict will probably die soon, means to determine the principle which is followed by the society which judges him"—a theorist of the French terror Saint-Just grandiloquently noticed, without noticing that he breaks not only the moral, but also the formal-logical law. The paradox of the French revolution, however as well as all others, is that, rebelling against cruelty, tyrants, suppression of citizens' freedom, they soon turned into even more cruel tyrants. It was perfectly shown by F. M. Dostoyevsky in his "The Grand inquisitor". "Scaffolds are perceived as altars of religion and injustice,—A. Camus writes.—The new faith can't stand them. But the time comes when it, having become dogmatic, makes own altars and requires absolute worship. Then again scaffolds appear and, despite altars, freedom, oaths of the Reason feast, the masses of the new faith will have to be said among human blood".[21]

As we see, justice and freedom are being equaled to cruelty as a result of ignorance, including awareness of elementary laws of formal logic. Continuing his logical illiteracy, Saint-Just gives a metaphoric definition: "monarchy is a crime". Execution of a king is considered by him as revenge for the murder of people. Thus, barbarous, unlawful, even non-state decision is brought by him to the level of the principle of building a republic of free people. It is familiar logic, isn't it? The murder of the imperial family, including a small child, the tzarevitch, in the cellar of Yekaterinburg, was also represented as the means to release the Russian people. Perhaps, this devil crime had crucial importance upon transformation of a revolutionary paradigm. Meanwhile "one must not be cruel even when it is necessary to be ruthless!"

However terror generates terror, violence—violence, cruelty—cruelty. It was known already by the ancient. The history confirms it. Both executions of French revolutionaries, and the destiny of the Russian Bolsheviks. The absurd phrase of Saint-Just "A scaffold is freedom!"—becomes the motto of many terrorists today. "death is more desired to us, than life is to them!" It is very alike, is not it?

Sincerely claiming to be called a philanthropist, another leader of the French revolution Marat exclaimed: "Who doesn't see that I want to cut off a few heads thereby rescue many others?!"[22] A few heads—it was said very optimistically. They say that by his calculations, it was necessary "to cut off" 273 thousand heads! "Brand them with red-hot iron, cut off their thumbs, pierce their tongues!"—he requires, admitting atrocities and murders as the main means of building the bright future.

Eventually, this forced, in their opinion, cruelty turns against themselves, confirming the words: "A revolt when it doesn't go alright, waves between extermination of others and self-destruction"[23]. The only way to rescue the weakening principles is to die for them. According to A. Camus's note, a revolt chops off own roots when it refuses any concrete morals.

The regicides of the XVIII and the XIX centuries were followed by the deicide of the XX century and "manslaughter" of the XXI century. Today they already use the special term "teocide" coinciding by the content with a suicide of a person.

Theodor Adorno in his work "The authoritarian personality" develops the Freudian thesis that the authoritative parent syndrome forms an unstable, neurotic, aggressive personality, what Eric Fromm called "sadomasochist character". "In the psychodynamics of "the authoritative" character,—he writes,—early aggression is partially absorbed, being transformed into a mechanism, partially it remains in the form of sadism, which looks for nutrient solutions in those with whom the individual doesn't identify himself, i.e. in a foreign group"[24].

Often a representative of a foreign nationality, religion, country, ideology becomes a substitute of the hated father or another authoritative tutor and all unmotivated aggression of the person restrained in the childhood pours out on him. Strict prohibitions of "Super I", going from a certain culture, can form in a person an unconscious need for punishment, and besides, both himself, and others. Not accidentally some religious people, sincerely preaching of the spiritual perfection, good and forgiveness, sometimes become the most ruthless executioners. It will just suffice to mention the courts of medieval inquisition which representatives very sincerely thought that an execution, i.e. physical destruction of the body, is the only way to save the soul of a whorish person! T. Adorno, quoting M. Linder, gives his reasoning on a psychopath and a fanatic: "a psychopath is not only a criminal, he is an innate fascist. He is a disinherited, deceived opponent, . . . whose aggression can be mobilized at the moment when he is offered a slogan which is well aimed and calling for frustration; that Fuhrer under whose tinsel sign unruliness becomes the law: the hidden and primitive desires become the cheaply purchased virtuous ambition, and instinctive reactions, always considered as deserving punishments, go to the agenda".[25]

A psychopath is described by M. Linder as a religious fanatic, a rebel who commits a crime because of his desire to satisfy the "almost sexual" need for punishment. And both "the enemy", and himself. He can overcome or at least reduce the feeling of the increasing fault only through punishment. "I have sinned against my father and must be "punished" is an unexpressed motive of the psychopathic behavior, and for this reason psychopaths often commit crimes which are never based on the desire of enrichment. Therefore, standing out of the general logic of an average mass man, they are difficultly predicted. Strange, but it is easy to fall in love with them due to their unpredictability. Not incidentally many terrorists hire women, using their "men's charms".

Hatred of psychopaths often has a paranoid character and an unusual form. Violence and pain act as hatred objectification in them. The paradoxicality of a psychopathic personality is shown also by the fact that aggression, rebelling against the authoritative suppression of his personality, is unconsciously caused by unclear even to him aspiration to subordination and to being manipulated. And at the same time they are overwhelmed with opposite passions to manipulation and dictatorship, to imposing of their will to as many people as possible. That is, they want both to subordinate and to submit at the same time and unconsciously search for a stronger dictator. Not finding him in their surrounding, they address sometimes to mystic and supernatural forces, completely subordinating their will to them, more precisely, their willfulness.

Hence the unclear, almost mythical love to dictators. Is not it surprising that at the heart of respect and even awe to dictators there is not only fear, but almost always sincere love is. Probably, not only from love to hatred there is one step, the opposite statement is also fair. Especially for psychopathic persons in whose life fear plays an extremely important role. It is metaphysical uncertain fear, and not dread.

Theodor Adorno notes that there is a potentially fascist structure of character which can develop as a result of, on the one hand, the suppressed inclinations of "It", and on the other hand—"Super I". "Alienation of "Super I" by the fascist character,—he writes,—connected with the unconscious sense of guilt which should be made silent at any cost, substantially promotes transformation and "cultural discrimination" into insatiable hostility fed by hostile instincts"[26]. In order to force out the sense of guilt disturbing self-esteem and just life, it is replaced with aggression.

The victim and the executioner are trading places. They begin to reproach the victim that it is itself to blame of what has happened to it. To the above noted case of the Jews genocide in fascist Germany it is possible to add also the genocide of the Greeks, Armenians, Bulgarians in the Ottoman Empire and other people in different countries during various historical eras. The history shows that hatred and aggression of executioners towards their victims after the committed crime only increases by the former. "A group of strangers,—T. Adorno writes,—that is, the selected enemy, is an eternal challenge. Until something in it remains not as it should be, the fascist character feels a threat irrespective of the fact how weak another one is.[27] The projection of the own forced-out guilt onto the victim leads to the desire of the executioner to completely eliminate the hatred object. Familiar logic—no man, no problem! Sometimes this scheme is used in relation to the entire people. "Discrepancy between guilt and punishment forces him rather to obey to own hatred in order to prove to oneself and to others that he "must be right . . . terrorizing others, he should terrorize himself as well"[28].

The socio-cultural analysis of the terrorism phenomenon assumes comparison of human society in general with a man, with a social organism and a social personality. Let's notice, the term "social organism" is widespread in the socio-humanistic environment while the concept "social personality" in view of its strangeness grates on hears a little. And might there be another personality, except the social one? In this case under the concept "social personality" a society as a personality is meant.

It is known that any comparison "limps". However, in our opinion, it is very fruitful to apply the analysis on an analogy method in social researches. For example, a child—an undeveloped personality can be associated with the primitive society, i.e. with the society at the earliest stage of its development.

We should note that a child becomes "a terrorist" still in the mother's womb, frightening her with various impacts (of course, unconsciously) on her organism. After the birth a child very skillfully uses such a reliable method of "terror" as crying. Parents are ready to do everything so that their dear child ceases crying. And the child knows it, at least, feels.

Interesting researches of aggression in different types of primitive cultures were made by Erich Fromm. Having studied more than thirty types of primitive cultures, he came to a conclusion that depending on the type of relations in them it is possible to divide these societies on vital, non-destructive and destructive. The latter are marked with high aggression, cruelty, destructive inclinations of its members (both inside the tribe, and in relation to other tribes). The aggressive spirit, hostility and fear reign in the society; insidiousness and treachery are widespread. The large role is played in general by the private property (if not concerning material values, then symbols at least) therefore rivalry (competition) is substantially developed. This society is strictly hierarchical, often wages wars.

Today more often it is possible to hear the phrase "Islamic terrorism". To understand the legitimacy or, on the contrary, the absurdity of such epithets which have settled in the public consciousness, we will deal, first of all, with the concepts. What religion is, almost everyone knows, but it is difficult to perform the substantial analysis of the religion phenomenon even for many religious figures. This is so much the case that some confuse the content of such concepts as "faith", "religion", "church".

The etymology of the word "religion" means (re—repetition, ligare—to link, to connect) restoring the connection of a human as a final being, with

God, representing infinity. A man as a part of a system, namely its thinking part, has a need to establish the link with the whole system. Only then the substantial essence of a man is implemented. Without religion the completion of forming the spiritual personality isn't carried out. Philosophy performs a mission of intellectual catharsis and spiritual ascension. Whereas religion is the sphere of feelings, faith. And no matter how much a person is developed intellectually, there is always a need of spiritual evolution remaining in him. However, sometimes this function is fulfilled not by traditional religions, but by their substitutes in the form of various theories, ideologies. But in this case they play exactly the religion role.

Attaching terrorism to any religion owing to inadequate understanding of the essence of both the religion, and the terrorism does serious harm to understanding of the problem. So, in Wikipedia it is possible to read: "Islamic terrorism is one of the variants of religious terrorism . . . Tactics of violent punishments of the opponents, which finds for itself ideological reasons and justification in the interpretation of the dogma as directed to protection of the Islamic world from influence or aggression of non-Muslim countries and ideology, in particular from the Western world". Although there are qualifications like "an interpretation of the dogma" in these definitions, nevertheless such an understanding obscures the problem more and complicates its understanding.

No traditional religion, especially the world one, justifies terror, murders, violence. Religion as a form of public consciousness regulates behavior of a man by means of belief in God, in absolute Good and Justice. In different religions this regulation is made by means of specific provisions. Let's not dwell here into the features of Buddhism and its difference from Abrahamic religions. The present references to the Koran, namely to the regulations on jihad, can be called only a misunderstanding of the skimmed reading or even a result of illiteracy. "Islam" in translation from Arab means patience, humility. And jihad means nothing else but the human right (of a Muslim) to defend himself with a sword if someone wants to kill him for the faith, i.e. it is a possibility to defend one's faith and life from physical encroachments. The same interpreters who consciously or unconsciously confuse "unbelievers" and "people of other faiths", without differentiating "jihad" from "murder" and terrorism, a sacred war from a criminal war, do irreparable harm to the consciousness of people.

The word "war" is translated as "daf", coming from the root "da-fa-a", a closer translation of this word—"to beat off, to repel", includes "resistance against any political and ideological oppression" The word "jihad" comes from the root "jahd". The word "mujahada" coming from the same root means diligence or effort to overcome own passions, body desires, lust, i.e. "nafs" (ego). Spiritual purification, "self-education for the purpose of self-control and obtaining of highly moral qualities", i.e. "jihad with its nafs is the biggest jihad”[29]. Such an understanding has nothing in common with the aggressive and terroristic interpretation of this concept imposed by some politicians and ideologists.

It is no secret that today in the Muslim countries the general educational censure is rather low and it is used by the theorists who turn religion into the means of ideology and policy. And intelligently narrow and morally dirty ideologists accompany it, turning people into “ludens” (toys). Instead of building bridges, they create theories of “collision of civilizations”. With a helping hand of S. Huntington this absolutely politically incorrect term has set it not only in the political, but also in the academic literature, and mentality of people.

What collision can be spoken about when a civilization is a certain stage in cultural development as the way of the attitude to the world? Collision is possible not between civilizations, and even not between contradictory ideologies but only between people, imposed with these ideologies who are maniacally trying to extend their influence on the larger amount of other zombies. “To frighten in order to enslave!”—here is their motto. And the more illiterate the people, the easier it is to frighten them. After all fear, as it has been shown, unlike dread, is first of all based on imaginations and ignorance.

It is necessary to build bridges, but not to dig abysses between different cultures and civilizations because the entire mankind, especially today, during the era of globalization of the world development is interested in it. The pleasure from the peaceful friendly existence is much higher, than from fear and hatred.

Having considered the main civilizational challenges of the pleasure of the 21st century and the ways to exceed them, we have closely approached the principal theme of the research—the ultimatum of pleasure. What does it consist of and how is it shown? What is its cornerstone? Why do we call it the most important challenge of the modern civilization and, the most important thing, is it possible to respond to the ultimatum? The following chapter is devoted to these questions.

3.3 PLEASURE IN THE GRIP OF DARWINISM AND FREUDISM-MARXISM

The 19th century was marked by the final victory of materialistic science. One after another scientific discoveries hammered another “nail in the coffin” of multidimensional understanding of the world, establishing domination of experimentally proved science. However, the question of purity of experiments and validity of conclusions often remained open. Minds of people were entirely seized by the Darwinian matrix of the outlook– the world appeared as a gladiatorial arena of survival. And one-dimensionality was inherent also to understanding of the tools of survival. Fitness acted as a new god of the modern era. Usually it was represented as physical force and dexterity or, at the worst, cunning allowing to deceive the rival and the enemy. By the way, the Darwinism provided the whole field of players of the process of evolution as rivals or even enemies. The strongest survives! And it is unimportant what the price for the victory was. There are no morals in nature! There is only the will to win. And pleasure from superiority. It is painfully familiar philosophy, isn't it?

But is everything really so primitive in nature? Or perhaps development of the techno civilization left its mark on scientific theories, in particular on the Darwinism which safely transferred the laws of survival to the divine nature? The answer to this question assumes more detailed consideration of the basic provisions of the theory of Ch. Darwin.

It is no secret that Charles Darwin proceeded from an idea of the world as of the sphere of opposite, even hostile forces where violence and death dominate. In his work "On the origin of species" he wrote: "From this war raging among nature, from hunger and death directly comes the highest result which the mind is able to imagine, it is formation of the highest forms of the animal life".[30]

The second wrong setting of Ch. Darwin was understanding of invariance of the environment and random changes in an organism which, having passed through a competition prism, were given to descendants. Variability—heredity—natural selection—this triad of Ch. Darwin, unfortunately, didn't count activity of the environment which didn't select ready copies of individuals at all, and, in fact, "grew up" them like a selector, changing itself. Being metaphorically expressed, if "mother" changed—also "child" changed. That is, the priority in emergence of new species was on the side of the system, but not the element and, especially, a blind chance. The system, changing, generates the element required for it, serving in its turn as a necessary means of its change. To some extent Jean Baptiste Lamarck noted the non-randomness of the changes happening in live systems and the role of the environment in this process, but with a shade of teleologism.

The Darwinian thesis: "The strongest survives!"—was, in fact, a principle of antagonistic society with transferring the slave idea of force as a capability to survive on any human community. As an objection to the thesis about survival of the strongest we will notice that sometimes no less force and courage is required to die. Unfortunately, we often see how the strongest and bravest die during wars. And what is the force for nature? Adaptability? And it is not always. Force and adaptability of an individual is one thing, and force and adaptability of a species is another. Not for nothing Thomas Carlyle called the principle of fight for existence "the philosophy of pigs".

In general, the triad variability—heredity—natural selection—is fair for intra-specific evolution, but not inter-specific one. Charles Darwin considered it right this way. A cockroach can compete with a cockroach, but not with a hippopotamus or a lion. And the ideas of cruel survival in nature and in the primitive society are too exaggerated as well as about the cruelty of the ancient. It is known that a primitive man spent several hours a week on fending, the rest of the time indulging into free pastime to his own pleasure. There are also cases known when primitive young people chewed meat for old men who already had no teeth. It means that they were not "beasts" at all as it is imagined sometimes! We are imposed that man is a wolf to man, quoting Thomas Hobbes, intentionally shortening the quotation and thus changing the sense to completely the opposite. Hobbes noted that man is a wolf to man only in the natural condition, i.e. without the state, without the laws of human existence. To be a man to a man is one of the highest pleasures.

Even among animals sympathy, friendship, mutual help and mutual assistance favor their survival and keeps the species. Ch. Darwin called these feelings sympathy. A lot of cases are known when animals help each other, save each other, sometimes risking own life. Once in Africa travelers with dogs were crossing a valley on which there was a herd of baboons. The baboons repelled aggression of dogs, climbed the mountain, but left a little monkey in the valley which was surrounded by the dogs and was calling relatives to help it. The largest and the bravest baboon went down from the hillside, passed between dogs, took the monkey, caressed it and left with dignity with the monkey in its hands. The dogs didn't even dare to attack it. Or there is one more rather recent episode which was uploaded in You-Tube. An antelope came to drink some water to a river where a crocodile has successfully hidden, pretending to be a log. While the antelope, without suspecting anything, was drinking water, the crocodile in a jump seized it by the throat and dragged off to the river. Suddenly, from nowhere, a hippopotamus appeared, snatched on the crocodile and rescued the victim. The hippopotamus in its mouth brought the antelope to the shore, put on the ground, then returned to the river, got some water into its mouth and sprinkled the antelope which recovered and with horror ran away. Such behavior is subject not to any human! And it is possible to give a great number of such examples; the main thing is that they demonstrate our simplified understanding of animals, their mentality and behavior. Animals derive pleasure not only from satisfaction of physical needs. Unfortunately, people sometimes are driven by not so much the thirst of the truth, but rather by the snobbish desire to separate from all other world.

O. Spengler specified that changes in science, in particular in mathematics, determine a certain type of culture. In a case with Ch. Darwin we see an opposite situation when changes in society, in culture lead to emergence of a theory, which in turn, affected the course of cultural- historical progress. And the fact that a man is a much more complicated being and that his development greatly depends on what he thinks of himself and in what environment he lives—is known to everybody now. Therefore it is necessary to develop the theories about humanity as a source of the highest pleasure of a man.

In his work "Man's search for meaning" Victor Frankl, psychologist and psychotherapist, perfectly writes about it. The author's wisdom is determined by the fact that a lot of things which he writes about were endured by him in the concentration camp. V. Frankl saw with own eyes, and didn't subtract from books how a man remained a man, despite inhuman conditions. Not the competition and fight for survival allowed people to survive there, but the fact that they had kept the sense of existence in themselves, love to relatives who wouldn't do without them, and own human dignity. Of cou rse, for S. Freud considering a man "a supplement to sexual glands"—all these are just fine words. But, pardon, for some reason we believe Victor Frankl who had experienced all this in life.

Ch. Darwin, certainly, is a great scientist who made a revolutionary contribution to development of biology, but he didn't claim for creating a new outlook and moreover a civilizational paradigm at all. However, as it happens to many scientific theories, his doctrine was fated to play the role which was not foreseen by its creator.

Another great doctrine of the XIX century was Marxism which turned into the real force which remade the world during the next century. The brilliant economic analysis of capitalism was completed with the social-philosophic and politological forecast about the inevitability of a new socioeconomic structure—communism with the basic principle: "to each according to his needs". Although in the same century, shortly before that, A. S. Pushkin wrote a no less genius small (in comparison with the four-volume The Capital) fairy tale *The Tale of the Fisherman and the Fish* in which he showed that needs of a man are infinite and can be even absurd. What he has will never be enough to a man. And the modern society of mass consumption with its absurd offers and needs serves more evidence to that. But unlike Ch. Darwin who had put DNA and its random change providing special survivability as the core point of the human evolution, K. Marx considered productive forces as the main factor of social and human evolution, that is, generally speaking—tools of labor and techniques. He had simplified the human essence to a set of public relations, thus having deprived a concrete person of his own, independent essence. "The essence of a man,—he writes in the known Theses on Feuerbach,—is not something abstract, inherent in an individual, but as a whole it represents the whole, the ensemble of the public relations".[31]

Marxism, to be exact, Lenin's understanding of it, has set the mankind free from any socio-natural regularities, having established in the consciousness of people a thought of possible change of the social and economic structure. For this purpose, according to Marxism, it is only required to socialize the means of production since the antagonistic societies were based on the private property on the means of production. An ugly form of such outlook was the doctrine of Michurin trying to create natural mutants—an apple-tree fructifying pears and vice versa. "We should not wait for any favor from nature! To take it by force—this is our task!"—is his notorious phrase. Where did such aggression and hatred to the nature come from? Perhaps, it came from the mental transfer of the offense on social injustice to nature. An important factor of creation of these theories, in our opinion, was the pleasure from awareness of own power, and sometimes just from violence. Both the Darwinism and Marxism idolize the competition force remaking reality. In the first case it is intra-specific competition, and in the second one—inter-class.

The most important world outlook doctrine of the XX century which not only affected minds, but also seriously changed the value system and the way of life of people was more than once mentioned Freudism. S. Freud made, certainly, a huge contribution to development of the theory of the unconscious which idea was developed by E. Hartmann and A. Schopenhauer, and other philosophers, having shown a huge role of the unconscious in human behavior. However he didn't avoid the fate of great scientists, having hypertrophied the role of the researched object. This is about the sexual power of libido with which S. Freud replaces all the psycho-physiological power of a man.

Having adopted the main idea of physiology from his teacher Gustav Theodor Fechner that all living beings, in fact, are thermodynamic systems which are charged and discharged, he saw almost the one, at least universal and the main method of "discharge", of dropping off the psycho-energetic intensity in the sexual activity of a person. This discharge allows a person to feel pleasure. However, by means of the concept "sublimation" Sigmund Freud tried to specify a variety of methods to remove tension, but the dominating meaning of sexual life of a human nevertheless remained in his doctrine. Inadmissibility of such simplification of psychophysiology of a man was perfectly reflected by the works of his followers, representatives of the school of psychoanalysis founded by him—E. Fromm, A. Adler, K. Horny and others.

The unconscious is of great importance in human life, learning of these impulses will allow to learn a lot of things about a man, but nevertheless it is wrong to reduce all human behavior to it. Especially wrong it is to narrow human pleasure only to physiological one.

The mankind shall be grateful to great scientists: Ch. Darwin, K. Marx, S. Freud, as well as to many other scientists, for what they have given to the world, but it is not right to idolize them, turning into an icon. It is said: "you shall not make for yourself an idol ". And we have made. This is why we have idolized the Force, class fight, material conditions of survival, sex, having formed the civilizational paradigm which is based on aspiration to pleasure from the feeling of possession and superiority. It isn't accidental that all world religions, trying to keep love and humanity in a person, were opposing that. That is why the 19th century, a century of rapid development of science and technology, was so greatly rebelling against religion, having offered Darwinism and Freudism-Marxism, in fact as its alternative.

The 21st century contrasted the rational pleasure from power with the absurdly irrational pleasure from despair expressed by the words of Ben Laden: "We love death more, than they love life".

Let's consider the paradigmal reasons of this despair in detail.

3.4 THE ULTIMATUM OF PLEASURE: CONSUMER CAPITALISM VS HUMANISTIC CULTURE

Throughout the whole book we have been describing the dependence of a person on pleasure. We said that it was impossible to make any action, to make any decision, without having weighed the expected pleasure beforehand.

Having demonstrated what sort of guiles the pleasure is capable of, we showed how it provokes a person to turn his sincere altruistic impulses against himself.

The pleasure behaves outrageous unconsciously, in the depth of our mentality. Its tricks have been perfected for millions of years of evolution to automatism and hidden in the most ancient parts of the brain. Homo sapiens are locked in a dungeon of their own physiology. The situation is worse than one can imagine.

3.4.1 Knowledge about Humans against Humans

It can become worse when someone starts using the knowledge of pleasure against humans. Imagine that enemies of the mankind have got the researches of neurophysiologists, psychologists, anthropologists about human mentality and behavior models fallen into their hands. Everything turned out to be in the hands of those who pursue benefits, paying no attention to ethics.

Imagine that these enemies of the mankind are so influential that they might launch shattering missiles against the planet Earth using all the knowledge about our weaknesses. Imagine that the enemies have captured the most perfect technologies, the information on each person wherever he lives: in Tokyo or Tbilisi, Naples or Samara.

They know what he buys, what he gifts, what he likes to listen and even to whom and what letters he writes, with whom, when and how often he speaks on phone. Humanoids have gathered all the data about us over the last ten years.

They can predict our actions prior we manage to think of them.

These beings, greedy for power, dream to turn us into a power source, same as robots turned people into batteries in the movie of brothers Wachowski[32]. Aliens are clever, they have managed not to give out their presence for a long time, their weapon was imperceptible. They have been exhausting resources from us, and we have not even noticed.

Do you think an unsuspecting person occupied with his affairs has a chance to overthrow the invisible tyranny, to throw off the invisible, but very heavy fetters?

It is unlikely.

The enemy was found!

Attention, we are giving an orientation: "It has no tentacles with suckers and no egg-like head as we were told before. It has not arrived by a spaceship. It has grown up here, together with us. We ourselves have generated it. An invisible blood-sucker is the market.

And its army is marketing specialists.

Now people know the true owner of the world.

But what can they do with it, if for 100 years of its government it has become so powerful that it is unapproachable now.

Today the scheme of a day of a metropolis resident has become similar to navigation in a shopping mall.

How did it happen?

It was very simple.

The best minds of the planet work for the Market. Indeed they understood long ago that you won't sell many goods. Why should a person have five suits if the first one has not been worn out yet?

One should sell something that a person can consume endlessly, something that a person pursues after, without knowing any limits and barriers.

Expansion of marketing reached the apogee when it had almost monopolized pleasure, having allowed people to get it only through purchases.

The society throughout all the history constrained the thirst for pleasure as the dependence threatening the intellectual and spiritual development. Ethical standards, religious doctrines and morals came to the rescue. There appeared a concept "a vice". To derive pleasure in touch with a vice meant to doom oneself to a sense of guilt and social censure. They are two faithful guards at the gates of pleasure.

In the last century, marketing stepped out on the stage, and the aspiration to pleasure ceased being a vice or demonstration of unworthy behavior. The companies by means of brands turned the aspiration to pleasure into a phenomenon which is socially encouraged and global. They launched overall sales of indulgences. The morals retired.

The market almost replaced air. In our memory there are more names of brands, than names of poets. Children start learning logos earlier, than they can say the first “mama”. In the USA there are more people visiting McDonald’s restaurants than churches.[33]

During planning meetings of marketing specialists it more often sounds the following: “the pleasure—something that a man is after by his nature, should not be free. The pleasure is the best of goods. This is what should be sold!”

The pleasure got on counters. They started selling it in car showrooms, in restaurants, in shopping centers, by mail, by means of sales representatives—everywhere and everyway.

Henchmen of the market were not limited to the market of real goods, after all pleasure is everywhere.

Everything turned into merchandise: knowledge, communication, personal contact, services, products, art.

We obtain more knowledge so that to sell something more expensively, it is a deal of purchase and sale.

We read books to be more interesting interlocutors. We buy and resell information.

We watch news to be aware of the situation and can educate colleagues, thus having won their affectation. Better say, buying their affectation.

We do our best at work so that the boss would give us a bonus. It is again a deal.

Having taken control of pleasure, marketing specialists took control of the essence of a person.

The great marketing specialist became the Great Inquisitor.

3.4.2 Easy Pleasure Became a Narcotic

For only a few decades an adult, mature, reasonable, successful individual turned into an exchanger of money, time and, we can say, all of himself into pleasure.

To get pleasure for money at the earliest opportunity became a norm of life.

Only few have the sense that having bought a product they won’t get the promised pleasure.

It seems to everyone that they need more pleasure. That they simply had outgrown over a certain level and therefore ceased to feel pleasure.

Instead of exposing the dopamine deception, they are accelerated in chasing their tail.

The global market outgrew the needs. Today desires make a demand. Satisfaction gave way to pleasure.

It is a seemingly simple replacement of words but how the world has changed as a tresult of it! Over the last 10 years, the world economy has grown twice more than for the previous decade.

Inventions, novelties, know-how ceased being achievements. Creation of innovations became an administrative model.

Everything got on a conveyor. The tape was rolled out, apparently, to a limit.

But no, every year it speeds up more and more. Is there a limit?

There are no limits to desires.

Marketing specialists lead consumers round the circle.

Everyone promises pleasure. But it is still missing.

Good marketing specialists know that selling desires, they should only tease people by pleasure. Not to allow them to be sated with it.

Even if the main dream of life comes true, and the lucky one buys a red Ferrari, at the very same time he has to want something bigger, for example, an advanced seat, or tires of the latest model.

Even the fastest car in the world doesn't satisfy a need for speed but only kindles it.

Desires have no limits, since it is possible to promise pleasure eternally.

To promise—here is a trick which marketing specialists learned on an ingenious, incomprehensible to the consumer level.

3.4.3 Between Pain and Pleasure

Here exactly a consumer has found himself. On both sides there are marketing specialists. They don't avoid hurting so that to sell quickly by themselves the anesthetics.

Martin Lindstrom, the guru of neuro-marketing wrote—"fear and wine are the best sellers". They sell sports cars to getting old bachelors, healthy food in metropolises with bad ecology, and expensive children's toys to bad parents as well.

Having a man hooked on a paid dopamine needle, corporations are getting able-bodied, motivated and seeking for professional development addicts, spending all the earned money for a next dose.

What will be able to stop this huge machine under the name "the mankind"?

3.4.4 The Ultimatum: a Man or a Consumer

The man is mighty. The will of one person is enough to change the world. But the consumer is weak. He is being led, he is a victim. It is his role.He lost the battle, without even joining it. The consumer was born to buy. It is possible that codependence is the best form of people's coexistence.During the evolution only the organisms most suitable for life remained. But what is about the phenomena?

If the codependence continues to live and gets stronger, does it mean that it is the best form of coexistence?

E. Fromm as far back as in the middle of the last century wrote a prophetical paper "Escape from Freedom" in which he stated that in the modern society people did not strive for freedom, but on the contrary did everything possible to avoid it. Seventy years ago it was a prediction, today it is a diagnosis.

Marketing turned into an interdisciplinary doctrine, having united in itself psychology, neurophysiology, economy, sociology, turned into a science on modeling the behavior of masses.

Today it is impending to turn into a planetary formation, into a new paradigm of existence of a man.

Can people learn again to receive pleasures independently, and with the same ease and in the same volume, what they receive in exchange for money?

A man is mighty! The power required for managing himself and the pleasure is initially input inside of him. But for its activation it is necessary to apply the will.

The will that won't appear until a man himself realizes a problem, until he understands it with his mind and feels it with his heart.

It is obvious that in the fight against the market aggressors not all will stand. Many will fall, without a victory over their pleasure. It is a required victim. Possibly, there will be not less than a half of them.But you shouldn't shed tears over the fallen. After all everyone has equal chances in this war, and a victory depends only on ourselves.

One shouldn't hope for a victory without having spent efforts for search, without troubling oneself with understanding and without overcoming fear to allow thoughts to the heart so that to experience new knowledge.

For further evolutionary growth it is not enough just to survive and give birth to the offspring, it is necessary to learn to control own nature.

Already today it becomes clear that the mankind will be divided into two big groups: the consuming majority and the creating minority. Over the centuries, and probably the millennia this distinction will become specific. It will be more and more difficult to pass from the lowest level of development to the highest one. What looks today as a crack in the soil, in a thousand years will become an insuperable abyss.

An opportunity to make decisions, without being led by the dopamine temptation, but on the contrary by the power of the clear mind to call pleasure at the moment when the decision is made, will become the most important difference of a free new person from the captivated one, painfully familiar to us.

Today the first fight in a war for a free mind is being conducted, the fight for the pleasure. The more the people would be able to win their right for pleasure, disallowing the market to replace all the pleasure sources, the more realizable the hope will be, that the victory in the final fight with psycho-physiology is possible.

Jack Trout, in his paper "Horse Sense," wrote about the importance of being able to anticipate trends and manage to take the correct positions.

In the war for pleasure, we take the part of people. We trust in the Homo sapiens who possess courage to be free.

Homo sapiens, who is not a victim of the psychophysiological mechanisms honed by evolution to sensations of pleasure, and chooses for himself the ways and means bringing pleasure.

However, not only a man himself has to choose what to derive pleasure from, but all human culture has to make people focus on pleasure not from mass egoistical consumption, but from creation of harmony giving pleasure from self-realization and unity of "Me" with the environment.

Change of the behavioral strategy of a man calls for the change in culture. We can endlessly focus a man on amending but if the nature of the existing culture is not being amended, transformation will concern only some people, thereby dooming the majority to existence in the consumerism captivity.

Now it is a high time to speak about a new civilization paradigm, about the new culture carrying the signs of the new humanism which will become an alternative to the consumer capitalism.

Difference of the modern humanism from the humanism of the Renaissance is that if in the XVI century it was required to come back from the outlook placing the God in the center of the universe to the outlook considering a human, the crown of the nature, as such a center, the modern humanism dictates a need to establish a human as a son of the nature. In other words, from the medieval theocentric outlook the society of the Renaissance passed to the anthropocentric one, and the era of environmental, eco-centric outlook has set in today.

The main condition of the new humanism should be the understanding that a man and the nature are not the object and the subject, but are the elements of the whole system that needs each other for the harmonious development.

The twenty first century has to finish the era of rationalism and, as a result of it, stop approving a man as an all-knowing being, and therefore "having the right ". Lucifer ambitions of a man have to be replaced with Christian love to all the surrounding. The way of sense has to concede the way of Heart.

Through an ecological crisis, the nature itself has bared a need of changing a man in this direction.We should notice that the way of heart was always close to both Russia, and India, and many other countries as well. The pleasure which is felt by a man is a mechanism of forming the unity of a man and culture.

Transforming the pleasure from consumption to the pleasure from creation, a man evolves from the being who seeks for competition into the being who wishes to be of assistance to others.

The mankind was searching for this mechanism outside, and it was hidden deeply inside of a man. A parable comes to mind, how the god wanted to hide from ungrateful people annoying him with requests. And, finally, lodged inside of a man, considering it the last place a man would look for him.

To disclose the essence of the new humanism even a separate book will not be enough therefore we will return to description of the new culture principles in the final chapter. For now, we allow ourselves to stop, finishing the narration by an illustration of humanism with the words of Confucius. Answering a question how a man should live, he said: "Don't behave with others in such a way that you would not want them to behave with you". It was in the 6th century B.C. Then in the 18th century Immanuel Kant added: "Behave such a way that the maxim of your will could become the general law". Paraphrasing these words in relation to the principle of pleasure, it is possible to say

"Behave such a way so that what brings pleasure to you would bring pleasure to all!"

Chapter Four

On the Way to a New Paradigm

4.1 A RESPONSE TO THE CIVILIZATIONAL CHALLENGE

The pleasure conducts a person like a guide of a blind man.

We can't get rid of it, but we can regain the eyesight and the right to choose independently our road together with it as well.

How to learn redirecting energy of a desire?

How to feel pleasure where it was unavailable to us before?

The pleasure is an emotional experience and a man is able to activate it himself.

To rise above pleasure doesn't mean to inhibit a desire inside.

To rise above pleasure means not to experience it from what doesn't bring benefit to a person, but to experience it from what he considers necessary.

For some time it was considered that scientists had found the center of pleasure in a brain of mammals.

Kelly McGonigal, a professor of the Stanford University, in her book "The willpower instinct," wrote about it in an easy and very interesting way.

"In 1953 James Olds and Peter Milner, two young scientists of the McGill's University in Montreal, were trying to understand one mysterious rat. The scientists had implanted an electrode in its brain and delivered current through it. They tried to activate a brain zone which, as other researchers considered, was responsible for a fear reaction of rats. Judging by the previous reports, laboratory rats hated electric discharges and tried to avoid everything that coincided with the moment of brain stimulation. But Olds and Milner's rat always came back to that corner of the cage where it had been electrocuted; as though it dreamed to repeat everything.

The scientists puzzled with the freakish behavior of the rat decided to check a hypothesis according to which the animal wanted those shake-ups.

They awarded the rat with an easy electric discharge every time when it made a small step out of that corner. The rat quickly saw through the trick and in a few minutes was already sitting in the opposite corner of the cage. Olds and Milner found out that the rat would move in any direction if awarded with a current rush. Soon they were operating the mouse, like a joystick. Were other scientists really mistaken about consequences of stimulating this area of rats' midbrain? Or the chaps had got a masochist rat? Actually they had groped an unstudied brain area—only by implanting an electrode inaccurately. Olds was a social psychologist, not a neurobiologist, but he had to work in a laboratory as well. He had poked a cable wrongly. By a mere mistake the researchers had found a brain zone which, apparently, provided a feeling of incredible pleasure upon stimulation. Or why would the rat go anywhere to get a current rush? Olds and Milner called the found brain structure the center of pleasure. But they did not realize then where they had got into".

The rat was feeling not pleasure, but desire.

As it became clear, dopamine only promises pleasure to us, but does not give it[1].

Rats, dependent on dopamine, were ready to run on the energized floor, receiving an extra portion of a neuro-mediator until their paws burned down. Is it worth saying that rats were easily refusing food for dopamine, even after starving for a whole day? When rats were given a chance to stimulate themselves independently with dopamine through pressing a lever, they were pressing it until fell down exhausted nearby.

Generally, rats would undoubtedly die out as a species if they could themselves obtain a neuro-mediator. Rats are lucky, they cannot.

And what about people?

Olds and Milner decided to test their experiment on people.

McGonigal writes "In the Tulane University Robert Heath implanted electrodes in the patients' brain and gave them a chance to stimulate themselves a recently found center of pleasure. Heath's patients behaved exactly in the same way, as Olds and Milner's rats. When allowed to stimulate themselves with any frequency, they gave themselves 40 charges per minute. They were offered trays with food during breaks, but the patients, although admitting they were hungry, didn't want to be interrupted. One patient was extremely indignant when the experimenter tried to finish the session and to disconnect electrodes. Another participant pressed the button 200 times after current had been disconnected until the scientist urged him to calm down".

What can make a man receive pleasure forty times in a minute?

Is it really often required more and more pleasure and a man will never be able to be sated with it?

Something is wrong with it. Satisfaction has to come along with pleasure then.

The doubts were confirmed by the fact of patients' confessions that their unceasing self-stimulation was provoked by anxiety over possible current disconnection.

Can really a person who has received pleasure feel anxiety, shouldn't he simply enjoy a present situation being satisfied?

McGonigal writes: "The remaining records of the patients themselves open up another side of this allegedly blissful experience. One patient suffering from a narcolepsy was implanted with an electrode and provided with the device so that he didn't fall asleep. The man claimed that self-stimulation was accompanied by the feeling of despair. Despite "frequent, sometimes violent, pressing of the button", he never felt pleasure which seemed so near.

Self-stimulation had caused anxiety, but not happiness.

His behavior looked rather as obtrusiveness than experience of pleasure".

And what if Olds and Milner's rats were exhausting themselves not because they were getting pleasure but because they wanted to get rid of displeasure, of pain?

McGonigal asks: "What if the brain area which they activated, didn't award them with a feeling of deep satisfaction, but only promised it? Perhaps the rats excited themselves because the brain was telling them, that they needed to press just once, and something marvelous would happen?"

Olds and Milner had not discovered the center of pleasure.

The area which they stimulated was a part of the most primitive motivational brain structure which had appeared to induce us to action. And dopamine played a major role there.

What scientists had considered pleasure turned out to be only an expectation of pleasure.

Here is how McGonigal herself narrates about the neurophysiological nuances of this process:

"When the brain notices a possibility of an award, it excretes a neuromediator dopamine. Dopamine orders the rest of the brain to concentrate on this award and to receive it by all means. Dopamine inflow by itself doesn't cause happiness—it rather simply excites.

We are cheerful, vigorous and keen. We feel a possibility of pleasure and are ready to work hard to gain it".

Neurophysiologists call the dopamine effect differently, for example: search, volition, appetency, desire, etc. But one thing is clear: it is not the experience of something pleasant—pleasures, delight or the award. It is only a desire, anticipation, expectation of it.

The researches have proved that it is possible to exterminate the whole dopamine system in the brain of a rat, but it all the same will demonstrate pleasure after sugar consumption. Only it won't work to allure the rat with sugar, it won't wish it. It still loves sugar, but doesn't want it.

In 2001 Brian Knutson, a neurobiologist from Stanford, published a convincing research in which he proved that dopamine was responsible for anticipation, but not for experience of being rewarded. The scientist used the experience of the experiment of Ivan Pavlov—dog and a bell. Knutson assumed that the brain also excreted some kind of saliva in anticipation of reward. In his research Knutson was putting the participants into a tomograph and forced their conditioned response: when there was a certain symbol on the screen, they could win a monetary prize. To get it, they had to press a button. Soon, when people saw a symbol, a supporting system was activated in their brain and dopamine was emitted, and the participants were pressing the button with all their might. But after the win, this area of the brain was calming down. The pleasure of a victory was registered in other nervous centers. Knutson illustrated that dopamine was responsible for action, and not for happiness.

All the matter is that we are insatiable in our expectation and chase of pleasure, but the pleasure itself can sate us very quickly.

Having received the object of desire, we don't want it any more. We are satisfied.

Soon a new desire seizes us. And so on endlessly.

If a person wants to cease running after "a carrot", it is necessary just to realize what he really desires: the pleasure itself or its expectation?

The difference seems insignificant, but it changes the world.

As soon as a man learns to concentrate on the object of pleasure, but not on its expectation and to devote all his attention to the pleasure from possession, but not from anticipation, he will be able to satisfy his unrestrained hunger.

A man will cease to burn paws like the rats, rushing through the life in expectation. Now he will be able to move quietly towards the objective, without limiting his eyesight to a keyhole of desire.

Exactly about this riddance of desires the enlightened are speaking about, Epicurus spoke exactly about such freedom from pleasure.

We should strive for pleasure, but we should not desire it.

It would seem a small difference in words. But absence of desire as expectation of pleasure gives us freedom. Having derived pleasure, we must be able to enjoy it. However while we are nearing it, we should be able to liberate ourselves from the passionate desire.

4.1.1 The Sense of Pleasure

The best questions which a person can ask to release from desire:

- What will I do with the pleasure I will get after the goal achievement?
- Will I be able to use it as a resource for further development?
- How long will I be able to be charged with the energy of that pleasure?

If there is no answer, it is the time to refuse the desire.

People are getting rid of desires not through a ban, not through violent will, but through awareness of the irrelevance of pleasure.

We will tell a bit later why "the iron" will is a distorted harmful term and why efforts "to make oneself knuckle under" continually turn into fiascoes.

4.1.2 The Pleasure Generates Desire and Stress

As a rule, we strive for pleasure in order to remove the itch which it itself has gifted to us. Yes, it is like that—the pleasure infects us with pain, suffering, stress, itch, desire, however.

Here is how McGonigal describes it:

"Researchers observed this combination of desire and stress in women who wanted some chocolate. When shown images of chocolate, they almost imperceptibly shuddered. This physiological reflex is connected with anxiety and excitement—similar as a predator is being noticed in the wild area. The women reported that they felt desire and anxiety at the same time ".

In other words, when the desire is born inside of us, we attribute pleasure to the object, possessing which is so necessary for us, and stress—to the fact that we don't have this thing.

However, we should emphasize that desire and a stress are children of pleasure.

The object of desire causes both anticipation of pleasure and stress simultaneously.

During an experiment it was revealed that shopaholics who reduce stress or lighten their mood by visiting a shopping mall, are the happiest ... guess during what period, prior, at the time of or after the purchase?

You are right—prior. On the way to the shopping center the mood of shopaholics is at the peak, since they anticipate excellent pastime.

The most interesting is that this feeling is changed by nervousness, itch when they are at a cash desk. Certainly, it is influenced by a pain from expenses. But it is not only that. It became clear, the longer the sales process is, the more nervous girls are. Why would they be? After all they are doing their favorite thing. Why should not they relax in a queue, not savor every moment?

There is nothing of that kind!

Instead of it there is only one desire: to pay off as soon as possible and to leave the boutique.

4.1.3 Dopamine Trace

What began as search of pleasure, as anticipation of pleasure, ended with stress.

Chanel, Manolo Blanic, Michele Kors promised unforgettable pleasure, and while a buyer anticipated it, he was happy.

But the closer the outcome was, the closer the object of your desire was becoming, the stronger a new feeling was arising—stress, tension, and itch.

A person paid with a card and fluttered out from a boutique.

Where is pleasure, happiness?

It is absent.

The brain doesn't have any concern about happiness. Its task is to force us to want, to start the process of chasing the goal; to bring us into a shop and to put in a queue. To create such a tension, living with which for long is simply impossible. We are getting rid of it! Mission is completed.

It is done. Good job. Dopamine has left the stage.

But we remain. We are waiting for the promised happiness.

However, happiness is no care of the brain. It's care of desires and their execution.

Was the bag bought? It was!

Any claims?

No matter if it is the tenth for this fall; if the credit card has reached the bottom; if there are 28 days left till the salary—those are not its problems.

Dopamine is the prehistoric replacement of "the willpower"

The task of dopamine is not to make you stop wanting.

The motivational system appeared in our organism millions years ago when the human brain was slightly more than a walnut.

You must admit that it is dangerous to give freedom of choice to such a being.

Therefore the nature has developed an excellent control mechanism.

An autopilot was input into us.

The nature has supplied a man with dopamine, the strongest driver of desires, which won't calm down until we get what we want.

While pursuing pleasure a man finds a relief from the pain which he feels from expectation of this pleasure.

It is the maximum that we can count on.

The primary expected pleasure remains unreachable.

It is like the horizon, always runs away from us.

McGonigal confirms this thought:

"We are concentrated, and constantly looking for what we aspire, we are ready to work—even to suffer—for the sake of what we want to gain. It seems to us that the object of our desire will make our happiness. We buy a thousandth chocolate bar, a new kitchen device, we order one more glass of drink, we exhaust ourselves searching for a new soul mate, the best work, the highest profit.

We confuse experience of volition to a happiness guarantee.

No wonder that we, people, are almost unable to distinguish the promise of a reward from any pleasure or an award which we are searching for. The promise of a reward is strong, and we continue to pursue something that doesn't give us happiness, and we consume those things that bring more sufferings, than pleasures. Since the pursuit of a reward is the main mission of dopamine, it will never order you to stop—even if the result doesn't correspond to the promise".

A man learned to get dopamine artificially as though there was not enough of it being discharged under natural conditions.

All marketing communications in the modern multinational companies are directed to make people start wanting.

Neuro-marketing specialists can start the process of dopamine discharge by means of a picture, a sound, a smell, a word and etc.

In order to get pleasure, and not to be deceived by its promise, one should always be alert and ask himself questions helping to realize our true motivation.

In other words to ask regularly a question: What is my pleasure like?

However, it is generally agreed that there are also things that bring pleasure, and not just promise it.

According to the American psychological association, the real pleasure is brought by:

- physical trainings
- game sports,
- prayer or visit of religious service,
- reading,
- music,
- time spent with relatives
- massage,
- walk,
- meditation
- yoga,

and of course, creativity.

And things which deceive with dopamine are:

- gambling and video games,
- shopping
- smoking,
- drinks,
- yummies,
- surfing the Internet,
- TV, uncontrolled watching.

How do these two groups of occupations differ?

What really reduces stress, does not lead to a splash of dopamine and does not rely on the promise of a reward, but increases discharges of such neuro-mediators, as "serotonin and GABA27," as well as a hormone of "happiness"—oxytocin.

These kinds of activities help to interrupt the stressful response of the brain to lower the quantity of stress hormones in the blood and to cause a remedial reaction of relax. They do not excite as much as the occupations provoking release of dopamine, and people are inclined to underestimate how well they feel during the minutes of occupation. We forget about these strategies not because they are useless but because our brain in a stressful state is constantly mistaken in estimates of what is required for it.

Ability to ignore desires and to derive long pleasure from the result of the decisions is a hard, but still possible to be obtained, skill.

You should not give up if you were born in Moscow or New York, and not in the mountains of Nepal, you should not put an end to the freedom of your spirit if you did not have to spend in meditations all your adolescence. To win over the principle of pleasure you should only distinguish your own pleasure.

Remind yourself daily what pleasure you seek to.

But, as it often happens, simple things are given with great difficulty.

And meanwhile, the decision is simple—to surpass the principle of pleasure one should learn to ignore desires and to feel long-lasting pleasure from the decisions being made.

Pleasure is in everything that brings less suffering.

Sometimes the pleasure and the enjoyment are considered synonyms, and the concepts are being easily substituted. Especially often it occurs upon translation of texts on foreign languages. Not by accident even such a well-known work of S. Freud "Beyond the pleasure" is sometimes translated as "Beyond the enjoyment ". Almost the same happened with the translation of the present work into English. However, we have succeeded in defending our understanding.

We will note that it is easier for Russian-speaking readers to catch a difference. It is felt in the mere sounding.

Enjoyment is a size of the pleasure which brings pleasant feelings.

Pleasure is a basic feeling which a person experiences.

Same as pain, for example.

The main difference between pleasure and enjoyment is that pleasure is not often realized and does not bring pleasant feelings to a person. A person can make hard decisions, never admitting to himself that pleasure is their cornerstone. Decisions might be different: to sterilize a cat today or to drown kittens in a year; to surrender the city today or to lose the country in half a year.

Everything that helps us to avoid pain, or to replace it by less pain—is pleasure.

Enjoyment can be characterized as the size of the pleasure bringing pleasant feelings. To eat a cake, to drive a forced car or to spend an evening with the beloved person—all this can give enjoyment.

Enjoyment is the realized pleasure giving us strong emotional experiences.

Enjoyment is always being realized.

The aspiration to pleasure is laid in our nature. But we strive for enjoyment deliberately, and we often call it a vice.

Absence of pain is enough for happiness

Substituting the concepts of pleasure and enjoyment, many people aspire to the last, believing that there is no happiness without it. It is a delusion. Absence of pain is really important for happiness, but it can provide the pleasure which has not reached the extent of enjoyment. The volume of pleasure should be precisely as much as it is necessary to eliminate pain, however, it should not be excessive to ensure pleasant feelings.

Happiness is a product of our perception. Of course, it requires objective conditions, such as a balance of pleasure and pain, but happiness lies not in the external object granting enjoyment and, moreover, not in the enjoyment itself.

The realized enjoyment gives freedom from desires

Many people, continuing the above given thought, find the role of enjoyment in human life harmful, assuring that all troubles are from enjoyments and therefore try to exclude them from their life, which results afterwards in a reverse pathological thirst for pleasant feelings, or in the existence deprived of joy.

None of those is a worthy example for imitation.

Enjoyment as a source of pleasant feelings is very useful for personal development, since it is an excellent assistant in building of the desirable behavior model and a way of thinking.

Taking into consideration natural aspiration to pleasures, a man can turn enjoyment into a self-encouragement element to develop the behavior model required for him.

Let us say, to quit smoking, or to start doing exercises.

For example, today many people feel a strong need for communication in social networks. It is possible to say that the Internet gives them enjoyment.

But, instead of turning the work in Facebook into a positive support for making an action necessary to them (to edit this chapter, for example), they uselessly spend hours without a break there.

Karen Pryor, a scientist-behaviorist, in her book "Don't Shoot the Dog: The New Art of Teaching and Training" writes that positive reinforcement upon successful experience is the strongest factor of remembering and repeating this experience. Stronger than the usual positive reinforcement it can only be the irregular positive reinforcement when enjoyment is occurring in various volumes and with different frequency. For example, when a dolphin gets used to receiving two fish for the executed trick, it can be given five fish next time, and the next but one—only one fish. Later, it is even possible to miss a reward a couple times. The dolphin will better try then to earn a bigger reward.

We are surrounded by a huge amount of enjoyment, and it can be placed to fulfill our conscious desires: to exercise abs or to learn a language.

Don't approach your phone or sketch-board until you finish your exercises. As soon as you accustom yourself to being rewarded by enjoyment for any useful activity, make it irregular.

Pull out from "a hat" notes with minutes for Facebook, indicating how many of them you give to yourself.

One day it can be 20 minutes, another day—40, and on the third day—0.

Before you know it, in 3–4 months, you will have a sculptured tummy and an excellent mood. Your life will be filled with both conscious result, and enjoyment.

You shouldn't avoid enjoyment. This is our great assistant.

Use enjoyment to grow a desire to achieve the required result in yourself.

We often speak about the future, about evolution of a man, about the new world on the pages of this book. A consecutive reader can ask us: if you consider, that instincts are relicts and they cause only troubles in the new world, then why not to get rid of them already on the biological level? Have a great mind to exterminate this dopamine; to implant a smart chip instead of it in order to activate the desires directed only on what is really necessary for us.

This is a good question.

Perhaps, sometime it will be so—people will learn to start "the system of volition" only for what is necessary for them. And to switch it off so that not to want what it isn't necessary. Then we will surely cease to want a red Ferrari, a Birkin handbag, a prize in one million dollars, and we will start wishing health and peace in the world. Well, and, of course, we will phone the mother, at last.

But while modern neuro-engineering makes its first steps it is early to speak about modeling of the brain. The only thing which scientists can make today is to remove completely the part of the brain which discharges dopamine so that we cease to wish at all.

An interesting case happened to a cheerful 33 years old guy. His name was Adam, just like the first man's on earth. Only he was the first among his friends by slovenliness and by the amount of drugs which he could consume. Once during the police raid he had eaten all he had at that moment: cocaine, ecstasy, oxycodone and methadone. Having obviously overestimated himself, he got to reanimation. But he survived by a miracle. Although he was discharged from hospital, temporary oxygen starvation all the same had an effect. Adam lost all inclinations to drugs and alcohol. He ceased to accept them at all, which was confirmed by medical tests during the following half a year.

Miracles! The guy hit the jack-pot: he wasn't imprisoned, he didn't die and he became pure.

But this miraculous metamorphosis wasn't a result of his spiritual enlightenment. In the coma he didn't meet Jesus, he wasn't charged with energy from the divine light. He didn't come to his senses and didn't realize that he had been wrong having such a vile, animal-like life—no! He only lost the desire to use psychoactive agents, and desire of anything in this world together with it. A man, who couldn't refuse himself of conniving at own desires, suddenly loses the ability to desire. Is not it ironic? We should tell about that to film directors. An excellent movie would turn out of that.

However, everything was not so simple in life. Adam had lost the pleasure from life, he could not think of anything that would please him. The enthusiasm disappeared, he became unsociable. But the most important thing is that together with an ability to enjoy, to be exact to expect enjoyment, he lost hope. The hope—one of the most important abilities of a man, abandoned him. Adam plunged into a deep gloomy depression.

How and why did he lose his desires?

Psychiatrists from the Columbia University treating Adam found an answer to this question, having studied the results of his brain tomography. Oxygen starvation during the overdose left scars in the system of reinforcement. Adam described his new life, as a set of habits without any expectation of pleasure. He could eat, buy things, communicate, have sex, but he didn't anticipate anything pleasant from it.

Together with the loss of desire, he lost motivation to do anything: it was hard to get up, go outside and be engaged in something.

Having removed the eternal itch from his desires demanding their implementation, he had got apathy.

No harmony with the world which is promised by spiritual religious literature.

Adam got rid of desires, including the desire to live.

Nevertheless, "riddance" is not the word which should be used together with desire. Be attentive in interpretation of Buddhist masters. Freedom and riddance are different phenomena!

To be suppressed, to be in a depression is not the same as to be pacified and to live in harmony.

Without desires a man loses liaison with the world, not finding it with the cosmos.

You can have desires, but do not depend on them. You can feel pleasures, but do not depend on their source. The point is in the true understanding of freedom.

Even in the Buddhism, after the third noble truth suggesting to be abstain from desires, the fourth truth follows—an octal way of purifying the desires. One should keep only the correct and pure desires which have passed through the light of reason and therefore are not burdening the karma.

Researches of neurophysiologists and psychologists show that the pleasures giving energy repeatedly increase their power with their semantic value. Two thousand years prior to them Epicurus was saying about that, dividing pleasures on short-term and long-term, physical and spiritual.

To understand what sort of pleasure brings benefit, we should remember that there is the infinite universe inside of us (the world of cells, for example).

But the world around us is the entire cosmos as well.

It is possible to call the true pleasure that pleasure, the aspiration which brings pleasure to both internal and external cosmoses.

And definitely doesn't harm anybody, unlike a person abusing alcohol who gets pleasure from intoxication, at the same time destroying his cells and tormenting neighbors.

Can a person refuse a pleasure, exclude it from the process of decision-making? No, these processes aren't under our control. They proceed, passing by our consciousness like the work of the heart or the liver does. Pleasure is required by a person for motivation and for a desire to make something.

We can raise a question only on how to learn to control desires.

The easiest way which comes to mind is to obey to own iron will. To make oneself knuckle under and to turn into a robot which will execute only what the reasonable and rational neo-cortex has decided.

A set of practices for increasing personal efficiency exist. Some mean that "me of today" is a subordinate to "me of yesterday". Every evening, a plan for the next day is being written, a video addressed to oneself of tomorrow is being recorded: Dear Sir Peter, today you should make this and that.

In the morning "me of today" switches on this record, from where a strict face of "me of yesterday" orders to do what he considers important.

Then "me of today" warms to his role of the subordinate and starts executing the objectives. Only after their execution, he can pass to solving the problems of the present day. And so on every day. It is very effective practice.

Someone writes for himself a schedule of actions for the whole day and imagines himself a robot. Literally, he has got in hands a minutely scheduled plan of the day which, of course, was born from preliminary observation of himself. People live according to this plan.

12.15–13.00 I'm writing a report.

13.00–13.05 I'm smoking two cigarettes in succession because for 45 minutes I have not interrupted,

13.15 I'm calling my mother to say that the sofa will be delivered at 19.00 and so on.

Each action which can be remembered is being documented the day before, and a person lives the next day as a robot. All divergences are equated to a task failure.

It is a good practice as well.

We have tested these and many other techniques built on self-checking.

All of them work. But they work only till a certain moment.

They work until a person falls down with fatigue.

In a week or two, different for each, the brain turns on a protecting mode, a function of protection against overheat.

A person is flaking out. It might be for any reason—a cold, a toothache, a stomach attack, heart or kidneys troubles.

Forcing can be used upon solution of only one task (to do exercises), but not to all the model of behavior. You have to admit, however, it isn't enough, since the needs of a man aren't limited to a nice abdomen. He also needs to make a good career, and to learn a language, and to read a useful book, and to watch a proper movie and a lot more.

Forcing won't be enough for all this. There will not be enough brain resources, to be more correct.

Someone falls after the second week of such practice, someone stands for a month and after that also becomes incapable: someone is able to stand for two days only, on the third day he already complains of a headache.

You have to agree, that it is not a very effective strategy. Work for three weeks so that to lie in a bed for eight days afterwards.

We should admit that a man can't force himself to live only by the command of sober reason for long.

He needs indulgences, spontaneity, divergences, freedom.

The brain was given to a man so that not to make him a slave deprived of any rights. It should be treated like a friend; you need to agree with it and to be on friendly terms. It knows a lot of things better than us, but in something we could point it to its mistakes. For example, not to allow confusing the pleasure expected in the long term with its total absence.

We will talk in the following chapter right about the difference between long-term and short-term pleasure.

People so often oppose "I don't want to" and "I ought to" to each other that have turned them into arch enemies. Animating the phrase "I don't want to", we turn it into a monster which is only dreaming to get us and to absorb in its insatiable belly.

But here a Jedi "I ought to" jumps out—a noble intergalactic knight. He makes a flip, then a somersault and cuts the spawn in half with his light saber. Green blood and bile are splashing, two halves fall to the ground and dissolve bubbling.

Here is what we have turned "I ought to" and "I don't want to" into! And it is not like that at all.

In fact everything is vice versa. Well, almost everything.

"I ought to" is the same "I want to"

Of course, we won't risk to blacken the noble image of "I ought to".

But still, to be fair, we should say that "I ought to" is a part of "I want to".

"I ought to" is the pleasure postponed in time, and "I want to" or "I don't want to" is short-term pleasure.

Everything that we don't want and for the sake of which we have to force ourselves, we, actually, want later.

For example, we don't want to wake up in the mornings and to go to school. They say "you ought to". But actually—we want. We want to get education, to get an interesting job and to do favorite things.

Hurrah, the dream has come true! Farewell, the boring Jedi! We have always empathized more to Darth Vader.

How good it is to live without the word "ought to"

"I don't want to, but I ought to go to work".

There is no more word "ought to"! You don't want—you don't go.

Give up work if it doesn't bring pleasure. What, you do not want? Are you afraid? It means that the work gives a feeling of safety, and together with it weak, but still pleasure.

Our duty, our obligations are our pleasure.

If "I ought to" is "I want to", it gives pleasure then

Our cross is our wings. If our wings can't lift us up, the problem is not in them, but in us.

We should have trained them, we should have let them grow.

We should surround ourselves with obligations of such a quality that we would feel the true pleasure from their fulfillment.

Who needs a crucifixion by means of which one would not rise to heavens?

We do not speak about the life after death. We speak about the pleasure which lifts the person over the earth. The pleasure from the debt realized.

I ought to go to school because I want to return to my yard on three multicolored Gelandewagen.

I ought to go to work because I want to buy up a new collection in Lafayette.

I ought to go to the gym because I want to have an athletic body. We do everything for the sake of pleasure.

And our "ought to"—is correct to call "I remember what I want".

When we speak about the long pleasure, we always remember the willpower.

This is the concept which is well-known and liked by many people. Talking about the willpower, we imagine it as a rider in shining armor.

Warriors of the "willpower" smash our impulsive desires.

We dream of such willpower after reading motivating books. In these books such authors as Walter Mischel are writing that willpower can be developed like any other ability.

All of these writers recommend simple exercises for training the will.

Surely, these exercises give good results.

But let us ask only one question.

"Why willpower isn't required for implementation of tasks which give us pleasure?"

What unknown force makes a man surpass his laziness, overcome fear and pain from disappointments and keep on going forth.

It is the desire.

But why a man has no desire when he needs to make an act bringing the same, or maybe even greater pleasure, only not at once, but after some time? Why don't people anticipate pleasure which will appear in a month or a year?

Everything is simple.

They forget about it. If somebody constantly reminded them of pleasure from the achieved objectives, everything would be different.

If every day before going to the gym when a person is lazy and looks for the reasons to shirk, somebody showed him the body he would have in four months of exercises, how girls would look at him, how a white shirt would fit him, he would easily remember what he really wants: to lie on a sofa or to go to the gym.

Instead of hard exercises on training the willpower which help to learn to do what people do not want to do, we would recommend them to train memory and imagination in order not to forget what they already want.

They should draw the most realistic images of their goals in mind and to repeat, repeat, repeat every day, every hour.

The energy of desire will itself deliver them to the goal then.

Scientists were puzzled long ago with this question: What is happening in the mind of a man when he struggles with temptation, in what part of the brain do impulses live, and in what part does that very "willpower" live?

It is considered that the limbic system, a section in the depth of the brain, is responsible for emotions. And the prefrontal cortex which is in the frontal part of the head is responsible for self-checking.

Here is how Kelly McGonigal writes about it:

"The prefrontal cortex controls that, what you pay attention to, what you think of, even what you feel. Thus it manages to control what you are doing better. Robert Sapolsky, a Neurobiologist from the Stanford University, proved that the main task of the modern prefrontal cortex is to incline the brain to "what is harder". When it is easier to lie on a sofa, your prefrontal cortex forces you to wish to rise and run about. When it is easier to say "yes" to a dessert, your prefrontal cortex remembers the reasons for which it is better to order just a cup of tea instead of it. And if it is easier to put off affairs, the prefrontal cortex helps a person to open the file and to work.

The prefrontal cortex has three main areas which divide among themselves the tasks "I will ", "I will not" and "I want".

One zone is in the top left part and is responsible for the strength of "I will". It helps to start and to continue to be engaged in boring, difficult or intense affairs, for example, to stay on a racetrack when a person prefers to go to the shower already. The right side, by contrast, is responsible for the strength "I will not" and doesn't allow to follow all impulses and desires without analysis. You can thank it that you had patience and didn't read SMS while driving. These two areas control actions of a person.

It is important to remember that the brain structure is variable, new neural connections are being formed in it and the amount of the gray substance is being thickening. Like a bodybuilder, loading his muscles, is capable to build an athletic body, it is possible to train the certain areas of the brain which are responsible for attention, memory, logical thinking, and "willpower". There is a scientific confirmation of the fact that different exercises on training the

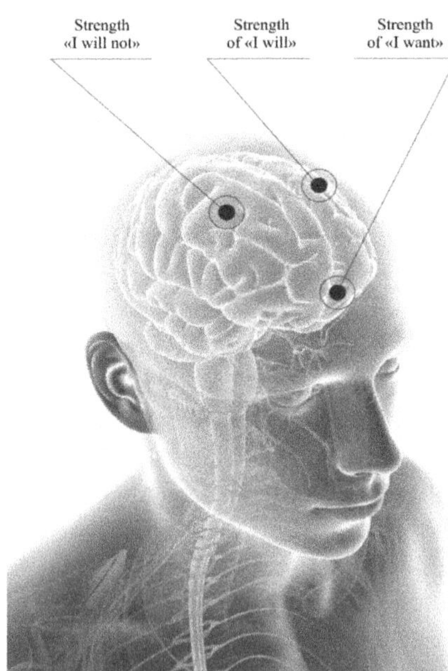

Figure 4.1. Three main areas in the prefrontal cortex.

will of "I want", "I will", "I will not" help to spend less energy for modeling the behavior in future.

We can put all responsibility on the prefrontal cortex and make it play a role of a strict gendarme responsible for self-checking, and we can just remember what we want, and then the powerful machine of the limbic system will take us away towards our desires, easily overcoming doubts, laziness and weakness.

Willpower can be trained as a muscle.

By means of special exercises it is possible to develop willpower.

The brain is dynamic. If memory is trained, then there will be relevant changes in the zone responsible for memories in due course and a man will receive a greater resource for memorizing on the biological level.

The same is true about the willpower and self-checking. Already in the middle of the last century, scientists understood that by means of certain exercises it was possible to develop iron will in oneself.

We have studied the most effective techniques and we provide their list in the present chapter. Also we have developed a number of our own exercises which will help readers in self-checking development.

4.1.4 Exercises from Roberto Assagioli. Desire Is at the Heart of Everything

Italian psychotherapist, philosopher Roberto Assagioli wrote about the willpower in the middle of the last century. In his applied book about reconstruction of the personality "Psycho synthesis" he gives a number of exercises for willpower, confirming the main theses of our research—everything starts with the desire.

Energy of desire is one of the strongest vital forces of a man, and it can be caused artificially for achievement of the actions bringing benefit.

"To gain success,—Assagioli notes,—it is absolutely necessary to carry out certain preparatory work and to create an initial incentive and aspiration. Such work should arouse strong emotional desire".

Let us consider an exercise which will help to reach such a state.

4.1.5 How to Arouse the Desire According to R. Assagioli:

1. To Imagine Troubles

Try to imagine as vivid as possible all those troubles which were caused to you and your relatives by the absence of your enough developed will. Study in detail each of them, trying to define precisely what is the core of it. Then write down the list of these troubles. Feel all those emotions which these memories and expectations have aroused in you: shame, dissatisfaction, a desire to avoid repeating similar behavior and a persistent desire to change the current situation.

2. To Imagine Pleasure

Imagine as vivid as possible all the advantages which the development of will can give you, all those benefits and joys which you and your relatives will receive from it. Study in detail each of these advantages. Try to formulate precisely each of them and then write them down. Give yourself completely to the feelings which these thoughts will arouse in you: pleasure from the opportunities opening in front of you, a keen desire to perform them, a strong desire to begin at once.

3. To Imagine Iron Will

Try to imagine as well as possible that you possess the strong and persistent will. Imagine how firmly and aggressively you walk, how resolutely you behave in various situations: you are concentrated on achievement of the conceived, you are able to mobilize all your efforts. Imagine how persistent you are, how well you can control and manage your behavior. Nothing is able to embarrass you. Imagine how you achieve success in the conceived. Try to select the situations similar to those in which you didn't manage to show enough willpower and persistence before. Imagine how you demonstrate the desirable qualities in similar situations.

4. Buy Books

Select literature for reading which would develop and support determination in you. It has to be encouraging, optimistic and dynamic literature stimulating belief in your own strength and inducing to action. However to make this reading really useful, it is required that it should be done in a certain way: read slowly, entirely concentrating on what is going on there, noting fragments which make special impression on you, and copying what will seem especially amazing and relevant to your case. It is good to re-read these fragments several times, to appreciate them deeply. Biographies of the outstanding people who had strong and constructive will would be the best option for this purpose, or take other books which are directly aimed at arousing the desirable internal energy. Having devoted some time to such reading, you will feel inside a growing, even a keen desire to get to work immediately. It will be the right moment to decide with all your available firmness to devote your time, energy and all possible means to your will development.

5. Keep Silence

By no means tell anyone about your decision even if from the best motives you want to persuade someone to follow your example. Talks usually weaken the accumulated energy required for action. Besides, if others learn about your purpose, it can easily cause skeptical and offensive remarks, which in their turn will sow doubt and despondency in you. Work silently. At least, there will be no harm from that.

4.1.6 Exercises to Develop Willpower by R. Assagioli Soul Gymnastics

Start performing the actions which aren't making any sense except for training the will. They can be compared to gymnastic exercises which make sense only for developing muscles and improving neuromuscular coordination and physical condition of a person in general. This technique was first offered by William James in his book "Talks to Teachers": "Maintain in yourself an ability to dare by means of a daily short, quite senseless exercise. Systematically show heroism in some unnecessary trifles: every day or every other day make something that doesn't make any sense rather than just overcoming an obstacle, and when the time of the real test comes, you will be able to meet it fully armed. Asceticism of this sort is similar to an insurance fee which we pay for the house and other property. Giving this money, we don't get anything in return, and it is very improbable that it will return to us sometime. But, should the fire happen in the house, the insurance will rescue us from ruin. The same is with the person who was daily in trifles developing his concentration, vigorous will and ability of self-denial. When everything around him starts staggering, and more coddled mortals surrounding him will be destroyed by elements, he will stand as firm as a rock"[2].

Boyd Barrett also resorted to similar practice. It is described in his book "Strength of Will"[3] .

4.1.7 Exercises to Train the Will in Everyday Life

The following group of exercises for will development is based on the use of numerous opportunities which are concealed in everyday care and duties.

Wake Up Earlier

Usual morning wake up can become an exercise on will training if to get up in ten-fifteen minutes prior to usual time.

Put On Clothes with No Rush

The same can be told about morning clothing if to set a task for oneself to make every move with concentration, quickly and accurately, without hurrying though. Simultaneously it is possible to develop in oneself a very important quality in life—to learn "to hurry slowly". Modern intensive life with all its stresses makes us hurry even when there is no need to, simply by force of habit. It is not easy to hurry without rush, but it is quite possible. If you could learn it, you will be able to work effectively and to achieve good results without tension and excessive tiredness. Such ability is being gained hardly. It demands almost splitting of the personality—on the one who acts, and the other who simultaneously watches these actions. But even if you just try to make it, such an attempt will become a good way of the will development.

Consciousness in the Routine

The routine cannot be avoided, but it is possible not to sink in it, but to slide over.

Remind yourself that the routine is an integral part of any, even the most creative work. Keep peace of mind, imagining, that even Michelangelo had to grind stones monotonously and methodically.

Overcome Impatience.

Catch yourself at demonstration of impatience, facing small troubles and irritating factors like, for example, when you are in the overfilled transport, when you wait for a door to open, or when you see mistakes of subordinates or injustice from the management.

Eat Slowly

This is useful not only for training the will, but also for health: control the desire or impulses to eat quickly when you think of something. It is necessary to make yourself chew the food well and to eat in a quiet, relaxed state.

Be Able to Stop.

Both at work, and at home, if it is possible, we must resolutely stop working, having felt tiredness, and stop the aspiration to accelerate in ourselves in order to finish the work quickly. It is better to give yourself a chance to rest smartly instead.

Short Breaks

It is more useful to make a short break, having only felt tiredness, than, having been overtired, to rest for a long time afterwards. When short and frequent breaks for rest were established in the industries, it considerably increased labor productivity. During such rest it is enough to do some physical exercises or to relax, having closed the eyes for some minutes. The fatigue caused by mental work is usually removed best by physical exercises. One of the advantages of frequent and short breaks is that a person doesn't lose interest and aspiration towards the performed work and at the same time overcomes fatigue and nervous tension.

Go to Bed in Time

For will training it is useful to try going to bed at a certain time, resolutely stopping fascinating reading or an interesting conversation. It is difficult, especially in the beginning, to achieve success in all these exercises, and if you undertake all at once and at the same time, it will easily lead you to being utterly discouraged. Therefore, it is better to begin with several exercises which would evenly cover the whole day. When you achieve success in them, add new ones, replace or change some of them.

Carry out exercises with interest and pleasure, with sports passion, noting success and failure, writing down all your achievements and defeats. So you will manage to avoid too rigid and over-organized life. Thus you will be able to make interesting and bright all that otherwise would turn into a tiresome duty. Besides, almost all who you would meet will become your allies. For example, a strict boss or a boring partner will become something like an exerciser on which your will to improvement of the human relations will develop. If the meal is not being served for long, it is a good chance to train patience and a peace of mind in yourself, as well as a fine opportunity to read an interesting book. Fans of chatting and simply talkative friends will help you to learn to restrain yourself during a conversation. Thanks to them you will be able to obtain an ability to refuse participating in an unnecessary conversation. The art of saying "no" is very hard, but very useful.

4.1.8 Physical Exercises for Training the Will

Physical exercises can be very effective if they are used especially for development of will. As a French writer Gillet said: "gymnastics is an elementary school for training the will... and serves as a model of educating the mind". In fact, any physical move is an act of will, an order given to the body. The persistent repetition of these actions made with concentration, diligently and patiently, trains and tempers the will. Simultaneously there is a feeling of inflow of physical energy, blood circulation increases—extremities become warm, mobile and obedient. All this makes a feeling of moral power, determination and perfection which increases the tonus of will and facilitates energy rush. However we should emphasize once again that exercise will give the greatest benefit only if we do them with the only one or, at least, the main aim—training the will.

Exercises should be carried out with big accuracy and attention. They must not be too energetic or too relaxed. Each move or a series of moves has to be carried out quite strongly and vigorously.

The most suitable exercises for these purposes shouldn't have a strength-building or over-exciting character; rather the exercises demanding from a person patience, calmness, and dexterity will do here.

They should be various and allow an opportunity to interrupt.

The majority of outdoors sports occupations are suitable for training of the will. Especially good for this purpose are golf, tennis, skating, walking and mountaineering. But even if you have no opportunity to do any of these types, it is always possible to select physical exercises which are suitable for solitary home practice, yoga for example.

The primary emotions at the service of willpower.

The most common difficulty is that people with weak will can make the exercise one-two times—and that is all. We face a vicious circle: in order to effectively perform exercises for development of will, the will is initially required.

In such cases it is useful to resort to techniques, offered by Baudoin. They use support of the person's motives capable to serve as a better incentive, than pure will. These motives do not necessarily have to belong to the highest level. It is possible to use the so-called "primary" or "primitive" inclinations and motives for achievement of the prime goals. Pride and vanity can be useful. Praise or rewards can render good service for development of will-power.

The incentives using "hazardous" instincts of a person, his inclination to games are working best of all.

A certain ability to misidentify is required for a game and competition with oneself, as "I" of a person "compete" with his sub-persons and inclinations. It is necessary to consider all this as a game, without taking it too much to heart, and like a real sportsman, just trying to win. The mere interest in game is already the incentive possessing appeal and not causing resistance or active counteraction which could arise upon violent use of will.

Applying techniques of will development, it is necessary to watch closely so that not to cause resistance of the unconscious, not to set it against exercises. One of the ways allowing to avoid such resistance is not to treat trainings too seriously, not to fall into pedantry and not to cause displeasure of the unconscious. On the contrary, the goal is to win the favor of the unconscious by making these exercises interesting and attractive. And this is exactly peculiar to a game.

4.1.9 Exercises from Kelly McGonigal

McGonigal is the doctor of philosophy, a psychologist and Stanford's professor, owner of the highest award of Stanford University for teachers. Her works about dependence of a mental and physical condition of a person, about stress science, about ability to achieve the objectives, overcoming the internal conflict, are widely known.

Breath

For instant increase of willpower: slow down your breath to 4–6 breaths per minute. Each breath will take from 10 to 15 seconds. Slowing down your breath, you activate your prefrontal cortex and increase variability of the heart rhythm which helps to transfer the brain and the body from the stress condition to the self-checking mode. In some minutes calmness will come to you, you will regain self-control and you will be able to cope with motives or temptations.

Five-minute Ecological Charging

Even five minutes of outdoors exercising reduce stress, improve mood and concentration of attention, increase self-checking.

Healthy Sleep

According to the results of researches, only one night of good, deep sleep renovates the brain activity to the optimum level. If you went to bed late all week and got up early, sleep off during the week-end, this will strengthen your willpower.

Pause of 10 Minutes

In her book "The Willpower Instinct" Kelly writes, "It seems, 10 minutes are not too long if you want something, but neurobiologists found out that this time changes our views on pleasure. If the instant pleasure comes with the forced 10-minute delay, the brain perceives it as postponed. The system of promising a reward is less excited, and a strong biological impulse decreases". Exactly the immediacy of the instant pleasure captures our brain and changes our preferences.

They tell about treatment of shopaholics who got addicted to the Internet shops.

They are asked before surfing the Internet to freeze their plastic card in an ice cube. Further they, as usual, browse gigabytes of handbags, pendants, dresses and choose what they would like to buy.

At the moment they are ready to pay the filled cart, they need to get the card from a freezer and to wait till it melts (it is forbidden to use a microwave). As a rule, most of shopaholics lose the desire to buy the reserved things. They satisfy their passion with the mere process of choice and selection. Happy and not ruined, they minimize all windows and start doing the daily routine.

To Take Away Tomorrow

As a rule, we justify our today's unsatisfactory behavior with the promise to correct it tomorrow. By means of magnet-resonant scanning scientists were able to prove that we treat ourselves in the future as another person. When examinees were asked to think of what they would do tomorrow, the part of the brain responsible for self-identification wasn't activated.

We imagine "me from tomorrow" not only as another person, but also as a person apparently possessing superpower. Because he can do everything that "me of today" can't. "Me from tomorrow" has no current issues, he has an excellent memory allowing to remember all necessary matters, he has iron will capable not to break the promise, he has the mind of a military strategist capable to schedule the time up to every second and, of course, he has neither laziness, nor feelings, nor a desire to live his own life.

Our invented "me from tomorrow" is a big problem. Psychologists understand that and therefore recommend "to kill him", to be exact, to take away the right to think that everything will be different tomorrow. The Exercise consists in obliging yourself to do tomorrow the same as you do today.

If today you ate too much sweet at night, tomorrow you have to eat at night as well. If today you missed trainings in the gym, tomorrow you are obliged to pass it by. Paradoxically such attitude doesn't lead to the vicious circle, but on the contrary makes people stop being lazy already today.

To Draw a Future Portrait

Communicate with people older than you by 10–15 years. No, not for the reason to learn their vital wisdom, but, on the contrary, to see what mistakes they had made 10 years ago and what it led to.

One allowed himself to eat after 21.00 and sported on taverns with a small beer tummy, now he has 30 extra kilos. Another one laughed at athletes and throughout all his life remembered the school boxing club, now he lies with a heart attack.

Having around you people older than you, you willy-nilly start to draw a portrait of your future, and to learn on the mistakes of others.

While the time machine is not invented yet, this exercise is its worthy replacement.

Not to Block, Not to Blame

Everyone breaks promises made to oneself. Absolutely everyone does. Both who achieve success and who give up the initiated. What is the difference?

It is in the chosen strategy helping to continue or stop exercising.

Guilt and self-flagellation relate to the second one.

Many people mistakenly consider that if they do not forgive themselves for their failures, if they blame and punish themselves, then, having broken themselves, they will be able to achieve success.

But the unconscious is often stronger than our conscious desires. Punishment of oneself can lead to self-deception. People will start to find the "objective" reasons demanding to stop: tiredness, illness, urgent matters and even admitting that the task was impracticable or moreover, completely unnecessary. Trying to avoid punishment, we will simply begin to deceive ourselves. Unfortunately, a man is a wizard in that. In order not to become enemy No.1to yourself, you should learn to forgive yourself and to remember that you are not obliged to anybody, even to yourself. Everything, that you are doing, you do at your own will. Not because it is required but because you want it.

After all it isn't important in the long run, how many times you have broken the promises made to yourself. It is important that you still try to fulfill them.

Progress

Often people give up the initiated after they see the progress.

Prompt success reduces motivation even stronger than a failure.

In order not to give up the initiated only because everything works out, try to remember not your progress and result, but the reason why you started doing this. As a rule, the reason is beyond the first success.

4.1.10 Exercises from Arsen Dallan

Little No's

Obtain a manual clicker (the device with which Ben Affleck's hero counted smiles of girls in a commercial of an Axe deodorant) and count all suppressed impulses with its help: to check the phone, to speed up a car, to say something in response to a rude driver, to buy a roll—anything.

During the day you can collect more than one hundred little "no's".

Measure yourself, but don't make changes in your behavior, just count. Then, when in two-three days you gather statistics, try to double the number of little "no's". Not at once, but within a week.

This very easy exercise works wonders.

In one research a team of psychologists from the Northwest University of the USA decided to find out, whether little "no" can play a big role in human lives, and measured connections of self-checking over small temptations and family violence. 40 people (aged from 18 till 45 years engaged in the romantic relations) were randomly divided into groups. Participants of the first group were asked to eat, to brush teeth and to open doors not with the control arm. Another group was ordered to avoid curses and to answer "yes" instead of "yep". The third group received no instructions. Two weeks later the participants of the first two groups significantly less often used physical violence in situations which previously provoked them, for example, when they were jealous or felt disrespect from the partner. No changes were observed in the third group.

To Control the Internal Monologue

We constantly speak about ourselves. The internal monologue takes 8–18 hours per day according to the estimates of scientists. In fact, we are silent with ourselves, only when we are speaking with others or sleeping.

Your task is to understand what you are talking with yourself about.

Start fixing subjects. Write them down in your smartphone. Choose top 5 of the subjects after two or three days. As a rule, they will be non-constructive cyclic thoughts of a primitive level: thoughts about sex, food, about plans for the future or memoirs. Don't block them, just start to count again with the same clicker, every time when you catch yourself at these thoughts. Over some time you will see how the time spent on internal dialogue about empty repeating subjects will decrease, and it means that you will release resources for constructive work and self-regulation.

"Me of Yesterday"—the Chief

In the evening, while planning the next day, turn on the phone camera and sound the list of affairs as you would make it if held a planning meeting with your employees via Skype. Don't joke, don't smile, be strict, but don't overact. Sound precisely the agenda and time of the tomorrow's report. During the day re-watch the video. As soon as it seems to you that current affairs are more important than the planned ones, turn on the video.

Imagine your "me of today" a subordinate of "me of yesterday". The main thing is to make what the chief told, and then it is possible to start with what "me of today" considers important. Repeat this exercise day by day and all your affairs will be done in time, and the will would become stronger.

The Exact Schedule

Make a list of affairs, not just the list, but the exact schedule. Plan everything with accuracy up to 10 minutes. For example:

I wake up at 7.30.
I read news in bed till 8.00,
I wash and have breakfast till 8.30,
I go to work till 9.30
I respond to letters till 10.30
and so on.

Carry out everything strictly according to the schedule. If there are any current affairs, plan them with the same algorithm for tomorrow or in today's white space, but don't break the schedule. All the Sense is in learning to arrange circumstances according to the plan, and not vice versa, not to re-arrange the plan under constantly changing circumstances. It is a very useful exercise for middle managers who want to become tops.

Surround Yourself with Generators of Desires

During the era of Facebook and LinkedIn it is unallowable to ignore an opportunity to surround yourself with useful people. It doesn't mean that you have to become a double-faced and mercenary person, no. Just fill your newsfeed with news from people who passionately want the same, as you. It was proved long ago that desires, as well as other emotions have a virus character.

Use this property and, of course, avoid those who don't want anything.

4.1.11 Other Exercises

Meditation

Meditation in its essence is not in getting rid of all thoughts, but in supervision over them. Behold what you think of and do not let the thoughts to carry you away. Let them appear and disappear, remain a mute observer. Duration of the exercise is 5 minutes. Frequency is 3–4 times per day.

Don't worry if you are distracted during meditation. Just come back to observation. It is proved, still with a magnet-resonant tomo-graph that the people practicing meditation have a much more developed prefrontal cortex, than the people managing without similar practice.

One of such people, a Tibetan monk, author of the best-seller "The Buddha, the brain and the science of happiness" Yongey Mingyur Rinpoche, in his work clearly and simply shared the secrets of meditation.

Meals

The brain consumes up to 20% of energy of the whole body and if the power sources are insufficient, the most complicated area of the brain—the cortex suffers first. Therefore we can't make hard decisions on empty stomach, we become irritable and excessively emotional.

It is necessary to eat 4–5 times a day.

Willpower depends on the level of glucose dissolved in blood. It was revealed, that even a single act demanding self-control decreases amount of glucose in blood, reducing success of the subsequent attempts of self-checking. Experimentally it was found out, that even a sip of sweet aerated water fixes these problems. Always keep some fruit (complex carbohydrates) nearby to restore the level of glucose in blood.

To Tease Yourself

If you already refused bad habits and you can easily live without chocolate and cigarettes, complicate the task for yourself. Buy a bar of favorite chocolate and put it in a prominent place, carry an open and half-empty pack of cigarettes in your pocket.

Tension of Muscles

Singapore scientists revealed that tension of muscles allows to strengthen self-checking. Not incidentally we clench our fists when we try to resist to a temptation. Use this knowledge when you train willpower. Ten pull-ups on a horizontal bar will allow you to extinguish passionate desire to swear at the sight of the hated singer on TV.

Intermediate Terms

Break the complex task which was constantly postponed into small subtasks. For example, you postponed cleaning in the closet all the time.

Week 1—to open the door and to take a view of the disorder in the closet; week 2—to clean everything on tops; week 3—to throw out everything that isn't necessary, and so on.

Developed willpower is the key to life in pleasure as each important decision will be made by a person consciously, and not dictated by circumstances.

But people do not make all decisions consciously, a lot of things we make automatically. These are the so-called habits. Unfortunately, the majority of them are formed chaotically, by the path of least resistance. Therefore, many of them are harmful. Sooner or later in search of conscious pleasure a person faces a problem how to change bad habits and to form good ones. We will talk exactly about this in the following paragraph.

Want Only What You Really Want

Is it possible to learn to derive pleasure?

We shouldn't be forced to do something that brings pleasure.

But what doesn't promise pleasure, no matter even if it is three times useful, demands forcing.

How to aspire to what is necessary for us if we don't want it?

Is it possible to learn to derive pleasure from something that seems to us not bringing it?

Yes!

Desire in the Service of Usefulness

The main thought of our research is that pleasure is a reaction of the brain which can be caused artificially for encouragement of the chosen decision.

A man strives for pleasure. It is a neurophysiological law and we cannot surpass it. We won't be able to rearrange the work of the brain, we can't forbid discharging of a neuro-mediator.

Desire will always force us to strive for the object of pleasure.

The rule "the pleasure generates the desire, the desire forces to act" works also when the pleasure is thought up by ourselves.

We can learn to derive pleasure from usefulness, and then the desires directed on achievement of pleasure will lead us straight to usefulness.

The Scheme of Moving towards Pleasure

The scheme shows the sequence of moving towards pleasure. In different routes we come to different results: development, fault or weariness.

Thanks to it the process of achieving the goals will stop being painful.

So, the answer to the question "how to want what you really want?" sounds as follows: it is necessary to learn to convince yourself that the pleasure is hidden in your goal.

Habits Are a Way to Learn to Derive New Pleasure

By means of simple habits, a man can learn to derive pleasure from something that didn't bring it before.

He can artificially provoke the dopamine discharge so that to wish something that he was not attracted by before.

We are already able to do it.

Actually all of us are already able to do unloved things with pleasure.

Remember the taste of vodka. Imagine how you make three sips in succession.

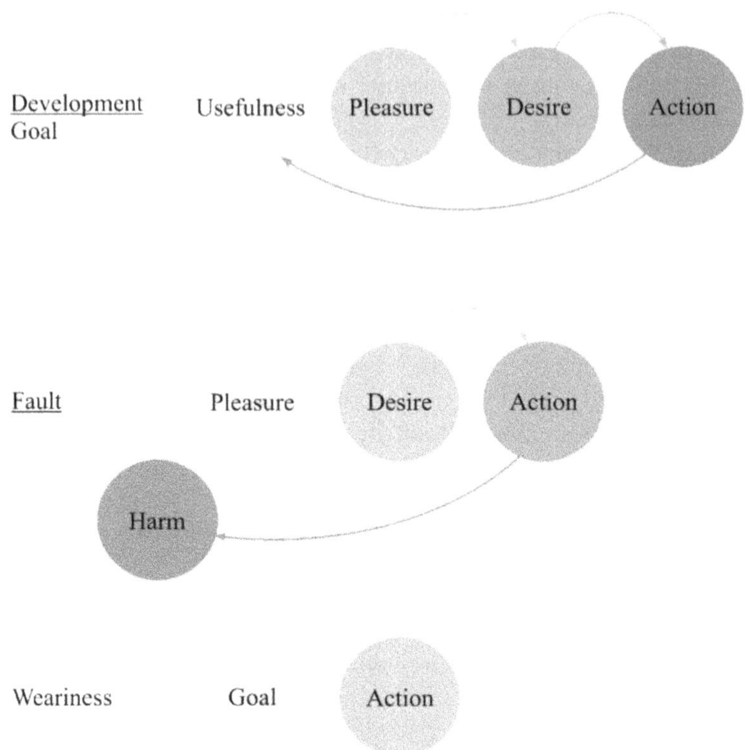

Figure 4.2. The moving to the pleasure.

For certain, you have frowned. The taste of vodka (whisky, rum, gin, cognac) causes rejection reaction in almost every healthy person. But it doesn't prevent it to be desired.

Remember the sight of the cold misted-over bottle, the sound of the opening cap, murmur of slightly thickened ice liquid and the anticipation of an excellent night with friends.

After these lines most of readers got an increased amount of dopamine, and had, maybe, a weak, but still a desire to go to a bar.

Desire had appeared, but we didn't stop to estimate the taste of alcohol beverages as unpleasant. However, it doesn't prevent us from wanting them.

We feel the same towards cigarettes, and coffee, bitter chocolate or spicy food.

How did we learn to desire what isn't pleasant to us?

We got used to anything. We don't doubt that it is worth to endure a few unpleasant minutes, and the pleasure won't keep you waiting.

Everything is the same as with the Pavlov's doggies.

Accustomed to feeding, right after the bell call, over some time they started salivating not only at the sight of food which is natural, but also from a sound "ding-ding" which, of course, is unnatural. Ivan Pavlov called it a conditioned reflex.

We call it a habit.

A habit has a lot of definitions.

Usually the behavior forms brought to automatism which aren't demanding continuous awareness are understood as a habit.

According to the psychological dictionary, a habit is "a well-learned action in performing which a man feels a constant need.

The habit appears after numerous repetitions of the same action—when it ceases to demand strong-willed and cognitive efforts. Here the result becomes not as much important, as the mere process causing pleasure ".

Don't have any pleasure? Create pain!

We will give our definition which is the closest to the principle of pleasure.

A habit is the acquired behavior model of a person upon breaking which he feels "pain", and respectively, successful implementation of the model leads to riddance of pain and, as a result,—to pleasure.

Simply speaking, if you can't derive pleasure from abs exercising, you start feeling pain from "not exercising".

Having put any action into the habit mode, a person starts feeling pain from its non-fulfillment. And avoiding pain will grant you pleasure.

A simple example is tooth brushing in the mornings.

It seems to be a natural action. For certain, many readers couldn't even imagine that in 1904, the vast majority of people on the planet didn't brush teeth. Although they had all reasons to do that—even in the developed countries, such as the USA, dental health of the population was so critical that the army commander entered this problem into the risk zone of national security. Despite all efforts of the doctors, only 7% of Americans had toothpastes in drugstores, and those who brushed teeth daily were even less than that. People didn't want to take care of their teeth. There were commercials On TV and radio, advertising tooth-powder, but everything was in vain.

Tooth brushing became an integral part of the morning ritual for 67% of Americans only after the World War II. Today we are so used to toothbrushing tooth brushing that we start to experience a very unpleasant feeling similar to itch should we miss the procedure. We literally feel physically the plaque on our teeth. The "itch" makes us count minutes, until we, finally, manage to get to the toothbrush with paste.

Let us take a fresher example—a visit to the gym.

Someone doesn't go to the gym and lives quite fine. Passing by a fitness center in the evening, where he sees silhouettes of running figures through panoramic windows, he, imitating Homer Simpson says: "Huh fools!"

But once such a person acquires a habit to run 3 km every evening, there will be a metamorphosis. The desire will change the behavior of a person. And now instead of a quiet evening with the smartphone on a sofa, he will choose to run in the park under the rain, snow, heat, wind—no matter. He will choose that because he knows that, having missed jogging, he will doom himself to suffering.

The itch from missing a habitual action will be so vile that no "games of thrones", no X-box and all the more no laziness will force him to miss jogging. Having written an SMS: "sweetheart, you are, of course, the best thing in my life, but I can't miss training", he will go to get rid of pain straight into the park. What has happened?

Our hero in sports pants and running shoes rushes towards the pleasure which wasn't even in mention half a year ago.

Turning down an occupation which isn't bringing pleasure into a habit you doom yourself to pain from non-performance of the action.

Thereby, you are generating pleasure from performance.

Thus you learn to use the system of dopamine motivation to your advantage.

How many times we undertook a new hobby, but few weeks passed and we quit the initiated. Why is it so hard to form habits?

Everything is simple—we avoid pain. Until the action became habitual, its performance requires forcing, and this is painful.

Sufferings which we have to experience today could be hardly covered by the pleasure which will occur only after some time.

We are afraid to suffer and not to get our postponed pleasure.

The opposite condition is much more pleasant for us: pleasure now and then pain. But it is a losing strategy. After all everyone knows that short pleasures are, as a rule, useless, and at times are even harmful.

In order not to get into stress from the pain of forcing, at first while you accustom yourself to a habit, we recommend to support each repetition with pleasant encouragement. It can be anything, from entering Facebook to a piece of cake.

4.1.12 How to Form Habits

We will give some recommendations below how to form a useful habit.

We hope they will be useful to you.

To learn to form habits it is necessary to understand the nature of their origin and structure.

The habit is a way to save the brain resource when performing the repeating routine actions.

Thanks exactly to that no thinking resources are required for habitual actions, we can tie laces and continue the conversation about a new book of Dan Ariely, or park our car and keep telling how we spent the week-end.

To make the brain learn when the repeating action begins, a trigger is required, which is an event which notifies about the launch of the block of repetitions.

Any habit possesses such a sign. Scientists found out that anything can serve as the sign. Nir Eyal in his book "Hooked" divides triggers on external and internal. External are any tactile prompts: images of sweet, coffee smell, a sound of the opening bottle of Pepsi and other, and internal are different feelings and personal experiences, for example, disappointment, fear of loneliness, need for social confirmation and many other things.

After the brain has distinguished the trigger, a habitual action is launched and this is the second component of a habit. Habitual actions can be both very difficult, and surprisingly simple (some habits, for example which are connected with emotions, are measured in milliseconds).

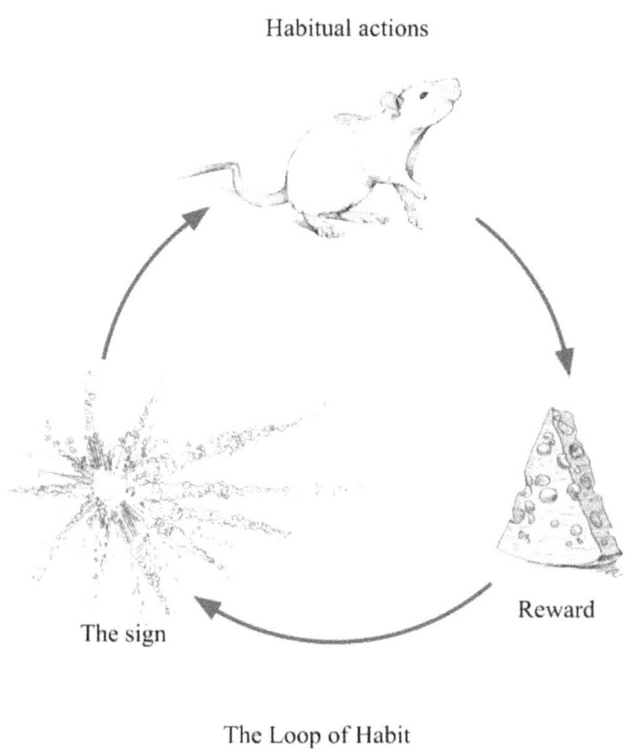

Figure 4.3. The loop of habbit.

An action always leads to a reward—the third part of the loop of habit. The reward can also be different: from food or drugs causing physical feelings to emotions.

In her book "Don't shoot the Dog" Karen Pryor, a scientist-behaviorist, pays huge attention to positive reinforcement, as the main instrument of modeling the behavior of a man.

So how to form or change a habit?

Answering this question Charles Duhigg, winner of the Pulitzer Prize, reporter of the New York Times and author of the book "Power of Habit", writes:

"It is easier to convince a person to accept some new behavior if initial and final stages are already familiar to him."

You should not change all steps of the habit.

It is more correct to change only the middle step—the habitual action.

Using the same sign and receiving the same reward, it is possible to change the habitual action and, respectively, the habit itself. It concerns almost any action. To prove his words the author gives a story from psychotherapeutic practice when a patient suffering from a habit of gnawing nails was able to rearrange her behavior after realizing that the trigger to action was slight tension at her finger-tips. After that she slid over nails with her thumb and unconsciously took fingers into her mouth. Having learned to identify the trigger, she began to hide hands behind her back or under herself if she was sitting on a chair. Two weeks later the habit tormenting her for years disappeared.

We can give an example from the personal experience. Spending evenings with the laptop, one of our acquaintances kept cookies nearby for a snack. In a month, he noticed that it led to appearance of excess fat on his sides. But the desire to chew something during the course of thoughts over a text was insuperable. Without it he was constantly distracted by phone. Then the high-calorie cookies were replaced with pits from dates. Each time he wanted to have a bite, he took one pit from a saucer. Only two weeks passed, and the fat on his sides disappeared, and the work was done faster.

Let us admit that you want to do push-ups regularly, the onset of precise hour might be the trigger then: 12.00, 13.00. If the clock shows zero—zero minutes, it means it is the time to do push-ups.

For fans of books, the trigger can be every twentieth page. Read 20 pages—do an exercise.

Well and here is absolutely extreme:

You firmly decided to jog in the mornings. Put your running shoes in the prominent place in the evening. The desire to put them away from there will be a trigger.

Having touched the shoes, you will already be on a half the way to jogging.

It is also possible to leave dumbbells in the most improper place on the floor in your apartment if you have decided to build arm muscles.

But numerous researches show that only signs and rewards are not enough to form a longstanding habit. The brain has to start to want the reward passionately—to seek to derive pleasure from accomplishing the loop of habit. Thus, we are coming back to the main subject of the book again—the ability to form expectation of pleasure by ourselves in order to achieve our goals.

Formation of desire can become the major skill helping to model own behavior.

To learn to do with pleasure something that brings benefit, will allow a person to achieve success with less pain.

Energy of desire helps to change ourselves and to become the one who we want to be.

However, there are a lot of ways barriers on the way towards that. A great number of factors are stealing conscious pleasure from us, and the desire along with it, destroying motivation to develop and pushing us to consumption of easy, short-term and useless pleasure. We will talk about the things that steal pleasure from us in the following chapter.

Not to allow to be deprived of deliberate pleasure

Under the expert redaction of Arina Skibinskaya, Psychologist, psychotherapist and journalist.

With the same speed a man was sating his life with pleasure and saving suffering as well. Along with the growing amount of easy and quick pleasure people started to experience heavy, unceasing, and only at times weakening pain more often.

It isn't surprising that a suicide is committed in the world each 40 seconds.[4]

Despite abundance of pleasure, people are surrounded only by its cheap substitute, and the true long-lasting pleasure is hidden deeply. In order to reach it one should reconsider some widely spread views on many public phenomena.

Fear Steals Pleasure.

Once upon a time there was a king. He had an interesting tradition. After a victory in a battle, he used to offer his prisoners either to stand in front of his archers and to face certain death from arrows, or to enter a frightful black blood-stained door covered with parts of human bodies, bones and skulls. It was horrible just to look at it, not that to open.

Everyone was choosing the certain, but familiar death from arrows of the archers. People were afraid of that black frightful door, afraid perhaps of uncertainty, imagining that not just death, but also terrible torments were waiting for them behind the door.

And then, when the war ended, one of the royal archers asked, shaking with fear: "Your majesty, do not be angry with me, but … what is behind this awful black door? The king answered: "Go and open the door". The archer, with his hands shaking pulled the handle and found himself in a field covered with flowers. The terrible door was opening a way to freedom.

The moral is simple:

The black door is our fears. If you make a step towards them, it is possible to find freedom.

Fear is an unusual feeling. It is in the basis of many feelings, defining the behavior and often the whole life. For example, envy, which is often mistaken to a desire to have something that another one has. Envy is the fear of own negligibility. Jealousy is the fear to lose the beloved one. Aggression is the fear of another one's strength, a desire to attack first because it might be late afterwards. Greed is the fear to remain without means of subsistence, hence the pathological pursuit of money.

The fear is diverse, and it should be distinguished from dread and anxiety.

The fear is a general state of apprehension, without a certain object.

Dread is the fear of a certain threat.

Anxiety is a constant unconscious state of fear expectation.

How the fear steals pleasure

1. In decisions

The fear reduces the expected pleasure, blocks decision-making. As a result we stay without decisions and without pleasure at all.

2. In life

The fear steals pleasure since it forms tension.

George Frankl in his book "The Unknown Self" gives an interesting example illustrating how the fear and anxiety do not allow a man to live and to get pleasure properly.

A young twenty two-year-old man suffered from an irresistible compulsion to comb constantly his hair to be sure that he looks good. He was afraid of the censure of public opinion, was afraid to look slovenly, shaggy. "This obsession,—G. Frankl writes,—didn't leave him for a minute while he was awake, all his attention was directed on this occupation, without leaving him an opportunity to join in any activity or to communicate with people as his anxiety that his hair was not in order was increasing at once, and a strong desire to brush his hair was appearing. At his workplace, or in a bar, or in any other public place he constantly had to go to the bathroom or somewhere else where no one could see him to put his hair in order. When he was with a girl, he couldn't think of anything, except his anxiety, and used the first opportunity to stay alone with himself and to comb his hair"[5]

After a psychoanalytic study it became clear that yet being a boy he tried to be constantly encouraged by his mother. Even sitting on a pot he tried to show himself and sometimes, in a rush of narcissism, even demonstrated his excrements to his mother. It is clear that his mother not only discouraged that, but also roughly showed discontent with her child. Since then the unconscious of the boy had kept the pathological desire to be liked by people in everything, a priori perceiving himself as a dirty, ugly person. He was quite an attractive young man in life though.

In pathopsychology there are a lot of demonstrations of tension from fear. One of them is codependency. The term "codependency" was introduced by Melody Beattie, an American psychologist-writer. The codependency is shown through pathological care of others when people consider that they are responsible for the thoughts, actions, choice, desires, requirements, wellbeing and destiny of other people.

The codependent people feel an irresistible desire to help, solve problems of another person and are angry when their help is not used.

They try to anticipate the needs of other people and are surprised why others do not do the same for them.

Such people find out that they say "yes", meaning "no", and do things which in fact they didn't want to do.

The fear of accepting oneself as an autonomous, independent personality is the cornerstone of the codependency. Fear of freedom.

No wonder why we call fear the main "thief" of pleasure", since it has millions of manifestations and forces people towards pathological behavior increasing pain and disappointment.

The deep basis of fear and anxiety of a man is his realizing of his own mortality. A man doesn't constantly think of death, but unconsciously, like forced-out information, these thoughts are terrorizing his mentality.

The fear is an expectation.

The fear is directly connected with a phenomenon of threat expectation. If there is no threat expectation, a man is not afraid of anything. Even if something happens, he won't be frightened. But on the contrary, if a man has a threat expectation, he will be afraid of everything, even of his own shadow.

The fear is unconscious.

The fear almost always includes fantasies, conjectures based on unawareness of what a man is afraid of. Therefore it is difficult to struggle with fear. The fear is irrational. A man cannot always explain what and why exactly he is afraid of. The fear can be unrealized at all. There is a famous text-book case with a maniac abuser and murderer whose psychoanalytical research established that his mother had had a difficult childbirth, and thus he received a patrimonial trauma. Having grown up, he was unconsciously revenging all women for the pain he felt at birth. In this case the fear, hatred and aggression had merged together in his unconscious.

We desire what we are afraid of.

In his "Diary" S. Kierkegaard notes: "the fear is desire of what we fear, it is sympathetic antipathy; the fear is an alien force which captures an individual, and yet he can't get free from it,—he doesn't want actually because he fears, but he fears what he desires. Fear makes an individual powerless, and the first sin always occurs in weakness; therefore it happens apparently as if unconsciously, but such absence of consciousness is the real trap" [2. p. 367]. According to Kierkegaard, the one who through fear came to a crime, on the one hand, is innocent since the fear and unawareness had forced him to do that, and on the other,—is guilty since he himself had plunged into this fear which nevertheless he loved, although he was afraid of it.

According to Theodor Adorno, exactly in the traditional societies where strict upbringing from the father's side based on fearing him is kept, there is the highest probability of forming aggressive and destructive in the future personalities. [3. p. 280]. In this case the hatred and aggression generated by the strict upbringing, frequent punishments, and at times even direct violence over the child's personality are merged together in his unconscious with love to his father. This love can automatically be transferred to a sense of fear. A person derives pleasure from the aggressive behavior since it relieves the tension in the unconscious sphere of his mentality.

Lindstrom in his book "Buyology" wrote that the main feeling forcing people to buy something is fear. The guru of neuromarketing is right; fear is the cornerstone of overconsumption. However not only the economy stands on fear, but also the policy, fear is the basis of a totalitarian political regime. To prolong the years of his board, the leader sometimes forms a situation of threat to the safe existence of citizens, inculcating in them that only with his help it is possible to cope successfully with the arisen threat.

Totalitarian regimes, limiting freedom of citizens, deprive them of many pleasures, sometimes even of happiness of self-determination and self-realization, but give a very deceptive feeling of safety, security by the strong management.

However, very few people guess that the dictator's behavior in turn is also defined by fear, the fear to lose control over masses, meaning the loss of power as well[6]. Thus, fear generates fear. The circle is closed.

No wonder that the main tendency of the modern society is hypertrophy of threat. Mass media successfully create people who are afraid of everyone and everything. The society of mass consumption represents the total industry of fear. Having paraphrased a known expression, we can say that if the fear didn't exist in the nature, it should have been invented. After all the power, especially the power of money is impossible without fear.

However, we shouldn't blame the system for everything. A man himself wishes to be afraid.

This way he tries to bring his internal fears and anxiety beyond his own essence, i.e. to transcend them into the environment. According to the second law of entropy, the system is kept by means of continuous removal of entropy out of its boundaries. Thus the system keeps the order in itself. In other words, being unable to win over his internal fear, a man is compelled to look for the objects outside. The demand for fear finds the offer and its consumption exponentially grows.

The fear creates tension, and tension as it was already emphasized many times, takes away pleasure. In this regard the belief in the afterlife of a man, the idea of the Heaven or the Buddhist idea about reincarnation looks especially attractive. If there is no death, there is also no fear, thus no tension.

Another way to overcome the fear of death is creativity which is making its author immortal. In creativity the author takes the God's place, creating his own world which will continue to live, even after his death. Therefore the people who devoted themselves to creativity are less afraid of death. A lot of such mentions can be found among poets from the Pushkin's "Exegi Monumentum" to the Shevchuk's song "That's all".

Fear is the strongest of the pleasure enemies. It gets invisibly, unconsciously into the soul through secret loopholes, blocking decision-making, preventing from pleasure expectation and forcing to refuse it. Only accepting the idea of death being non-dominative over the space and time allows to get free from fear and to direct energy on creation, granting the highest of all pleasures. But, unfortunately, not only the fear steals pleasure. The way to it is also blocked by another one's will.

Another One's Will Steals Pleasure

No decisions—no pleasure from decisions.

If there are no decisions, there will not be the greatest part of pleasure as well. Unfortunately, modern life is full of different circumstances that considerably influences our decisions. Sometimes their pressure is so insuperable that we are compelled to assign the choice to an unknown force.

Obtaining the result by a decision which a person didn't make, he still gets pleasure and calmness: his efforts are compensated, however the effect is so negligibly small, as compared with the pleasure he could get if he had made the decision himself.

We can give numerous examples when the same action brings different pleasure depending on the degree of its being realized. Pleasure from the made decision differs from pleasure without decision making like a different kind of hits in billiards game. One thing is to hit at random and to score the ball by chance into the first available pocket, and another thing is to state that the ball with number six will hit in the upper right corner.

The structured life doesn't demand decisions.

Unfortunately, today more and more people allow circumstances to influence the decision-making process, and at times even to define it.

Study—often the educational institution is chosen by parents.

Work—many people go where they were called to,

Family—as a rule, people stay with those who it worked out with.

People not only forget about their pleasure when the matter concerns decision-making, but sometimes also confuse their feelings.

"People often assign the decisions to circumstances,—a psychologist, Arina Skibinskaya writes,—because they forget or never knew what exactly brings pleasure to them. Along with it they quite often do not completely understand their own feelings, this is called alexithymia among psychologists. Such people are not only unable to name their own feelings, but also confuse one to another. For example, when you ask a person feeling guilty "what do you feel?" he might answer "I understand that I wasn't right". He expresses the sense of guilt through "understanding", and it is not a feeling, but a thought form with all the ensuing consequences.

And people with emotional dependence, for example, often confuse fear with love. Answering a question: "How do you feel love?" they describe feelings similar to fear: "Tremble, tightness in breast as though everything turns over inside".

So how can a person make a choice by himself in favor of his pleasure if he doesn't recognize it? To do so, we teach people to observe their feelings more often and more attentively, to learn to recognize them. As psychologists note, 70–80% of people suffer from alexithymia!

Many people postpone decisions until there are alternatives left. All this is a voluntary hedonistic diet. It is a certain way to deprive life of pleasure. Unfortunately, this is the way of majority, who are losing huge part of pleasure going this way. It is interesting that in doing so it is often possible to hear that life is full of sufferings and pain. It is not surprising, since the pleasure, required for happiness is being voluntarily rejected.

We observe how everywhere people, having got rid of the pleasure- giant and, having faced pain, begin to collect pleasure—dwarfs tenderly like beads. Having got rid of really important decisions, such as the choice of the field of activity, a company which to work in, a desirable women to live with, that is, the decisions capable to grant pleasure for the rest of the life, many people try to replace it with the pleasure from small, meaningless decisions. Such decisions, for example, how to buy a plasma panel with an 80 cm diagonal for 30 thousand rubles or with a 110 cm diagonal for 40 thousand rubles.

No wonder a person is suffering as a result.

Sometimes people assign important decisions to circumstances, but almost always they rely on a surrounding situation when the matter concerns everyday decisions: to tell the truth or to keep silence, to make a remark to a solid man who entered the notary office without waiting in line, to go to another shop or to buy suspicious goods in this one and millions of other decisions.

"Circumstance" is our constant friend. We love mister "Circumstance", resorting to its help at every opportunity.

Freedom is the greatest of pleasures.

Modern life is so structured that it seems that no active participation will be required from a person soon.

Once the words "a man is the creator of his own destiny" sounded as a statement.

Now it is rather a hope.

An artist is really a creator, and the one who collects a puzzle—hardly is.

Making vital decisions is more similar to writing answers in a test. The same questions are set, and the same answers are offered for selection.

Probably, we should be glad that there are several options.

They are our freedom of choice.

What would it look like to live in a society which not only unbinds in answers, but also asks no questions at all? You yourself decide what questions it is necessary to answer and which ones are not worthy to think of.

To choose questions by yourself—here is the true freedom of a man. This freedom is forgotten by many people, but it is still real.

The decision is a pleasure forge. The more significant decision is made, the more pleasure it brings. Unfortunately, people more often make a decision not on the fulfillment fact: if it is necessary to do something or not, but on the way of fulfillment: to make it this or another way. Such an approach takes away the most part of pleasure from a person.

Will the remaining part be enough to live a happy life?

It is a good question if we consider that circumstances are not the only thief of pleasure. In the following chapter we will tell about the phenomenon already familiar to us—the automatisms, their dark side, unlimited potential for destruction of pleasure.

Automatisms Steal Pleasure.

Every day people make thousands of decisions.

Repetitive and simple decisions are usually made on autopilot, unconsciously.

To get to work by a habitual route, to go to lunch to a cafe—all this is done unconsciously.

Scientists consider that up to 95% of decisions are made this way.

Of course, these are not the most important decisions—everyday fuss, insignificant and repeating actions. But the irony is that they basically make our life. Life, unfortunately, consists of small things.

Unfortunately?

Maybe fortunately, after all the more the decisions, the more chances to get pleasure. Life spouts with pleasures, but people turn away from them.

If meaningful, and important decisions people often assign to the system or circumstances, small ones are within the power of automatism.

If a person understood that each decision, even the most insignificant one, was a resource for receiving pleasure, probably, he would change his attitude towards them.

The decision is oil, pleasure is gasoline.

Burning oil, a man, strangely, complains of gasoline shortage.

Once you remove a habitual action which isn't bringing any pleasure from an automatism zone, it starts bringing pleasure as if by magic.

You don't believe? Let us do a small experiment.

Try not to brush your teeth today.

Eat sweet, salty food, drink coffee. In the evening pass by your tooth brush as well. And in the morning first of all go to the bathroom and clean your teeth.

You feel pleasure. Don't you?

Having spent more time than usually you will make all this especially thoroughly.

This principle is universal, and it works practically in everything. Let's take another example. Go to work by the subway tomorrow, having left your car in the yard. Arrange a week of public transport for yourself.

How will your feelings change when you find yourself again in the warm salon with a pleasant smell and favorite music? You will place yourself in the comfortable seat, enjoy the engine growl and the obedient wheel. What a pleasure it is!

The ability to realize automatisms granted additional pleasure from decision-making

Another one's violent will

When the decision is imposed from the outside, any action even seemingly, capable of bringing pleasure in other circumstances, will be rejected. There will be no pleasure, and the efforts will seem excessive. It concerns everything, from slave labor to excessive care.

Possibly, it is the best way to disaccustom a person from bad habits. A smoker will quit smoking if he is forced to smoke a cigarette in the precisely allotted time, a sweet tooth will refuse sweets if only a certain portion of chocolate is imposed daily.

However, the opposite is also true, forcing a person to refuse the established behavior model, it is impossible to achieve long-term results.

Let's remember the practice of alcoholism treatment in the USSR when there were medical and labor dispensaries to where people were banished for alcoholism for 2 years; their efficiency made only 2–3%. While Dovzhenko's method assuming a conscious very strong desire to get rid of alcoholic addiction shows efficiency of 80%.

A psychologist Arina Skibinskaya gives an example from the life of her client, with all her heart hating bananas. It turns out, that being young she had to participate in a competition on high-speed eating of this fruit. Having eaten too much of them once, she still can't look at them. Though, apparently, many years have passed since then.

At first sight it might seem that there is a contradiction here, since it is known that some people run away from the freedom of choice, so how is it combined with the thesis that another one's violent will steals pleasure?

To understand why "another one's will" steals pleasure, and at the same time it can sometimes bring pleasure to a person, it is necessary first of all to answer a question: "Does another one's will remove psychophysiological tension from the person to whom it is imposed or, on the contrary, strengthens it?" If a person can't relax, and another one's will, relieving his tension, helps him to relax, in this case it gives pleasure. If it makes him nervous that others make decisions for him, it is clear that in that case another one's will would deprive the person of pleasure.

Therefore, main point is how a person understands freedom and how he treats it. Freedom, as we know, is not a possibility to act as a person would like to, to do whatever he wants, but is the dependence on his own "I". Exactly not just independence from others and dependence on himself, but namely dependence on his own "I". After all both an alcoholic, and a drug addict can depend on themselves, their body, but you won't call them free.

If another one's will goes contrary to "I" of a personality, it steals his pleasure, and if it doesn't contradict it, the character of his personality accepts the offered condition as normal, the person derives pleasure then.

We will elaborate it in detail.

A man like any gregarious animal is ready to submit and be in a crowd, to obey the will of the leader and the majority.

He gives with pleasure his right to choose and allows to be led, thereby releasing himself of the difficulties connected with decision-making.

However, it is necessary to differentiate pleasure from submission and suffering from another one's will.

People must have an option. They give reins of government of their decisions, only if they think that it is their personal decision. People must be sure that they themselves control the situation and at the first need are capable to regain their right to decide. Whether they will use this right is another question.

But understanding of the possibility changes polarity, turning pain into pleasure.

Slavery will turn into release from the need to decide if an ephemeral, unsupported illusion of choice and control appears. The western democratic model is built on this principle. The power can be usurped not less than in the monarchy, but if there is an illusion of choice, people will no longer feel oppressed.

It is useful to adhere to the principles of democracy not only for politicians, but for ordinary spouses as well. It is known that the first of the five main reasons for disagreement in couples is that everyone tries to control the other, at the same time being afraid to lose own free will.

Wars for control in different manifestations are a basis of the conflicts of people relations. The effect of the spring triggers—the more you "press" on a person, the more he "bounces".

Absence of Sense Steals Pleasure

Senseless actions aren't very rare. It doesn't mean at all that they are reckless or irrational. The meaning can be lost due to a lot of rationalizations, prejudices or repetitions.

To watch TV, to dress fashionably, to drive a jeep over the city, to make selfies, to scroll Facebook—all this in the majority is senseless.

Nonsense has filled the life not because it is overflowed with unnecessary things and phenomena but because the necessary things are forgotten.

Spiritual development can't be resold, like, for example, the business, education or work experience. What isn't demanded within the market exchange is assigned to the supporting roles today for which in the long run there is no time left at all. Unfortunately, such attitude produces nonsense, since eventually we always stay alone with ourselves.

Thus the existential vacuum is born.

But back to pleasure and pain.

The history knows a lot of examples when one and the same action could bring either suffering, or pleasure.

A psychologist Bruno Bettelheim imprisoned in a fascist concentration camp during World War II remembers in his book "The Informed Heart" the tortures which the prisoners were exposed to. Digging a hole was one of such. People were forced to dig the ground, despite cold, sleets and diseases. Nearby the convoy was standing and shot everyone who would dare to refuse. As soon as the holes reached the required depth, the second order was given—to fill them up. People spent the rest of the day and strength to return the platform to a former look. Again and again, day after day, month by month people were forced to do the work, meaningless for them.

Many people could not stand that and rushed under bullets. Others went mad.

At the same time in the back of the Red Army, women and old men were digging entrenchments.

They did that voluntarily. In very severe conditions, they also were dying of cold, falling unconscious from exhaustion.

However, nobody threw away the shovel at his will, nobody went crazy from the hard work because with each dug meter the defenders imagined how they are coming closer to the Victory. Their work made great sense. They believed, and it is fair that without them the USSR couldn't defeat the fascist evil.

Looking back at the work done, they received pathetic, but still a portion of pleasure.

The understanding of sense granted the result, and thus the work was encouraged by the brain.

No sense, no system of motivation, no result, no encouragement. A man goes crazy. Some prisoners of concentration camps understood that and invented their own sense of digging the holes. They convinced themselves that the more they would dig and fill out the holes, the more chances of a victory the allies would have. Of course, in such a belief there is not an iota of rationality but if it helps to survive and stay sane, it is the most reasonable choice.

Viktor Frankl, describing evolution of prisoners of a concentration camp, says that if the first phase of their change is the fear and horror, the second phase is adaptation, and the third one is the loss of the personality if, of course, a person doesn't have inside of him that very sense which allows him to resist senselessness and hopelessness of his existence. The choice of the prisoner varies between suicide on a barbed wire through which the current passes and a gas chamber to which he will be sent sooner or later. The main thing in the adaptation stage is not to lose the sense of psychological resistance and not to become indifferent to everything that happens around and, first of all, to own destiny. Objecting to S. Freud, V. Frankl all the time claims that a man isn't only physiology, "an application to sex glands", but first of all he is what he thinks of himself and what he does with himself.

Citing an example with two brothers who inherited such a quality as ingenuity he says that one of them became an inventive criminal, and the other—an inventive investigator. So a man is free to dispose by himself of what the nature gives him.

There are feelings and there is an attitude of a person towards these feelings.

There are values and there is an attitude of a person towards these values.

There is pleasure and there is an attitude of a person towards this pleasure.

And if he doesn't see any sense in them, he loses them. Therefore the attitude towards sense is what makes a man a man.

Something of this kind happens after the war. Of course, it happens not in concentration camps, but in impressive skyscrapers from steel and glass.

Having missed the true sense, many office employees have also lost pleasure from the result of their work.

Life of many people reminds the same fascist torture—digging in and out the unnecessary holes.

So what to do?

A good answer was given by Goethe; "How can we learn ourselves? By thinking—we never can, only by acting. Try to do your duty, and soon you will learn what you are. And what is your duty then? It is the requirements of every day".

To do the same that women and old men did during the heroic work in the back of our Homeland, the same that the prisoners did in the heart of the fascist Germany—to invent the sense and every day to come closer to a victory.

It is not important, what you are fighting for, for own mind or for a victory in the war. It is not important, what weapon you hold in hands, an AK-47, a shovel, or a smartphone. Every single day has to bring us closer to a victory. Maybe, we, like 30 million of our compatriots won't live up to the Victory Day, but the victory itself is not so much important, as the belief in it.

Thus, pleasure is personal experience which has little connection with the objective reality, which can be produced independently, with the purpose to direct the energy of desires on achievement of something that brings benefit. One should also extinguish pleasure to get free from its expectation, upon possession of the unnecessary object. Therefore in the following chapter we will talk how to control our attitude towards pleasure and what is required to be changed in our beliefs to do so.

To rethink the system of values

We like what we consider good.

And we do not like what we consider bad.

In other words the moral is in the base of our feelings—a form of public consciousness regulating people's behavior through a system of standards developed by public opinion. We consider good what is considered good in our culture. However, it is like that if the biological level of the super complex human being doesn't contradict his mental and sociocultural level. For example, a person might like a deviant form of behavior, or for example a dishonorable man. A woman can love a man although he is drinking, hanging around, and sometimes even letting his fists loose, not to mention the fact that he might be a criminal at all. Let's consider this situation in detail.

We like what is good. However it doesn't mean that everything we like is good. Every person differently interprets goodness and evil, good and bad. Today many people constantly emphasize the relativity of moral values. In response we usually emphasize that relativity is also relative, and it should not be seen in absolute terms. There are also universal values which any normal person can't and shouldn't ignore. The problem is in another thing. Firstly, the system of personal values isn't static, and it can change during the life. It is a continuous process influenced by thousands of factors: from education to news on television.

All this leads to that a simple, at first sight, rule "we like what we consider good", risks to lose its applied usefulness.

Secondly, a personality consists of multi-personalities which can sometimes be in conflict among themselves. One multi-personality likes one thing, another one—other things. Or a person wishes one thing on the biological level, and on mental and social levels—another thing. For example, he likes wood-carving and would eagerly be engaged in it professionally, but, considering such work socially non-prestigious, he becomes a lawyer from which, eventually, both the society, and he himself suffer. It once again proves that we can wish what we do not like.

Sometimes it is expressed in innocent weaknesses, such as a piece of chocolate at night, but it sometimes leads to tragedies, such as alcoholism and drug addiction.

In the book "Control Pleasure!" we described in detail, the difference between "I like" and "I want". Even different areas of the brain are responsible for these processes.

We hope that scientists will be able to dot all the I's in the next years and reveal a formula with fewer exceptions. We hope that we will be able to predict the behavior of a person more precisely in the future, knowing his value coordinate system.

Already today significant steps have been taken to define the profiling of an individual to identify his reaction in certain situations. For example, whether a client will honestly pay the loan or will fall into arrears. One of the leaders of behavioral profiling study in Moscow, Oleg Klepikov writes the following in his presentation:

"We have developed Psycheya—a system of profiling consumers with the aim of predicting their behavior. Both individuals and the groups united by a social, religious or ethnic criterion. Other characteristics, such as aesthetic preferences or even elements of expression which can be observed in the consumer can also be the criteria. Both the consumer and the indirect facts can be a source of such information: his handwriting, photo, biography, and of course, credit history and history of the social networks profile".

The rule "I like what I consider good for myself" explains why the share of happy people is larger in the totalitarian countries.

In such countries the morality of the individual is formed by the state propaganda, people grow up with the programmed system of values. It is natural that further they will aspire to what they consider good, which means to support the values established by the authorities.

In the context of these reflections some scientists wonder about the freedom of choice.

As if we call freedom a possibility to do whatever they like—it means that in the totalitarian countries people are freer. Sounds absurdity, but everything is logical.

The moral concepts "good and bad" are created by political ideology. People aspire to the good. The state doesn't preclude that, but on the contrary only supports them, because it is within its interests.

In democratic societies, there is a great risk that personal understanding of what is "good" and what is "bad" will differ from both the state ideology, and from every separate social group which also has the right for identity and self-realization.

As we have already emphasized more than once that if an action needs to come easily, it should promise pleasure.

Knowing what a person considers good helps in modeling the behavior, Personal and others'.

Since we are more likely to get pleasure from what we like.

To make a person like this or that object, it is necessary to place it in the scale of "good".

While aspiring to get free from pleasure, some people surround themselves with the living conditions which in their opinion can't bring any pleasure. For example, subject themselves to isolation, submission, sufferings. It is a trap. Paradoxically, but the pleasure exists even in such extreme living conditions. Moreover, the pleasure forces them to take such radical measures. We will talk about the pleasure traps in the following chapter.

4.2 A NEW CIVILIZATIONAL PARADIGM

4.2.1 Power or Love?

Overcoming the own nature is an evolutionary way of a man.

Controlling own pleasure is a matter of time.

There are no doubts that there will come an era in which people will learn to cause pleasure as encouragement for their conscious decisions, but not to aspire it, burning down in blind desire.

The energy of desire will be directed on achievement of the intended result, like the energy of wind and light today.

The only question is what will happen afterwards?

How will a man use the received energy? What goals will he set to himself?

As well as the energy of nuclear disintegration can at the same time give light, and destroy all living things, the energy of desires can become a basis

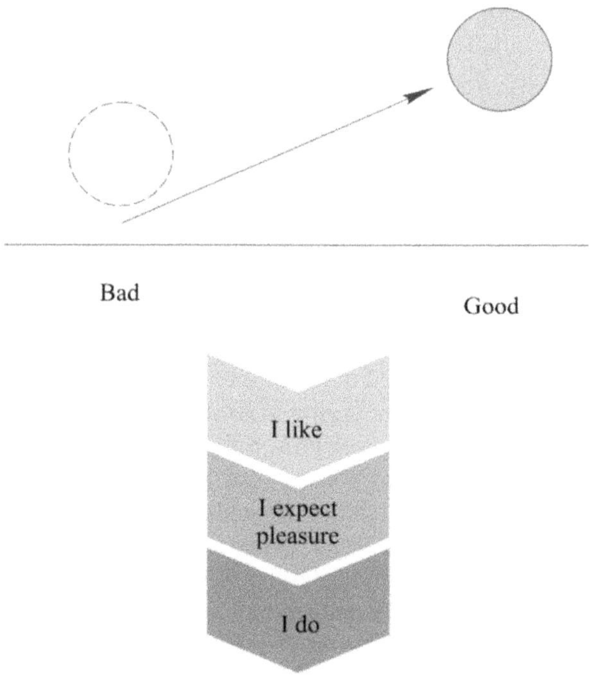

Figure 4.4. One of the ways to create artificial desire.

for general development, and can be usurped by the minority for suppression and manipulation of the majority.

Responsibility for the vector of development falls on the will of a man.

Will it be the true will or the domination over oneself will lead to the triumph of willfulness?

In the global scenario being realized today the development is a prerogative of the elite capable to overcome the press of the mass ideology and the dictated way of life. This way assumes opposition of a person to the society. A person is doomed to deprivations, loneliness and misunderstanding, a need to oppose everybody, having the risk to be booed and whistled. All this together with gaining control over the desires can lead to the change of morals of a person.

Those few people who will surpass the principle of pleasure risk to rise not only above pleasure, but also above the good and evil, having turned into Man-Gods, recognizing only force and aspiration to power, considering others as means to serve own purposes.

Such an outcome has a lot of prerequisites, but the most important thing is that seemingly this process has already begun. So the ideology of globalization is a consequence of the western outlook based on the idea that a man is an almighty conqueror, having the overall right, a superman.

From the very cradle the western culture considered a man as a rival to gods. Having stolen the fire from gods, Prometheus actually authorized a human right to make own fate, gradually taking away, and sometimes even stealing the means of such self-determination. The idea of possible theomachy in the western culture actually gives a carte blanche to willfulness which is shamelessly pushing aside the true will of a person.

Identification of willfulness and will is that very Rubicon, having passed which a person follows the way of the Man-God, about whose appearance Nietzsche had notified the world, having declared that for the subsequent development a man had to overcome his humanity by means of enormous development of his will cleansed of the morals.

Nietzsche loved his creation, urging to feed mercilessly the will to power, cultivating it to superhuman proportions. Subjecting all previous philosophy to the most severe criticism as the "school of slander" based on Socratic rationalistic moralism and Platonic transcendental idealism he declares life, not its separate sides or properties, the ultimate goal and the supreme value of a man. Exactly life, according to Nietzsche, is the only goal of the will as the will to power, might, force and domination.

In his brilliant metaphorical style, Nietzsche shows the stages of evolution of the human spirit: a camel, a lion, a child. He shows transformation which happens to a man upon achievement of a certain level of freedom and understanding of his essence.

"What is the weight?—the spirit asks, kneels like a camel and requests to be properly loaded"[7] .

But in the lonely desert where the camel runs away to, there is a transformation: "here the spirit becomes a lion, it wants to gain freedom and to be the master in his own desert". The strength of the lion is capable to gain the freedom required for new creation, but it can't create new values yet.

Only a child can, as "innocence and oblivion, a new start, a game, a self-sliding wheel, an initial move, the sacred word of the statement. The spirit wants its own will now, its abjurer finds his own world"[8].

It is important to understand adequately the third transformation. According to Nietzsche, the child rejecting old values symbolizes a man who refused the stamps and stereotypes imposed to him by the society and rediscovers the world, proceeding from own spirit. In his consciousness there are yet no values imposed by the society, there is no pronounced desire.

This is the man capable to get free from the pleasure imposed to him—the Superman, the embodiment of the highest manifestation of the will to power. Freedom from desires gives impetuous energy. How will he dispose of it? Nietzsche himself answers this question.

"Free, from what? It is none of Zarathustra's business. But let the light of thine eyes answer me: free—what for?" [9] . Free for the world domination. This is what F. Nietzsche said by Zarathustra's lips, thus generating an era of worshipping force and cruelty and the triumph of the "Man-God".

He calls kind people weak and sick, and angry ones- strong because they can cross the line. Criminals and geeks are called heroes and strong personalities since they not only proceed from own will, but also can impose it to people around. He explains hatred to Christianity by hatred to weak and degenerating people. "What is more harmful than any defect?—Active compassion to all losers and weak:—Christianity ….[10]

And the conclusion following these thoughts is natural: "Weak and unfortunate people have to die: the first provision of our philanthropy. Also it is necessary to help them with it". It is terrible philanthropy according to which the author of "the Antichrist" himself should be destroyed.

Nietzsche opposes the superman, speaking by the words of the author, to the "idiot" who voluntarily ascended to Golgotha in order to rescue people from the spiritual death. Moreover, he was praying for mercy of own executioners because those "didn't know what they were doing ". The author of "the Antichrist" writes that F. Dostoyevsky was the only one who had discerned the true essence of Jesus. A man who had founded a new European morality was, according to F. Nietzsche, neither a genius, nor a hero. He was an idiot. This thesis of F. Nietzsche is a necessary step to the following conclusion that any morality is idiocy. He calls Christianity a disease and its triumph in the society he explains by decadence.

It is interesting, that the author of "the will to power", and the author of the will to life (A. Schopenhauer) and the author of the "Crime and punishment" independently from each other come to a common denominator—impetuous will to self-affirmation which we call willfulness, leads to moral and physical self-destruction. Unfortunately, F. Nietzsche, unlike others came to it not through his works, but showed it with his own life. Believing neither Schopenhauer, nor Dostoyevsky, he had paid with his health and life, and not only his life...

It is pertinent to remember Joseph Brodsky's words: "Who spits on God, spits first on a man". Nietzschianism is spittle, first of all, in a man.

Because, without moral guidelines a creature calling itself the Homo sapiens turns into an animal.

Perhaps, F. Nietzsche would be right, if a man had possessed only physical essence; if life made sense only as the life of a single and independent person, separate from all of mankind. But then this being would be another species of the animal kingdom.

All history of mankind is the biography of formation of a whole being—a Man. Love is what unites not only two beings for human reproduction, but also all people feeling and realizing their inferiority without uniting into one humanity.

And if such a talented man as the author of "Thus spoke Zarathustra" did not understand that, then, probably, his life was lacking of those love, care and compassion which the Christianity hated by him calls for.

Spiritual and heavenly culture of the despotic East and intellectual and strong-willed one of the "democratic" West in a proud privacy were modeling a man for a long time. Distinctions of the eastern and western cultures are associated with the cross symbol. The vertical line symbolizes the eastern culture which is dissolving a man in the spiritualized cosmos, up to abnegation, identity removal; the horizontal line is the western culture, granting autonomy of the will of a person aimed at the total gain of the outside world.

For an eastern man only the soul is valid. The world, being only visibility, is similar to a dream. For him the deity is present in all things and, first of all, in a man. Therefore by means of yoga and meditation an eastern man, "removing" the outside world as illusion, through release from external feelings,

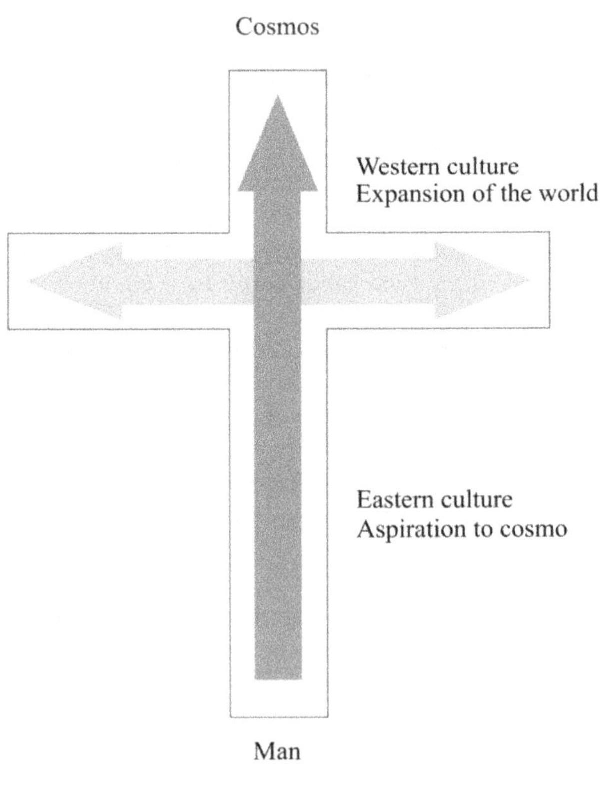

Figure 4.5. Decoding Christ symbol.

from the selfhood distorting the consciousness, experiences himself as the only real being and, developing evolutionarily, comes nearer to the God-man. The value of life for him consists in the possibility of transformation into the atman, i.e. deprived of selfhood, and therefore having left the sansara, the circle of reincarnations caused by karma. Coming back to the maternal bosom of the nature, an eastern man goes deep into the unconscious, trying to break through to his essence, to his "I" which is merged with "I" of the nature. Gloss of the land of Amitabha replaces the sleeping and dissolving individual-selfish "I" in the infinite ocean of the absolute Brahman.

This is the eastern way to the God-man.

Only the physical cover remains human here.

A serious place for a problem of the God-man is allocated by Nikolay Berdyaev in his work "Sense of creativity," where he emphasizes that each person through Christ stays not only in the beasty world, but also in the Deity. Therefore, the human nature is God-mundane, and not just mundane. According to N. Berdyaev, a man after the fall turned into a purely natural being. "In an absolute man,—N. Berdyaev writes,—"the human nature remains in the highest, divine spheres of existence while in the fallen natural person it plunges into the lowest spheres of existence to take him up to the highest level"[11].

Now the seemingly absurd, at first sight, fact of theophany (manifestation of deity in human form) becomes clear. A man after the fall lost his divine essence, and the God following him, like the father ought to do, went down exactly in human form in order to take a man up to the highest spiritual spheres, having shown an example.

According to N. Berdyaev, the divine essence of a man has to be shown in creativity, in his Spirit. "Where the spirit is, there is freedom as well,—he writes. In the Spirit the secret of creativity is being revealed, in the Spirit the human nature is being realized"[12].

In creativity a man himself opens the image and God's likeness in himself, finds the divine power input in him.

The Russian philosopher's words are remarkable that the God-man is revelation of not only the divine, but also the human greatness, and implies faith not only in God, but also in man. The God has hidden the truth from a man so that the latter in free creative boldness would reveal it. Therefore, a man is the coauthor of existence. And therein lies the great mystery!

The third revelation,—N. Berdyaev warns,—is impossible to be awaited for, it should be made by a man himself, living in the Spirit, he should make it with a free creative act. A man is absolutely free in his creativity, and in this "terrible freedom there is all godlike dignity of a man and his eerie responsibility"[13].

Not only a man needs God, but also God needs a man for implementation of his plans just like a system self-realizes through its parts, like the father continues his creativity through his son.

N. Berdyaev introduces an interesting idea of mutual creation of a man and God, opening one more aspect of god-humanity. "… In God,—he writes,—there is passionate longing and yearning for a man. In God there is a tragic defect which is compensated by the great gain—the birth of a man in Him. Mystics were teaching about the mystery of the birth of God in a man. But there is another mystery, the mystery of the birth of a man in God.

There is a call of a man so that God was born in him. But there is also a call of God so that a man was born in Him. Only by human hands God is fully able to realize himself. This is the mystery of Christianity, the mystery of Christ, unknown to mysticism of Hindus, Plotinus and all other abstract and monistic mysticism. God and man—are more, than one God"[14].

Is not it an anthem to a man whom the orthodox philosopher puts in one row with God, giving us an original interpretation of the God-man as the system "God—a Man?

The works of another great Russian philosopher—Vladimir Solovyov are also important to understand the idea of the god-man. He spoke about the need of forming not only the god-man, but also the god-humanity. According to V. Solovyov, Christ had won through the evil of egoism in the center of a man, and it should be done in the humanity as well.

Therefore, it is necessary to develop the god-humanity, and not only one god-man. From the Christophany, according to V. Solovyov, the true history of mankind begins, to be exact its first part. The second part will begin with emergence of the one whole Christian state—the Kingdom of Christ in which the Goodness should be realized through the mankind history.

V. Solovyov considers that the god-man is a creature, who first of all, has transformed his will, having replaced egoism with Love to all the surrounding.

A serious impulse in understanding of a man was N. O. Lossky's philosophy which, quite corresponding to traditions of the Russian religious philosophy, was based on the ideas of overall unity.

According to Lossky, originality and value of each "I" is not in its isolation, but in acceptance of the whole world with God at the head, and in readiness for conciliar creativity.

Thus the abyss between the sunny god-man who, "shining to others burns down himself" and the ahrimanic man-god burning others to shine himself, is the abyss between the true will, on the one hand, and willfulness—on the other.

The will of the god-man is the will of the divine and majestic nature, an individual form of existence of the environmental will while the will of the man-god—is only private will imposed to the whole.

And therefore it isn't even truly human will, in the best case claiming for willfulness.

The man-god derives pleasure from realization of the will to power, from the feeling of domination over others, while the god-man derives pleasure from serving to his environment, from awareness of own usefulness to people and the surrounding world in general; from breaking through to the true, highest "I" which is in harmony with the nature in general, like a part and the whole, an element and the system.

The true will of a man assumes amending of human culture towards its humanization and ecologization which are seen by us as the main reference points of the universal culture change. The steps which the society can make towards the god-man will be described in the final part of the present research. Now, summarizing, we will emphasize once again that having learned to control the principle of pleasure, a man releases huge energy, responsibility for using which is conferred on his will. The true will, promoting self-realization of the surrounding world, creates general harmony while the willfulness fixed on own ego, trying to subordinate the world to its ambitions leads to wars and destruction.

4.2.2 The Will and Its Role in Controlling Pleasure

The role of the will in the civilizational paradigm dominating today is not enough considered. Is not it because the Schopenhauer's sleeping will to live of one people and the Nietzschean awake will to power of others are satisfied with the existing differentiation of people on dominating and submitting ones? Including also by means of creating an agiotage in the process of pursuing pleasure. However, what is the will?

It is reasonable to begin the research of any phenomenon with its proteostasis, i.e.to study the genesis of its formation. We suggest to recall an ancient esoteric symbol—a snake swallowing its tail. It is not only an eternity symbol, but also the balance formula representing the closedness of the cycles in nature. The wasted energy at the exit under own weight falls on the entrance and awakes "the snake" starting its eternal work. Similar to the snowball effect a small perturbation of the equilibrium system can lead it into "the rage" of the non-equilibrium state. Perhaps, the myth about Sisyphus which was brilliantly used by A. Camus represents right this infinite work of the Nature.

The will is required for the system to exit from the equilibrium state, and then for maintenance of this state at a higher level as well.

The non-equilibrium state characterizing all living is the result of aspiration of an element to the lacking "friend—foe" in order to form the one system. For the lifeless at the macro-level centripetal backbone impulses are characteristic from a broader system which is pulling together the elements into the whole. While an element at this level is itself indifferent. In the process of complication of the level of organization the backbone impulses are interiorized. The deep basis of the genesis of the proto-will lies exactly in this non-indifferent attitude of an element to the environment, in readiness to percept its impacts and reaction to them, in our opinion. The protostasis of pleasure represents an equilibrium and safe state of an element in the system owing to harmonization of the centripetal and centrifugal forces. The true pleasure, as well as the true will, being at the same time the means of exiting from an equilibrium state and its maintenance at a higher level, promotes the development of both the element, and the system in general.

Not a thing is manifestation of the will, as A. Schopenhauer noted, but the nature of its activity. Another thing is that the system may contain several levels of activity. So, Hegel singled out three levels: intra physiological, intra mental, social. It would be possible to add also socio-natural activity, noting its being mediated by the social one itself.

If to understand a potentiality to self-organization, self-realization and self-positing as the will, then the proto-will represents "another one's will" since the backbone benchmarks of development are set from the outside in this case. A possibility to cardinally change the way of living activity is very limited. In the course of evolution the will is being interiorized, i.e. there is transformation of the external, someone else's information-program into the own one. Into the program of own true "I", into the means of implementing the essence of a man. Regulation of the behavior of a man by means of his "I" distinguishes the true will from the willfulness representing an impulse of needs and desires of a person. The true will is understood by us as a measure of presence of the essence of a man in his acts.

The system view allows to understand evolution not only as the process of "devouring" the environment by the private will, according to Schopenhauer, manifestation of a blind rush of the will to live, or, according to Nietzsche, of the will to power and might, but also as the process of "feeding" of a daughter system by a broader maternal system. The environment delivers "a child" necessary and corresponding to its requirements.

Such a view results in the need of creating a new environmental paradigm. A man acts as a certain synthesizer of horizontal (spatial) and vertical (temporary) reality, and his will acts as a special realization channel of the general by means of the single. As the means of universalization of the local reality and localization of the Universum.

The environment interiorized by a concrete subject generates in it a condition similar to "pregnancy" which ends up with the emergence of activity, new actions. The energy of activity required for the birth of something new, is the basis of the proto-will as a mechanism to implement the program, the process of its coordination and control.

The backbone factor of the will as a bio-psychosocial phenomenon is the social one which doesn't belittle the importance of its psycho-physiological bases requiring special consideration at all.

The Psychological Aspect of the Nature of the Will

According to special researches, the psycho-physiological basis of the will is integrative work of the highly differentiated central functional and dynamic systems of the brain. The subcortex (hypothalamus, reticular formation, thalamic nucleus and others) which sends the ascending, specific, activating excitements to the cortex acts as the power basis. Experiments of P. Dell and his colleagues have shown that such components of the internal and external environment of an organism as adrenaline, oxygen, sex hormones, carbon dioxide, nutrients selectively affect the reticular formation and the hypothalamus and by means of the activating influence of the reticular system organize the activity of the cerebral cortex, leading to emergence of the specific adaptive behavior[15]. Thus the conditions of transferring the needs of an organism into the corresponding behavior are formed.

The will is usually considered as the level of mental regulation by an action. And, although the will isn't just a regulation, besides not only by an action, it is fair that not every, but only a certain level of mental regulation can be called the will. Some authors specify as one of the main characteristics of the will the suppression of the desires and impulses arising in this situation. It is noted that the true will arises when a person is capable to a reflection of his inclinations.

The mentality refracts the information of the present through a prism of the past for the purpose of forming the future. The lever of "switching" the realities is the will storing information on the previous subject and object "transfusions" in its memory. A preliminary step to such transformation is emotions as reflection of the object properties, vitally significant for the subject. As a result of realization by the subject the insufficiency of the object there appears an ideal image of the object amended according to the person's needs, and also of the transformation process, i.e. the purpose which peculiarity is its direction into the future. An important psychological component of the will activity is interest as the axiological attitude to the object of the subject's need. Interest highlights those sides of the objective reality which, corresponding to the subject's nature, are necessary for it. According to the fair note of Schlegel, "We are brilliant in what it is interesting to us." After all, interest is manifestation of the inner, deep essence of a person, his "I". Therefore we derive pleasure from what it is interesting to us!

Thanks to the motive, the purpose acquires a personal sense. In psychological literature numerous experiments are described illustrating direct dependence of the level of the will regulation on the significance of the motive as an immediate incentive reason of an act. The significance of motivation affects first of all the dynamics of the claim level of a person. Higher motivation leads to increase of the claim level of a personality and to setting more difficult goals, requiring the corresponding greater will efforts. There might be an impression that a person by means of high motivation and will efforts goes against own pleasures. In fact there is a preference of one pleasure to another. Exactly the control of pleasure! And thanks to it the personal growth takes place.

Increase in motivation especially by means of creating some beliefs, leads to ignoring failures. For this reason the external manipulating of a personality assumes formation of these or those beliefs in it. We have illustrated it on the example of religious fanatics.

The esurient self-consciousness, according to Hegel, is "destroying" and "selfish"[16] . The attitude of desire relation to the object is certainly the attitude of selfish destruction, but not the attitude of creation. Therefore the will activity directed to receiving primitive pleasure is only willfulness which is absorbing, sometimes destroying the object on which it is directed for the purpose of satisfaction of own singularity. Such a person is a slave to his, and to a greater degree to others' needs. "the will of a slave,—Hegel writes,—here refuses from itself and is given to the will of the master; the content of the slave's will now becomes the purpose of the master who, in return, allows into his self-consciousness not the will of the slave, but only care of maintaining his natural vitality".[17]

At different levels there are various types of pleasures demanding the diverse will attitude towards them. In the relations of a single person and the natural environment bio-psychophysical pleasures and willfulness as ability of self-control and self-mobilization are formed. Then there appear socially imposed pleasures and another one's will when a person seems to act freely, without anyone's coercion, however is guided by someone else's information imposed from the outside, falling, according to E. Fromm, a victim of the automating conformism. And only in the attitude of a person to his "I" the will of the person reveals as his self-realizable and self-creating potentiality. Therefore the true will is closely connected with creative rushes of the soul because creativity as ability to create spiritually is supplemented with "physical creativity" as an ability to create materially. But, first of all, the creative essence of the will is shown in self-creativity, in the need of self-updating and self-creation. Therefore the will of a personality as its substantial quality, represents the most important means of transformation of pleasures from destroying into creative ones and first of all self-creating a person as a creative free being.

The Socio-cultural Content of the Will

Phylogenetically the will of a person was formed as a result of the self-organizing, negentropy need of the society. Emergence of a being, possessing considerably greater degree of freedom in relation to his environment, initially meant a threat of its destruction. External bio-spherical mechanisms of regulating species and population upon unprecedented multiplication of a possibility of the behavior individualization turned out to be insufficiently effective, requiring compensation by the internal social regulators of activities.

Originally such regulators were taboos, standards of behavior, rituals which observance was vitally important to keep the integrity of a certain social community: genus, tribe, etc. Therefore violation of these compiled laws was strictly punished, as a rule by death or exile from society. Experimental psychological studies show that self-regulation was preceded by a stage of external regulation of behavior of a man. It is convincingly illustrated by the dependence of behavior of a child on the external environment. Following rather precisely the instructions of an adult, a child at an early stage of its development isn't capable of independent regulation of its behavior. Similar paralysis of the will can appear also in adults, who were always obliged to follow the instructions of the administration.

Interiorization of external socio-cultural regulators of behavior gradually has led to forming of an internal personal—individual mechanism of behavior regulation. Today the society of mass consumption on the contrary forms a gregarious being, paralyzing individual will. Traditions, customs, taboos already practically don't exist. A man turns into an economic erythrocyte which is manipulated by forming expectation of pleasure. Evolution for the mass person goes back. Media, TV, supermarkets, various shows and all glam culture lulls the will of an average consumer.

Development of willfulness to actually the will assumes moving away from oneself the subjectively egoistical desires, passions locking a personality within the frames of egoism pursuing pleasures. Unlike Schopenhauer's such resignation means not death of the will, but on the opposite, only a prerequisite for its birth and development. The following stage is awareness of needs of broader systems (a family, a nation, mankind, the biosphere, etc.) and assistance to their improvement. Biographies of great persons perfectly illustrate the fact of "involving" the will of a personality into the interests of society. However there might be also a manipulation of the will of a person by means of imposing a "mission" alien to him. Therefore today each person has to realize his great mission—to remain a man, despite the active work on his transformation into the Matrix element. "Let the one who can be himself, be nobody else!"

In the process of development a man scoops the program of his behavior and the pleasure from it already in the system of the social relations. K. G. Jung's idea about "settling" of the evolutive hierarchy of social practice in the mentality of a person as archetypes of the collective unconscious, in our opinion, should be expanded. Not only social but also natural—biological factors of the environment settle in the mentality. Not only the mentality, but also the entire human body (including society) represents the concentrated objectivation of historical memory, environmental links and influences. Therefore the expression "a man is the folded Universe" isn't as aphoristic as it may seem at first sight. A man, figuratively speaking is "the DNA of the environment" both real, and historical. There is a paradoxical situation—the environment, acting as the basis of the will of living beings, generates, "crystallizes" a being which is potentially carrying "the burden" of the environment's will.

The will and culture act as help for each other. The former one creates the latter, and the latter one determines the former. Pleasure should become an intermediary between them since the perception of the way of formation should become the highest pleasure of a person.

Culture as an adaptive—willed mechanism of society, acting as "a will of the will" (according to Schelling), is interiorized in the individual will as its archetype, making one more round of individualization of "folding" the environment. In fact, the culture in the society carries out the functions similar to the will of a person, acting as a bridge between the worlds, as the means of negentropy development of the subject and the system in which the subject is included. Being some kind of the above-individual will, it directs the will of social subjects, creating "a sheaf" of the choice options.

There remained a Xenophon's story about the tragedy of Athenian strategists who rescued their city in a cruel fight with the sea forces of Sparta which is brightly illustrating the dependence of strong-willed behavior of people on traditions and laws of society. The battle happened during a strong storm. Chasing the enemy, required for a clear victory, in these conditions prevented the Athenian naval commanders to pick up corpses of the dead and to provide them with a funeral ceremony. Such non-compliance with the ancient custom aroused indignation of relatives of the dead, and as a result the heroes were condemned to death by the Athenian meeting. It led to the fact that during the next fight the commander of the fleet cared about corpses more, than about the victory, and the beheaded Athenian fleet a year later had a catastrophic crash near Aegospotami, which, eventually, turned the beam of the Peloponnesian war.

An important role in determination of the willed behavior is played by the ways of public regulation by individual behavior. It is known that the most efficient way of such regulation in the primitive society was ritualization. The focus on the shared values was fixed by following the traditional way of actions, the whole of acts and procedures driven almost to automatism upon execution. Morally valuable information was directly interwoven into actions which were determined mainly by ready stereotypes of behavior (tabuation) violation of which was strictly punished. Social evolution was accompanied with the growth of the freedom level of the will.

Psycholinguistic researches show accurate dependence of behavior of a child on the form of the language instruction, and the greatest impact on the will of a person is made by the statements relating to the type of exclamation, an order, a request, a question. The degree of impact on the interlocutor, his motives to action might be regulated consciously, choosing this or that type of the language shape. It is also fair for the self-control. Depending on how a person addresses himself, with what intonation, the degree of intensity of the will depends significantly, upon the control of pleasures as well. The attitude towards the speech source is very important. Information passing through the filter of trust or mistrust is accepted only when the source of information inspires trust. Therefore in case of the willed control of pleasures the self-esteem is very important.

In case of the willed control of pleasures it is necessary to be guided by the initiative purposes, that is, those purposes which a person sets himself in the course of his activities. Only then the purpose obtains its incentive, regulating and backbone functions when it is perceived by a person as vitally important.

Then the will of a personality belongs to its true "I" which has the power over pleasures.

The priority value of the subject which is recognized by the environment and the subject himself acts as his force. According to E. Fromm, "the highest strength of an individual is based on the maximum development of his personality, and it assumes the maximum understanding of himself. "Know thyself"—is one of the main precepts of the strength and happiness of a man"[18].

Understanding of the power as dependence of the will of one subject on the will of another one, and hence the responsibility for him, is an important point of social development. "When we speak about power,—H. Morgenthau writes,—we mean the control executed by a person over the consciousness and actions of other people"[19]. "Power,—M. Mann writes, is a capability to overcome and achieve these or those objectives by means of mastering the environment". Therefore power is strengthening of the will by means of absorption of the surrounding into itself: people, animals (domestic), natural forces (substances and energy) for the purpose of implementation of its goals. The same is fair in relation to the power of a person over himself and his pleasures.

The structure of the power organization, which is dominating in the society, leaves its mark on the nature of the social relations. In the totalitarian society the feeling of blind subordination to the impersonal power is formed.

The sphere of needs and motivation, formulation of the purpose and decision making here are spatially separated from their execution. The principle of feedback existing in the nature is broken. Instead of it the power functions in the unilateral direction, so the energy flow runs only in one direction: from the pyramid top to its base. Therefore the tension accumulated in the lowest strata of the totalitarian society is forcedly directed horizontally, inside the stratum, causing various social collisions—diseases, rise in crime, degradation, revolts and revolutions or "are grounded" through the natural environment, destroying it.

Unilaterally directed power or energy and will flow, being violence, generates aggression as a social pathology arising due to truncation of the human will deprived of such its major component as creativity. There is a connection between pleasure, productivity and disruptiveness, i.e. between creativity and a possibility of its implementation and aggression, hatred and destruction. "There is an impression,—E. Fromm writes,—that the degree of disruptiveness is pro rata to the extent of blocking the development of a human capability[20]. If on the way of the tendency to growth and life activity there is a barrier,—he continues,—then the blocked energy undergoes changes and is transformed into destructive energy. Disruptiveness is a result of restrained and thus distorted life"[21].

Thus, the unrealized will to live owing to a strong obstacle which was met on its way can be transformed to destruction, i.e. its vector might change to the opposite. And disruptiveness in itself is nothing else but the truncated, empty will; the will which has kept the energy force, but has lost the creative, demanding-motivational, target, moral content. The normal productive life bringing joy and pleasure to a person when blocked can develop into aggression and escaping into impetuous pleasures.

According to E. Fromm the paralysis of aspiration to growth and productivity existing in a normal person is a symptom of mental disturbance. Obstacles for a possibility to use the energy (bio—psycho-social) result in dissatisfaction, called "depression of being unused"[22]. If the excessive being in demand and self-devotion can lead to premature burn up of a personality, then the opposite, i.e. impossibility of self-devotion—to painful decay.

A man is often tormented by a dichotomy to live in consent with the world and at the same time with himself. This contradiction is solved in productive creative activities. However the consent with oneself and the consent with the world often contradict each other. For example during critical and unstable for society eras, when a desire of a man to keep himself puts him on the edge of physical and social death, and vice versa, a desire "to keep afloat" leads to the loss, fading of his "I". Then the role of the will as the means of self-preservation and self-organization, self-determination and self-positing is being actualized. As a bridge between "I" of the personality and the environment surrounding it to its true "I".

In the context of the paralysis of the productive capability, sadism and masochism as perverted forms of getting pleasure are explained. It is interesting to consider sadism as exploitation of the appropriated will up to destruction of its object, and masochism as exploitation and destruction of own will, voluntary refusal of it and transformation of oneself into a victim.

There is close connection between virtue of citizens and the extent of implementation of their productive capability. "If the society,—E. Fromm writes,—is interested in its members being virtuous, it shall be interested, therefore, that they were productive, so it shall be interested in forming of conditions for development of their productivity"[23]. In fact, a person shall eliminate obstacles preventing to receive pleasures from creativity both in himself, and in the environment. Only then there will be no threat of self-alienation. As Ortega and Gasset notice, we are half what surrounds us. Therefore much attention should be paid to the environment, selecting it by the principle of similarity. And at last, the most important condition for development of creativity of the will is democratization of the society.

All this speaks about the need of forming of a new civilizational paradigm –New humanism.

4.2.3 Humanization and Ecologization of Culture

We have shown that at different stages of the human culture evolution there were various types of cultures, with different attitude towards pleasure. The society of mass consumption created by the modern capitalism turned pleasure into the means of degradation of a man. Multiplied by technicalization and kibernetization of the society it leads to a threat of transforming a man not only into an animal, but already into a mechanism, a gear of the world machine. Erich Fromm called such a creature an automating conformist. It actualizes the need to determine the essence of the New Humanism, a new civilization paradigm which would affect all spheres of human activities.

"The New Humanism,—Aurelio Peccei writes,—should not only be conformable to the power acquired by a man and correspond to the amended external conditions, but also should possess firmness, flexibility and ability to self-update which would allow to regulate and direct the development of all modern revolutionary processes and changes in the industrial, socio-political, scientific and technical areas"[24].

The humanization of culture assumes its ecologization, but these processes shouldn't be perceived by people as something external what they are compelled to obey. We must do it with pleasure!

This is our message—through pleasure to blessing!

To rescue others is not a duty of a man. This is the highest blessing. To rescue oneself, others and the natural environment is the highest pleasure from gaining and implementing own mission!

Centuries-old social evolution vainly tried to create a being living in harmony with its environment. Throughout all the previous history a man wished to dominate over everything that surrounded him, to derive benefit from everything, subordinating it to his egoistical thirst of pleasure from consumption. It generated cruelty, violence, and, eventually, had led to the change not so much of the environment, as of the man himself.

Attempts to re-educate the man weren't successful. On the contrary, a man is blinded by individualism. The society is blinded by consumption. And the habitat is on the threshold of an environmental disaster.

Thus, the current state of the environment acts as a hint of the need to change the global strategy of human development where the will to power would be changed by the will to unity and Love.

Move from the blind pursuit of single pleasure towards conscious pleasure from harmony of the internal and the external.

These are the reference points of the New Humanism.

The most important condition of the New Humanism is the cosmic expansion of the subject's borders, up to removal of differences with the object. When a man realizes himself as the Nature, and the Nature as himself, it will remove the need of subject and object vision of social-natural relations, preventing "to see the wood behind the trees ".

As B. Devall and G. Session note, the "subject–object" distinction disappears—really, a man appears beyond all conceptual knowledge and feels "the merge of consciousness with all nature". And, finally, a man comes to "the direct immediate perception excluding all attempts to conceptualize the feeling of absolute uniqueness of each individual thing"[25].

If we understand the activity carrier as the subject, the relations with the nature should be classified as subject—subject. "The level of the consciousness which is deeper, than the ego-consciousness,—M. E. Zimmerman writes,—stimulates deep activity and provides fuller existence of a man, than his ego consciousness does"[26].

The transition to the environmental consciousness will allow to restore the lost Nature-Human and Human-Nature harmony. Then the question of pleasure expands its borders too.

The pleasure of a man is transformed into the pleasure of the system including both a man and the natural organism surrounding him.

At first glance this question may seem strange: "Does the nature feel pleasure?" In our opinion, of course it does. The nature is not only realizing the world by means of human brains, but also enjoys it by means of all living things. Maksimilian Voloshin's words are interesting in this regard, he says that the nature is admiring itself with the eyes of a man.

A man, having called himself the wreath of nature, has erected a wall between himself and the whole world.

The story about the Overweening pupil of God, who had considered himself equal to God and thus was expelled from the God's kingdom is the prophecy symbolizing the destiny of mankind.

Imagining himself the force at first resisting to the nature, and then dominating over it, he, becoming a bit sober, is searching for the ways to return to the paradise by means of the outlined threat of a global disaster. However, sadly, he looks for these paths not where he should. Not through pleasure and even not through repentance, humility, prayer and awe of the Nature, but still only through the technological development, self-strengthening, increase of wealth and fame. It is desirable that the opposition of the Vanity blown up by youth and the patient Wisdom would end with the return of "the prodigal son" to the generous father.

And meanwhile the techno-sphere being between the Man and the Nature and, having its own logic of development, transforms them.

The caution of science fiction writers about the danger to be destroyed by robots is more relevant than ever. However, a threat of people transformation into robots isn't less real. A concept "post-humanism" already exists and actively develops.

Humanization and ecologization of technology should lead to the evolution of human culture in the basis of which, strangely enough, is also the principle of pleasure, as the preservation of the natural environment of a man saves him the opportunity to enjoy life.

Formation of ecological culture is carried out by means of ecological education, teaching and training, which purpose is to make people understand the ideas of optimum interaction of the society and the nature.

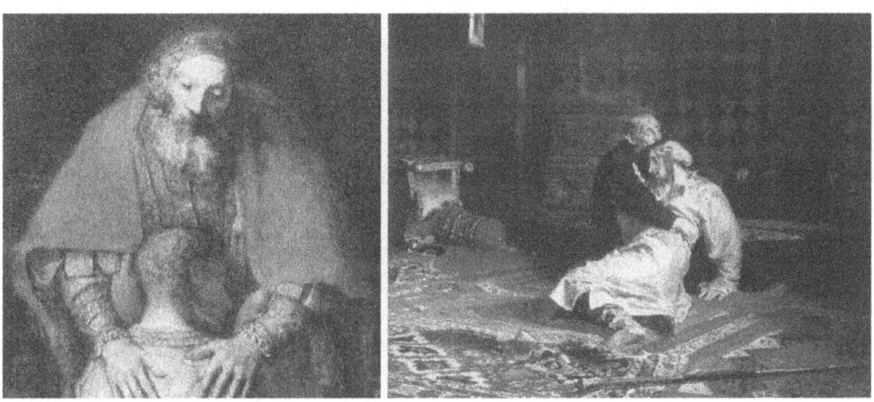

Figure 4.6. Rembrandt's vision (on the left) would be closer to reality in that case, than Repin's one (on the right).

However, understanding of any idea by people is imagined rather as a private moment of education, than its purpose. Besides the cognitive components of education it is necessary to remember also about the strong-willed and sensual ones. After all the purpose of ecological education of a person is formation of a complete personality.

To do so it is necessary to change not only consciousness, but also the will of a man as means of his unity with the world. It is possible to form the new humanism only through the unity of intelligence, feelings and will.

The most important layer of culture is the law like "the will of the will" (using Schelling's expression). Therefore formation and development of the corresponding right is the necessary means of creating new culture.

So that a public law becomes an internal law of a person, it has to comply with the following principles:

- To be objectively justified, which means to contribute to optimum functioning and developing of a person, and the society, and the nature.
- To be "close" to the subject, that is, what is approved by the law has to coincide with the desire of an individual. A man should execute the laws with pleasure.

It is possible only when in the center of the right there is a person to whom these laws serve. The constitution and the Civil Code turn into the Bible of a citizen.

Unfortunately, many legal laws including those regulating ecological behavior of a man, are directed, in the best case, on elimination of consequences of human activities.

As it was shown earlier, the most important determinant of behavior of a person is the belief.

Recently there are works appearing in special literature, which are devoted to connection between religion and ecology. The ecological perspective can become that very topic which would allow to integrate science, philosophy and religion. But religion as we noted, transfers pleasure to the sphere of service to God. We think that development of pleasure from harmonious existence of a man in the world could be one of the major directions in it.

The will to unification has to cement the outlined integration processes, having led to creation of the whole planetary house.

Integration has to include all faiths. The will of wise Vivekananda: do not try to entice a traveler to one's side, but help him to reach the Truth on his own way, fairly pushes towards awareness of the need to create an integrated ecoreligion which does not contradict the religious feelings of either a Christian, or a Muslim, or a Buddhist, or a Jew. As a matter of fact, each of these religions comprises the code of the norms and precepts aiming people at observance of ecologically focused rules. This is one more aspect of the overall unity which Vladimir Solovyov spoke about.

Pleasure shouldn't break the natural harmony. On the contrary, there should be a pleasure in the creation of this harmony.

A criterion of development of the social-natural system is input to a man. This is the secret of the great consecrated. This means to become Buddha—the awakened. To live with pleasure in a paradise garden, without picking fruit, without breaking the established harmony. And to derive pleasure from the understanding that you don't break, but you create, you restore the natural and cosmic harmony.

We got used that religion promises rescue after death to a man, suggesting to put up with the pain, injustice and sufferings during the lifetime. What if the rescue is possible in this life, and not through pain and sufferings, but through pleasure? No need to persuade a person to be with God, it is necessary only to teach him to derive pleasure from harmonious life.

It isn't necessary to control the world, it is necessary to control only own pleasure!

Conclusion

In the last century, the "operant conditioning chamber" was invented, which subsequently received the name "Skinner's box", showing dependence of behavior of a living being on the corresponding award—expectation of pleasure. Today, during the era of consumerism and advanced technologies, the possibility to control incentives and remunerations increased so much that the whole world appears as an analog of the Skinner's box. Having realized it, "the kings of marketing" skillfully use technical capabilities to control daily decisions of people. In fact, we are entering a new era of blind mass consumption. Modern technologies already created unmanned vehicles, but they also promote creation of drones, the so-called "auto-piloted society".

Dependence of a man on technical means turned advanced technologies into the intermediary between manipulators and manipulated. In response to techno-imitation of social interactions, the brain of a man excretes the substances bringing pleasure and forming habits. As it was shown, the triggers are inside of people. These are existential feelings: boredom, curiosity, loneliness, fear, etc. But the strongest is the expectation of pleasure which is specially cultivated by the society and especially by the techno-civilization. By causing psychological dependence in people, they actively manipulate with expectation of pleasure, and, not only with economic, but also political purposes.

There is a threat of transformation of a man into a cyborg controlled from the outside. Do we accept such an alternative—to gain power, having lost freedom and will? And the problem is not with the technologies at all, but with the level of development of the people setting the mainstream of the social development, i.e. in the dominating civilizational paradigms. Therefore, today it is necessary to change the paradigm of blind mass consumption. The will to power and possession shall be replaced by the will to self-improvement and integration. From the blind pursuit of the pleasures imposed from the outside to the pleasure from harmony of the internal and external.

Notes

1. PLEASURE AND THE VECTOR OF CIVILIZATIONAL DEVELOPMENT

1. Lacan J. Relations of objects. Paris. 1956
2. Foucault M, The Use of Pleasure. New York: Vintage book. 1990, p. 304
3. The Discourses of Epictetus. 1904. New York. D. Appleton and Company. Book 2, ch. 20, p. 180
4. Russell B. History of Western Philosophy. New York. 1945, p. 287
5. Cyril Bailey. The Greek Atomist and Epicurus. Oxford. 1928, p. 249
6. Ibid
7. Russell B. History of Western Philosophy. New York. 1945, p. 244
8. The Roman Stoics: Self, Responsibility and Affection. Chicago: University Of Chicago Press. 2006, p. 167
9. Russell B. History of Western Philosophy. New York. 1945, p. 260
10. Seneca. On Blissful Life. The Roman Stoics. 2006, p. 194
11. cited in Russell B, 1945, p. 273
12. Plato. Phaedo. London. Cambridge, MA, Harvard University Press. 1966. V. 1, p. 21
13. Aristotle. Nicomachean Ethics. London. 1893. b. VII, ch. 11–13, b. X, Ch. 1–5, 7, 8.
14. Ibid. ch. 11, p 118.
15. Spinoza, Ethics. Murfreesboro. MTSY. 1997, p III p. 508
16. Fechner Elements of Psychophysics. Holt. 1966, vol. 1. p. 227
17. Freud. S. Beyond the Pleasure Principle. London. The Hogarth Press.1955, p. 149.
18. Fromm, 1990, p. 142
19. Bataille, Accursed Share. Paris, 2003, p. 102
20. Goethe, 1958, p. 7
21. F. Nietzsche. The birth of tragedy from the spirit of music. The Preface to Richard Wagner.
22. O.Spengler. Ibid. P. 71
23. M.Ossovskaya. Knight and bourgeois. Researches on morals history. M.: Progress. 1987. P. 82.
24. E. Fromm. Man for Himself. M: Collegium, 1992
25. Dante Alighieri. The Divine comedy. Collected edition. v. 1. M. Literature; Veche, 2001. P. 656.

26. According to the American Psychiatric Association, the number of sociopaths in the world has grown from 3% to 5% for the last years
27. 2015 Global Games Market Report, the researchers estimate that the 2015 games market will jump from $83.6 billion in 2014, to $91.5 billion in 2015.
28. Growth of the corporate games market makes from $1.5 bln in 2012 to $3.3 bln in 2015. http://venturebeat.com/2013/08/16/with-a-mobile-boom-learning-games-are-a-1-5b-market-headed-toward-2-3b-by-2017-exclusive/
29. J. Huizinga. Homo Ludens. Or Man the Player. M.: Iris press. 2003. p. 496
30. According to the Phonanist application, an active resident of the metropolis, a manager of the administrative unit, checks his phone 150 times per day on average.
31. Dr. Catrine Tudor-Locke is on the hunt for the answer. Her study, published in "Medicine and Science in Sports and Exercise" in 2014
32. There is a famous experiment of 1951 by a psychologist Solomon Asch, where the people were changing their opinion saying the same which was sounded by the crowd.
33. Teachers' favorite question: what if all had jumped off the bridge, would you jump as well? We used to have no answer to that. Now we know it: Yes, I would jump. Moreover, you, Mrs. Lydia, would also jump, if our head teacher, principal, prefect, mayor and the whole district had jumped!
34. According to the data of the Federal Drug Control Service of the Russian Federation
35. See Bernard Barber. Science and the Social Order. Glencoe. The Free Press, 1952, and also Bernard Barber, R.K. Merton. Brief Bibliography for the Sociology of Science. Proceeding of the American Academy of Arts and Sciences, 1992. Vol. 80, P. 140-154.
36. Merton R. Social theory and social structure. M.: ACT. 2006.
37. See Perspectives of social psychology. M.: EKSMO, 2001. p. 343. Daly G.A.and Wiemann G.M. Strategic Interpersonal Communication. Hillsdale, NY, Eribaum, 1994.
38. Mc. Cann C.D. and Lalonde R.N. Dysfunctional communication and depretion. American Behaviorial Scientists, 1993. P. 271-287.
39. Brzezinski Z. The Grand Chessboard: American Primacy and Its Geostrategic Imperatives. M., 1998 C. 12, 53, 234. Friedman Th. Understanding globalization. The Lexus and the olive Tree. NY. 2000. P. 109 Foreign Policy. September—October, 2000. P. 34. Panarin A.S.Global political forecasting. M., 2000. p. 88–89. UtkinA.I. Globalization: the process and reflection. M.:ACT, 2001. p. 97.
40. Bataille G. The Accursed Share. M.: Logos, 2003. p. 208.
41. See: Dolgov S.I. Globalization: a new word or a new phenomenon. M., 1998. p. 10.
42. Paxman J. The English. A portrait of a People, L., 1999. P. 7.
43. Toffler A. The third wave. M.: ACT, 2002. p. 277.
44. Ibid. p. 278.
45. Toffler A. The third wave. M.: ACT, 2002. p. 280.
46. Zinovyev A. The global humant hill. M.: Algorithm, 2006, p 10.

2. PLEASURE AS A CATALYST FOR DEVELOPMENT OF SOCIETY

1. W. Reich. Character Analysis. M.: Republic. 1999, p. 283.
2. M. Weber. Economy and Society, ch.1, par.16
3. A monster, which image Thomas Hobbes used to personify the state
4. T. Adorno: The Authoritarian Personality. M.: Astrel, 2012.- p. 473.
5. (p. 275–276) one of the reasons for emergence of the pathological thirst for domination and submission Adorno calls violence in the family happening in the early childhood. So the examinee declared that his father had been punishing him and beating almost to death. And right there admitted "I was always punished for a good reason, and my father was always right and could listen and talk to me at any time".
6. According to the WHO in 2014

7. The first part of the surname "raskol" means "a split"

3. CIVILIZATIONAL THREATS OF THE PLEASURE PARADIGM

1. Kuhn T. The Structure of Scientific Revolutions. M.: ACT, 2003.
2. Spengler O. The Decline of the West. Novosibirsk: Nauka, 1993. p. 70.
3. Spengler O. Op.cit. p. 108.
4. The Big encyclopedic dictionary. M., 1997. p. 817.
5. Dahl V.I. Explanatory Dictionary of the Live Great Russian language. SPb. , 1863 – 1866.
6. Big explanatory psychological dictionary. M.: ACT, 2000. p. 71.
7. Kierkegaard S. Fear and Trembling. M.: Republic, 1993. p. 144
8. Kierkegaard S. Op. cit. p. 367.
9. T. Adorno "The authoritarian personality". M.: Astrel, 2012.-p.280
10. Baudrillard J. The Transparency of evil. M.: Dobrosvet, 2000. p. 48.
11. Baudrillard J. Op. cit. p. 50.
12. Baudrillard J. Op. cit. p. 50.
13. Ibid. p. 52.
14. Reshetnikov M.N. Social activism and terrorism in Europe. Philosophic sciences. M., 2006. No 4. p. 10.
15. Camus A. The Rebel. The myth of Sisyphus. M: Polit.literature, 1990. p. 25.
16. Ibid.
17. Ibid. p. 25.
18. Camus A. The Rebel. p. 39.
19. Horny K. The neurotic personality. M.: Progress, 1993. p. 140.
20. Ibid.
21. Camus A. The Rebel. M.: Politic literature, 1990. p. 208.
22. Ibid. p.210.
23. Camus A. Op.cit. C. 215.
24. Adorno T. The authoritarian personality. M.: Astrel, 2012. p. 274.
25. Adorno T. Op.cit. p. 282.
26. Adorno T. Op.cit. p. 54.
27. Ibid. p.55.
28. Fromm E. The Anatomy of Human Destructiveness. M.: ACT, 2015. p. 223.
29. Bulac A. Jihad. Islam about terror and acts of suicide bombers. M.: Novy svet, 2005. p. 127-128.
30. Darwin Ch. On the origin of species. SPb.: Nauka,1991. p. 431.
31. Marx K. Engels F. Op. Ed. 2. V. 3,.M.: Politizdat, 1955. p. 1–4.
32. they were brothers then yet.
33. M. Lindstrom "Buyology".

4. ON THE WAY TO A NEW PARADIGM

1. Oxytocin and endorphins are responsible for pleasure— they are called "the body's own narcotics" or "hormones of pleasure". So far 18 varieties of opiate-like substances have been identified in the human brain.
2. James W. Talks to Teachers. New York: Henry Holt, 1912, p. 75–76.
3. Barrett E. Boyd. Strength of Will. New York: Harper, 1931.
4. According to the WHO in 2014 http://www.interfax.ru/world/395021

5. George Frankl. The Unknown Self. M: Astrel, 2007, p. 299.
6. Read more about the role of fear in totalitarianism in the work of T. Adorno "The authoritarian personality". M.: Astrel, 2012–p. 473. Erich Fromm "the Anatomy of human destructiveness". M.: AST, 2015 - p. 618
7. Nietzsche, F. Thus spoke Zarathustra. Works in 2 Vol. M.: Mysl' 1990, vol. 2, p. 18
8. Same, p. 24
9. Same, p. 123.
10. Nietzsche F. The Antichrist. Works in 2 vol., M.: Mysl, 1990, vol.2, p 633.
11. Same work, p. 97.
12. Same work, p. 112.
13. Same work, p. 124.
14. Same work, p. 139.
15. Dell P.C. Some basic mechanisms of the translation of bodily needs into behavior. Neurological basic of behavior. London, 1958, P. 200.
16. Hegel G. Encyclopedia of the Philosophical Sciences. M.: Mysl'.V.319, p. 233.
17. Ibid. p. 245
18. Fromm E. Escape from Freedom. p. 208
19. Morgenthau H. Politics. Among Nations. NY. 1967. P. 26. Ray J.L. Global Politics. Boston, etc. 1987 P. 164.
20. Fromm E. Psychoanalysis and ethics. M.: Republic, 1993. p. 166.
21. Ibid.
22. Fromm E. Op.cit. p. 175.
23. Ibid. p. 176 .
24. Aurelio Peccei. The Human Quality. M.: C.
25. Devall B. Session G. Deep ecology: living as if nature mattered. - Salt lake City, 1985, p 239.
26. Zimmermann M.E. Quantum theory, intrinsic value and panentheism. Invironmental ethics, 1996, N 1, p 30

Index

www.ingramcontent.com/pod-product-compliance
Ingram Content Group UK Ltd.
Pitfield, Milton Keynes, MK11 3LW, UK
UKHW020256051026
15470UKWH00020B/116

9 780761 869436